NAZI PROPAGANDA THROUGH ART AND ARCHITECTURE

'The arts cannot thrive except where men are free to be themselves and to be in charge of the discipline of their own energies...What we call liberty in politics is freedom in the arts...Crush individuality in the arts and you crush art as well.'

Franklin D. Roosevelt at the opening of the Museum of Modern Art in New York, 10 May 1939

NAZI PROPAGANDA THROUGH ART AND ARCHITECTURE

CREATING THE MYTH OF HITLER'S THIRD REICH

NORMAN RIDLEY

FRONTLINE
BOOKS

First published in Great Britain in 2024 by
Frontline Books
An imprint of
Pen & Sword Books Ltd
Yorkshire – Philadelphia

ISBN 978-1-03610-021-6

A CIP catalogue record for this book is available from the British Library.

Typeset by Lapiz Digital
Printed and bound by CPI UK

Pen & Sword Books Limited incorporates the imprints of Atlas, Archaeology, Aviation, Discovery, Family History, Fiction, History, Maritime, Military, Military Classics, Politics, Select, Transport, True Crime, Air World, Frontline Books, Leo Cooper, Remember When, Seaforth Publishing, The Praetorian Press, Wharncliffe Local History, Wharncliffe Transport, Wharncliffe True Crime, White Owl and After the Battle.

For a complete list of Pen & Sword titles please contact:

PEN & SWORD BOOKS LIMITED
47 Church Street, Barnsley, South Yorkshire, S70 2AS, England
E-mail: enquiries@pen-and-sword.co.uk
Website: www.pen-and-sword.co.uk

or

PEN AND SWORD BOOKS
1950 Lawrence Rd, Havertown, PA 19083, USA
E-mail: uspen-and-sword@casematepublishers.com
Website: www.penandswordbooks.com

CONTENTS

Chapter 1

NAZI PROPAGANDA TECHNIQUES

> 'Propaganda does not have to seek objectively for the truth...but exclusively has to serve our interests.'
>
> Adolph Hitler, *Mein Kampf*

In 1622, Pope Gregory XV issued the Papal Bull *Inscrutabili Divinae* establishing the *Sacra Congregatio de Propaganda Fide* (the Sacred Congregation for the Propagation of the Faith), with a mission of winning back those who had been lost to the Church in the Reformation. In this way, the Catholic Church introduced the first systematic application of propaganda aimed at the masses by promoting its subjective worldview as absolute and unquestionable truth. The technique of mass persuasion then took on a very different guise during the First World War, when the British government had engaged in what is probably the first organised and sustained campaign of official film propaganda. They saw no peacetime use for the practice, however, and abandoned it when the war was over.[1] Latterly, the word propaganda has been used almost exclusively to mean dissemination of a message deliberately aimed to exaggerate one aspect of the truth while denigrating another side or, purely and simply, by lying. The tool is usually associated with tyrannical or authoritarian regimes, but democratic regimes have developed a great affection for what might be called 'soft propaganda', where the message is more muted and where regimes claim they are much more scrupulous in its use, but their methodology remains the same. Relying on selective truths rather than fabrication to persuade people to accept their argument seems to be a less contentious application, but their presentation of the facts is rarely as balanced as they would like their listeners to believe.

Propaganda may contain blatant untruths but can still be effective by suppressing access to contradictory information or simply by making it dangerous for anyone to challenge its message publicly. For a message to be called propaganda it should normally have a deliberate purpose and a clear target audience, which would normally safeguard it from being employed unintentionally or by accident. This, however, does not allow for the possibility that a message, which is not initially put out for propaganda purposes, might be used by others to give it political significance, and an innocent message might, in other circumstances, also acquire propagandic value in a particular context that had not been foreseen. In neither of these cases is there a clear connection between its purpose and eventual use. It might be said, therefore, that in these instances the actual message is not, of itself, propaganda, but the way it is used contrives to make it so. There is also a risk that a message, embodied say in the plot of a film, produced and directed for non-propaganda purposes and seen to be non-political in its contemporary setting, might be interpreted as propaganda by critics who evaluate it in the context of another time and a different political and aesthetic environment.

Propaganda may have varying levels of success which is measured against the way it can 'give force and direction to…popular feeling and desire'.[2] Manufacturing a new value system and altering opinions and attitudes in a radical way can usually only be brought about during times of crisis, but appealing to pre-existing prejudices and aspirations through allusion rather than assertion is like seed sown on fertile ground. The most effective propaganda is also subliminal in the way that it leaves room for the audience to believe it has arrived at its own conclusions, oblivious of the manipulation of its existing social, psychological and cultural prejudices. The less the audience is aware of being manipulated, the more likely it is to accept the message. The Nazi propaganda chief Josef Goebbels explained his concept of subtlety and disguise when he said that 'Propaganda becomes ineffective the moment we are aware of it'.[3]

Joseph Goebbels had been a small, sickly but extremely bright child. Born with a foot defect that required him to wear a supporting brace, he walked with a pronounced limp and was teased mercilessly at school.[4] He attended Bonn University to study literature and philosophy before moving on to Heidelberg University, where he earned his PhD in 1921 at the age of 24. During his time at university he had become interested in the writings of Marx and Engels, but was also exposed to extreme right-wing politics when he spent some months in Munich during the winter of 1919–1920.

Leaving university, he seemed to lack any sort of ambition other than wanting to be a writer, and later became depressed. It was at this time that he started his diary, which he assiduously kept up for the rest of his life. Eventually, after three years of idleness, he found employment as secretary to the Reichstag deputy and local Nazi leader Franz von Wiegershaus, contributing articles to his publications. It was while working for von Wiegershaus that Goebbels broke out of his despond and found new ambition through the discovery of his aptitude for debate and oratory. At this time, Hitler was not yet the undisputed leader of the National Socialist German Workers' Party (NSDAP) and it was with Goebbels' help that he gained the support of the northern wing of the party. Goebbels formed a powerful, unconditional attachment to Hitler that was personal as well as professional. 'Adolf Hitler, I love you', he wrote in his diary on 19 April 1926.[5] For his part, Hitler was impressed by Goebbels and appointed him as *Gauletier* (chief) of the small and hitherto chaotic and quarrelsome Berlin section of the NSDAP.

Goebbels set to work immediately by expelling all the troublemakers, making good use of the *Sturmabteilung* (SA, the original paramilitary wing of the NSDAP) stormtroopers at his disposal. Through his editorship of the weekly newspaper *Der Angriff* (The Attack), he provoked confrontations with communists on the streets and in the beerhalls, where his 'ferocious band' of ex-*Freikorps* fighters used extreme force. His penchant for propaganda was evident when he exhibited heavily bandaged 'victims' of communist violence beside him on platforms when addressing crowds, and he is also believed to have been the one to introduce the 'Heil Hitler' salute between party members. His tactics, however, brought about an eleven-month ban by the Berlin authorities against public speaking in an attempt to curb street violence.

One of his early propaganda successes was the immortalisation of one of his most brutal street gangsters as a martyr and hero of the party. This drunken womanising pastor's son, Sturmführer Horst Wessel, was shot and killed by communists in Vienna in 1930. In *Der Angriff*, Goebbels called Wessel 'A Christian Socialist [who] calls out through his deeds [and who] set an example and offered himself up as a sacrifice'.[6] Goebbels made sure that the Nazi leadership was well represented at Wessel's funeral, but Hitler, ever cautious about the communist threat in Berlin, was not among the mourners. The 'Horst Wessel Song' later became the official Nazi anthem in January 1933, when a regulation was passed into law requiring singers to raise their right arm in a Nazi salute when the first verse was sung. It would also be sung after Hitler's public speeches alongside the national anthem.

In 1928, Goebbels had been one of the few Nazis to win election to the Reichstag. Even before the Nazis came to power, he had taken on the role of Nazi propagandist and wrote of his ambitions in his diary in 1932 that 'My department will be something immense…something the world has never seen before'.[7] When Hitler appointed him Minister for Public Enlightenment and Propaganda, Goebbels found himself in a position in which he excelled. 'Politics is no more the art of the possible but for us the wonder of the impossible', he wrote in his diary. His propaganda machine inexorably tightened its grip on the German public as an essential tool in the dismantling of democracy in the country.

It was the ambition of the Nazis not simply to change the government but to foment a revolution that would fundamentally change German society. This was certainly no easy process and they would need all the tools at their disposal. Having taken steps, sometimes three forward and two back, towards their goal, the party took a giant leap in January 1933 when they captured the authority of state control, and the machinery of government that went with it, and this became the means by which they effected the next development. It allowed them to manipulate the system of laws to undermine democratic freedoms and implement their policies, while at the same time employing widespread terror and coercion to force the population into obedience. To counter this shadow of fear which they deliberately spread, propaganda was widely used to promote a positive image of what could be achieved in a society striving to recover from the multiple setbacks of inflation, economic depression and unemployment, all beneath the lingering pall of military defeat and the humiliation of the Treaty of Versailles.

In the context of Nazi propaganda, the idea of myth was always a powerful component. A myth might be described as a story in which meaning is interwoven with a narrative that, ideally, is already familiar to the audience and accepted as true or, at least, feasible. The purpose of myth is to help a society or body to overcome class divisions and coalesce into a functioning *Gemeinschaft* (community) bound by common traditions and values to which all can relate and draw strength from. It is a means of elevating language to a level where it transcends everyday meaning and takes on a power of its own. That, of course, leaves much room for truth, half truth and fabrication to coexist in varying combinations.

Nazi propaganda was aimed at all sections of German society, both those in high public office, who were persuaded to see advantage for themselves in the rise of fascism, and the mass of people below, who were made keenly aware of the dire consequences of resistance.

It was, however, still a means to an end and not, of itself, the cause of fascism in Germany. Propaganda has no power in a vacuum, it only has meaning in terms of a people's hopes, fears and prejudices. German soil was already sown with the seeds of fascism long before the Nazis came to power. The role of propaganda was to apply the fertilizer to help it grow. Many people in Germany were suffering from unemployment and impoverishment resulting from Germany's extreme vulnerability to the Wall Street Crash in 1929, which drained it of American investment. The people were filled with resentment, all crying out for someone to blame and someone to lead them out of the morass. In that regard they were open to the seductive messages that promised a better future for them and their families. The negative consequences of succumbing to powerful propaganda are rarely apparent, except in retrospect.

The Nazis made much use of the concept of a link between the peoples of classical civilisations and the concept of a modern 'new man' of the Reich. This new man would be an ideal citizen created by the adoption of a classical aesthetic propagated using the tools of propaganda. The state could draw upon art, advertising, radio transmissions, public speeches and spectacles, easy-to-remember slogans and catchphrases to create the perfect Nazi subject, fanatically devoted to 'Führer, Volk und Reich'.[8] The first essential component of moulding a society was to give it a history, so the Nazis bestowed upon the German people an entirely fictitious narrative of a common Nordic and Indo-Germanic heroic past, linking it with an obligation to duty in the present. This version of a glorious past and racial history was disseminated everywhere by means of art, architecture, film and public ceremony, and constituted 'a racist seizure of classical Greek and Roman identity that was annexed in the service of the Nordic race'.[9]

In his paper *'Propaganda Techniques within Nazi Germany'*, Julius Yourman describes seven main propaganda devices used by the Nazis in the 1930s:

1. Name Calling

This is used to encourage people to form a judgement about a person, group or race without examining the evidence on which it is based. This devise employs endless repetition of a particular message using emotive words that are imprinted on the public mind, and appeal to hatred and fears that have already been stirred. It was used by the Nazis to eradicate support for trade unions and liberal democratic institutions that were equated with malicious communist and Jewish cabals. Liberals were depicted as weak and unprincipled people, whose evil democratic governments had taken the ship of the German state into perilous waters from which the Nazis would guide it back to a safe harbour.

2. Glittering Generalities

In this the propagandist identifies the positive qualities of the regime using 'virtue' words such as love, generosity and brotherhood. The German people are celebrated as possessing traits such as honesty, decency and goodwill as their true characteristics. Particular words such as labour and sacrifice are used repeatedly in the context of a fabricated mythology of racial purity where virtue reigned and will reign again under the Nazis. It was normal also for some words, such as science, to have their meaning distorted so that public faith in them was eroded. This permitted the regime to redefine certain concepts and, in effect, create a new reality that seemed authentic but was actually subversive and pernicious.

3. Transfer

This involves the carry-over of authority, sanction and prestige of something already respected by the audience onto something the propagandist would have them accept. This is most obvious in the linking of Hitler and religion. While Nazism itself is irreligious, it is clear to its leaders that religion still had a powerful hold on the national psyche. Where there is acceptance of 'divine' authority within the Church, the strategy is to transfer that same power to the Führer and so endow his policies, practices, beliefs and hatreds with the stamp of irrefutable truth. Baldur von Schirach, the Hitler Youth leader, wrote a prayer for his young men to learn, it begins 'Adolf Hitler, we believe in Thee'.

4. Testimonial

The opinion of a figure of authority and positive reputation, who is presented as someone who knows better than anyone else, is used to persuade the audience to accept an idea. The most important figure of authority was Hitler, who can promote or deny any idea even if it means inventing a wholly new 'scientific' principle of racial hierarchy. Only art and practices that are specifically designated as acceptable by supreme authority can be allowed to exist in the German state.

5. Plain Folks

Leaders present themselves as 'one of the people' to gain the confidence of their audience and convince them that their programme has the wellbeing of the ordinary people at its heart. Here the Nazis try to bring off the supreme irony of promoting Hitler as a god-like authority figure at the same time as showing that his humble beginnings also make him a man of the people who enjoys simple pleasures. He wears ordinary clothes, is rarely seen bemedaled and seems to lead a quiet, secluded life appearing in public only rarely at important functions. 'My whole life belongs to the people', he said in a self-effacing moment.[10]

6. Card Stacking

The propagandist employs underemphasis to avoid certain facts and overemphasis to promote others and create a narrative that distorts the truth. Misrepresentation is one of the most powerful of all propaganda devices. The first aspect of this is censorship, where facts thought to be unhelpful to the regime are rigorously suppressed by threat of arrest and incarceration. The other side of the devise is the ability of the state, through its control of communications and media, to promote falsehood without fear of contradiction, again because of the iron-grip of the Gestapo. Public opinion can be misdirected as in the example of when the Molotov-Ribbentrop Pact brought Germany and the Soviet Union into an alliance. Immediately, all commentary in German media stopped demonising communism and instead attacked the 'war-mongering English'.[11]

7. Bandwagon

The propagandist creates the impression that 'it must be right because everybody is doing it' to encourage the individual to join in and follow the crowd. All propaganda devices point towards, and are brought together, in this one. To resist climbing on the 'bandwagon' was tantamount to treason and guaranteed near 100 per cent 'yes' votes in all Nazi plebiscites. Probably the most potent bandwagon was the anti-Semitic one. Jews were lumped in with communists and liberals as enemies of the state, all of whom were condemned by 'gigantic crowds of people, massed ranks of uniformed troops, bands playing patriotic and martial airs [with] swastikas everywhere'.

The two most important methods of disseminating the Nazi message were newspapers and radio. Leftist and liberal newspapers were targeted as early as October 1933, when the Press Law was enacted making editors and journalists responsible to the state with draconian punishments for those who continued to promote leftist views. All the major news services were merged into the *Deutsches Nachrichten Büro* (German Press Agency) and all newspapers were obliged to use that to obtain international and national news stories.

Germany had lagged behind other industrial nations in radio ownership during the Weimar years for a number of reasons. The cost of receivers was prohibitive and the lack of electricity supplies to rural areas were the two main factors. Goebbels, knowing full well the power of radio, took immediate steps to increase public ownership of radio receivers. The first thing was to approach electrical engineer Otto Griessing to design a radio that was technically simple, easy to mass-produce and inexpensive. He came up with the *Volksempfänger 301* (People's Receiver VE301), which had an attractive art deco-inspired design.

Goebbels pressed twenty-eight German radio manufacturers, including Philips, Siemens and Telefunken, to manufacture it. It quickly went into production in spring 1933 and sold for about half the price of a conventional set. It had a limited range, which had the advantage of not being able to pick up foreign stations, but to improve reception of German transmissions larger German radio transmitters were constructed in the countryside. In some towns and villages, radio receivers were placed in public places so that those who could not afford to buy one could go and listen free of charge.

Early in 1933 Goebbels had taken control of the *Reichs-Rundfunk-Gesellschaft* (Reich Broadcasting Corporation). On 18 August 1933, he proclaimed that,

> We want a radio that reaches the people, a radio that works for the people, a radio that is an intermediary between the government and the nation, a radio that also reaches across our borders to give the world a picture of our character, our life, and our work.

He was acutely aware, however, that to be effective and to become a fixture in German homes, radio would need a regular programming schedule of operas, classical concerts, light dance music, games, jokes, and popular arts. In *News from Germany*, Heidi Tworek remarks that the Nazis used entertainment programmes to lure more people into listening to Hitler's speeches. During the first year of Nazi rule, more than fifty of Hitler's speeches were broadcast.

It is hard to evaluate the true effect of propaganda on the German people given that from 1933 onwards, as the Nazis tightened their grip on the country, it became ever more dangerous to criticise the regime. Goebbels was clear about the importance of integrating propaganda into mainstream activities. His idea was that propaganda should be addressed to large masses of people and create a uniform response so that each individual was reinforced in their received views by the reaction of those all around them. In this way, the people were swamped with endless newsreels in movie theatres, broadcasts on the radio, and saw propaganda posters wherever they turned.

In her book *Propaganda of Terror*, Sylke Wunderlich looks at posters and considers their effectiveness concluding that, in terms of how they advanced the Nazi message, they were very successful. It is clear from her research that the Nazi graphic artist Ludwig Hohlwein often copied the style and iconography of the most effective socialist and communist strategies, where the faces of Rosa Luxemburg or Karl Liebknecht could easily have been replaced by the face of Hitler. Neither were the Nazis averse to using *Bauhaus* artists such as Herbert Bayer, despite their aversion to the movement. Many incorporated techniques of photographic collages, clear lettering and pictorial language that clearly appealed to the people as modern and different.

The education of children was of profound importance to the Nazis and an essential part of their propaganda drive. Flying in the face of all Western tradition, they adopted an anti-intellectual approach, rejecting the pursuit of knowledge for its own sake. Teachers were instructed to abandon objectivity and value judgements, while embracing dramatization as the new format for historical education. Instruction, they claimed, should not focus on development of the individual either as a starting point or ultimate goal. Man was not a fully autonomous, self-sufficient unit in society but an inseparable member of a group. It was no longer the role of teachers to educate the individual but to shape the individual according to the needs of the state. Eminent professors and scholars of the ancient classical world were unquestioningly obedient towards this complete makeover of the curricula and revolutionary reform of the schools. By rejecting 'liberal ideology and its anaemic, hypocritical objectivity once and for all',[12] the study of antiquity should be accepted as a paradigm of proper values for the youth of the new Germany. Hitler said of history that he did not want to learn it but to be instructed by it. Study of the past would be little more than a political template for the future. The new ideology was summed up by Fritz Bucherer when he wrote, 'Subjects, professors, and schools exist for the students, but the students, both boys and girls, exist for the state'.[13]

On 15 March 1934, Alfred Rosenberg proclaimed that the new German education system would follow the Greek way that abjured the seductive and sentimental 'humanization of mankind' as 'a desiccated and overly cerebral rationalism' that was 'completely contradictory to all the laws of race'.[14] The Nazis, however, had to be more selective of exactly which aspects of the classical tradition to follow. It was necessary to separate out the Indo-Germanic influences on Classical Greece from the Semitic impact of Orientalised Hellenism, 'the twilight of racial decadence [and] a vehicle of an anti-Nordic spiritual heritage', which had caused the dissolution of the Nordic peoples of antiquity and 'still remained a destructive poison'.[15] Ancient history, as taught in schools, would now reassume its rightful place in the new Germany and encompass the full historical and cultural measure of the Nordic race. Through comparison with the other Nordic peoples of antiquity such as the Hittites, Persians, Greeks and Romans, the German people would see how the Nordic race had achieved a global reach.

Hitler had been fascinated by history since his days studying under Dr Leopold Pötsch at the *Realschule* in Linz. He wrote of his tutor that he 'knew how, quite literally, to conjure up the past, to breathe new life into it and give it rebirth through the inspiration and education of his students'.[16] 'Even today', he wrote in *Mein Kampf*, 'I think back with gentle emotion on this grey-haired man who, by the fire of his narratives, sometimes made us forget the present; who, as if by enchantment, carried us into past times and, out of the millennial veils of mist, moulded dry historical memories into living reality. On such occasions we sat there, often aflame with enthusiasm, and sometimes even moved to tears.'[17]

In the eighteenth century, the 'father of art history', Johann Joachim Winckelmann, had pioneered the study of Greek and Roman art that led to the birth of the Neoclassical movement at that time. His influence of artists was described as 'the tyranny of Greece over Germany'. It was under Winckelmann's influence that German architecture adopted a Neoclassical style and inspired Klenze, Gilly, Schinckel, and their ilk to plaster Munich and Berlin with neo-Grecian buildings and sculptures.[18]

In 1933, the writer Roger B. Nelson had an opportunity to personally interview many top Nazis and was surprised by the speed and efficiency with which their party had reorganised the political apparatus of Germany only a few short months after the November Federal elections had seen their electoral prospects fading. He concluded that it was the result of a carefully planned and executed propaganda campaign in which specific German conditions were systematically exploited. Leopold Pleichinger, the Nazi strategist, admitted that they had learnt much from the Soviets in this regard by probing for weakness in the bourgeois democratic system.

Nelson's observations led to him to conclude that the Nazi propaganda machine was particularly effective because of three fundamental characteristics:

- They acted as if all the world was a stage upon which great dramas were acted out and the people were invited to become heroes in that process.
- They always held the initiative as proactive purveyors of something new and interesting, controlling the political agenda.
- They always sought to understand how things looked to the people and endeavoured to express themselves in language and deed that the people would easily understand.

Nelson reflected that German had a military spirit as a consequence of Prussian domination, and this was evident throughout the population in the way that all classes like to play at soldiers and office-holding. Within the party, even the office of doorkeeper became a coveted role. The Nazi clerk in the party bookshop acted as if he was 'working in the commissary of an army division'. Asked why party members saluted so much, one replied that it 'infused them with solidarity [and] feelings of comradeship in the cause of rebuilding a strong and beautiful Germany'. One essential feature introduced by Goebbels was to dramatize circumstances and situations. As another of Goebbels' staff put it, 'The masses want it. We can and must give it to them. We must see through the eyes of the masses.'[19] The whole aim was to weave generalisations, illusions, promises and prejudices around the everyday interests and activities of the people.

Goebbels explained to Nelson that,

> It is an old lesson of history that when a young party sure of its aim wrecks the rule of a corrupt and inwardly foul system…it gives the responsibility to a dictator. That is what we are going to do.[20]

The means of promoting that dictator were various and imaginative. A pack of *Kommando* cigarettes had a *Hakenkreuz* (swastika) and eagle emblazoned across it and would contain inside a note that the cigarettes had been packed by hand 'to help overcome German unemployment'. Other brands, such as *Kameradschaft, Sturm, Trommler, Alarm* and *Neue Front* all depicted Nazi emblems. Ironically, while sales of cigarettes boosted party funds, Hitler tried to ban smoking, and certainly nobody smoked in his presence, but nationwide his bans were widely ignored. Visiting the Nazi Party headquarters, Nelson found every wall plastered with the *Hakenkreuz,* flags, pennants, banners and posters, while the bookshop was filled with postcards for sale of Hitler, Goebbels, Rosenberg and Göring, alongside images of great German heroes of the past.

Always, the propaganda machine appealed not to the individual but to each as part of 'the people' and it was this mythical concept in whose hands the whole future was to be grasped. The 'people' must choose between a future controlled by 'money-speculators and swindlers' or one in which 'honour and responsibility' should be the basis of a well-regulated life.[21] There was essentially only one enemy. That enemy was variously called, communists, socialists, liberals or Jews, each title being interchangeable and encapsulating the whole. Whichever title was used it was soon understood that it included all the others, and Goebbels demonstrated his mastery of propaganda by also lumping together all those who were not the 'enemy' into a single entity. 'We do not want to think any more in terms of classes', he said to a rally in the *Lustgarten* of Berlin. 'A great common cause welds us together. The day of freedom and bread is drawing near.'[22] Another Nazi strategist, G. Starck, told Nelson,

> Political propaganda is quite different from advertising though it uses the same methods…it seeks systematic education to win followers for a *Weltanschauung* (worldwide philosophy).

'The Nazi propaganda machine is generally considered to be the greatest peacetime organisation of its kind on earth.' So wrote L.F. Gittler in 1937, but he went on to observe that although the Nazis had used the 'greatest insight, intelligence and intuition' to impress [the crowds] with their rallies and festivals, they have come up short when it comes down to 'hypnotising' the individual. While a person might give in to 'abject submission' in the face of gigantic demonstrations 'unsurpassed in primitive appeal', they are much more sceptical when reading a book or newspaper, watching a play or film or listening to the radio.[23] By 1937, local agents were complaining to head office that the people were completely fed up with going to meetings and having to listen to 'boring mouth-pieces' reiterating the same old message that had been 'rumbling on' for years. 'Nazi propaganda is slowly deteriorating in the absence of a veritable enemy', Gittler noted. It would not be long before that changed.

In Gittler's view, Goebbels was 'the greatest press agent the twentieth century has ever seen (up to 1937) by raising all nazi activities to the epic and heroic levels'. He had 'a clever way of turning phrases to the hilarious enjoyment of his audiences' and his newspaper articles were filled with wit and sarcasm, but Goebbels had a reputation for being malleable in his views and was seen as hypocritically self-important by many.

It was always an appeal to the masses that conditioned the propaganda message. In *Mein Kampf,* Hitler had contemptuously written,

> Propaganda belongs to the mobs and multitudes and therefore must be popular in its leaning and appeal; it must grasp the sentimental imagination and idolatry of the wide masses whose receptive capacity and understanding are narrow.[24]

New recruits to Goebbels' ministry were taught that propaganda was an art form whose eternal truths they must learn. These were that all messages must have a completely one-sided viewpoint and all dissenting views were to be suppressed absolutely. Simply put, everything they said was true and everything that contradicted it was false.

Chapter 2

HITLER AND ART

'A truly great German is unthinkable without artistic trait; of the men who in the course of centuries were able to shape the destiny of our nation, Adolf Hitler is not only a unique phenomenon, he is both the first leader and the first artist of our Reich.'[1]

Baldur von Schirach, National Leader of the Hitler Youth, Christmas 1937

As a boy, Hitler was a reluctant scholar. He hated school and was determined to thwart the ambitions his father, Alois, had hoped for him to join the civil service. Frustrated by young Adolph's resistance, Alois beat him on the flimsiest pretext, especially when he was drunk and had to be brought home from the inn by Adolph, whose humiliation at such times was intense. This was probably where he developed his aversion to alcohol. For his mother, Klara, however, he felt only love, and she 'adored her son', making sacrifices for him to further his education after his father died. At Hitler's confirmation, which had 'disgusted' him, his godfather found him 'gruff and obstinate' but Dr Bloch, who tended at the time, thought him 'quiet [and] well-mannered'.[2]

Living in Linz, in his mid-teens, Hitler began frequenting the theatre to see Schiller's plays and Wagner's operas as often as he could. Of particular importance in terms of influence was Wagner's *Rienzi*, a work which required a large orchestra and crowds of extras. Each act worked towards a thrilling climax during which the performers repeatedly cried out 'Heil!' A friend Hitler made at the time, August Kubizek, who accompanied him to the theatre, recalled Hitler being transported when Rienzi sang 'if you choose me as your protector of the people's rights, look to your ancestors and call me your people's tribune', after which the cast roared out 'Renzi Heil!'

In September 1907, Hitler left home aged 18 and moved to Vienna, hoping to gain entry to the conservative Academy of Visual Arts in Schillerplatz. He passed the first part of the entry examination successfully, but the next stage, drawing, found him unable to impress the examiners. He had to take two three-hour exams in which he was asked to produce a number of freehand sketches on topics chosen from a list. The examiners noted his almost total lack of figures and returned a judgement of 'Drawing exam unsatisfactory'. He had shown some talent for architectural drawing, they said, but showed no aptitude at all for painting.[3] Hitler returned to Linz, where his mother was seriously ill with breast cancer. She suffered an extremely painful decline before dying on 21 December 1907, aged 47. Hitler sketched her as she had lain dying. Dr Bloch later said that he had 'never seen anyone so prostrate with grief' as Hitler was at his mother's funeral.[4] With a small inheritance to sustain him, Hitler returned to Vienna in February 1908 and tried once more to enter the Academy of Visual Arts. This time he did not even get past the preliminary test and never got a chance to sit the examination. The rejection left him humiliated, angry and despairing.

He was able to obtain a letter of introduction to a painter and Professor of Fine Arts, Alfred Roller, at Vienna's Court Opera. Hoping to gain entry to the Court Opera as an assistant in Roller's stage and costume design department, he was unable to find the courage to attend an interview with the professor, perhaps anticipating further rejection. When his friend, August Kubizek, was accepted at the Vienna Music Conservatory, he joined Hitler in his accommodation at 29 Sumpergaße but found it 'wretched and shabby'.

The two attended as much opera as they could afford, in standing areas only, and sometimes arriving at the theatre on a freezing cold night without a hat or coat to avoid having to pay for the cloakroom. Hitler studied the performances avidly. He tried his hand at writing stories and stage plots about German mythical heroes and even, despite his musical training having comprised no more than four months of piano lessons, attempted musical scores that Kubizek had to transcribe for him. The mechanics of actual performances such as the revolving stage, trapdoors and lighting effects fascinated him, and he would recall and discuss them enthusiastically and in great detail throughout his life.

The architecture of Vienna also captivated Hitler, especially the 2.5-mile long *Ringstraße* (boulevard), which oozed a sense of imperial power, albeit at a time when the Austro-Hungarian Empire itself was in decline. He particularly admired the Hofburg Palace, which fills much of the southwestern quarter of the *Innere Stadt* (centre), and the Neoclassical parliament building. Some days, Hitler would attend parliamentary debates, later claiming that it was here he began to loathe democracy. He considered the Court Opera House to be 'the most magnificent opera house in the world, with superb acoustics'. Kubizek recalled Hitler reading endless tomes on the history of architecture. He would sit up all night writing about it and making sketches of buildings he had seen but showed no interest in discussing the subject with anyone at all, learned or otherwise. All he was interested in were his own ideas and Kubizek had to endure hours of lectures on the subject. For him, unlike others, he told Kubizek, teachers were not necessary.

Hitler cannot fail to have been influenced by the rampant anti-Semitism in Vienna at the start of the twentieth century, which became associated with anti-Modernism by figures such as Richard Wagner. Modernism was also interchangeable with 'internationalism', which the Viennese keenly saw as an insult to their imperial heritage. 'Art is not international' said the *Alldeutsches Tagblatt* newspaper, 'it is Völkisch'.[5] Many modernist artists, of course, were not Jewish, but critics spared no effort to delve into their ancestry to find some Jewish connection, however spurious it may be. It was certainly true that Jews played a prominent part in the arts in Vienna at this time, both as promoters and audiences, and Hitler was one of those who urged a new emphasis on education in the arts for what he saw as culturally lazy 'Aryans'. In the view of many, this Jewish Modernism was little more than a trick played on the people by unscrupulous businessmen who were out to make money from gullible people.

The term *entartete* was fashionable in Vienna at the time and was used in connection with all areas of life. It is often translated as 'degenerate' or 'decadent' but would also be used to describe behaviour that was contrary to nature. Women's emancipation was *entartete* because it was against their traditional role. Modern Expressionist art was *entartete* because it depicted people and situations that were inimical to natural form. Loose morals were more easily associated with the term, which came to encompass all behaviour and expression that was hostile or contrary to beauty and nobility. It would become necessary to 'wage a merciless cleansing war [against] cultural disintegration'.[6]

By 1909, Hitler's funds were running low, and it is likely he joined the many hungry and homeless by availing himself of help from Jewish charitable organisations and soup kitchens. His later writing shows how much he had been humiliated by these acts of charity and by what he called snobbish condescension of fashionable women and their philanthropic flim-flam. As a desperate measure, Hitler begged money from his aunt to buy paints and paper so that he could start painting postcards depicting city buildings to be sold to tourists. The idea had come from Reinhold Hanisch, whom he had met in the homeless shelter and who agreed to go into taverns to sell the postcards for half the money earned. The slight upturn in his fortunes now allowed Hitler to move into a modern six-storey men's hostel at 27 Meldemanstraße in Brigettenau, where he was able to paint comfortably and make a living wage.

This prompted him to expand his market and offer to paint pictures for shops that sold picture frames, thus meaning they would have something to fill the frames in their shop window. Lacking any formal art training, Hitler had developed whatever talent he had in a closed and claustrophobic environment. He mostly copied scenes of romantic idealised bucolic landscapes painted by his favourite artists such as Anselm Feuerbach, which were empty of all except pompous theatricality. He would otherwise draw urban scenes featuring buildings he admired, copied this time from Carl Schütz and Rudolf von Alt, but these would be characterised by an almost total lack of people. Where people were included, critics would later say his figures were like 'tiny stuffed sacks' or would remind some of 'comic strips'.[7] Most of the pictures he painted of places like St Stephen's Cathedral and the Parliament buildings were copied from other works and, according to his patrons, were of poor quality. He tried to keep up a rate of production of one painting each day but failed due to the fact he would spend much of the morning reading newspapers from front to back, and then if any sort of political discussion started up in the hostel, he would weigh in and hold court with interminable lectures. Hanisch pressed him to paint quicker, which annoyed Hitler to the extent that he agreed for another man, a Jew called Josef Neumann, to peddle his pictures also.

Hitler tried a third time for entry to the Academy of Visual Arts in 1910. This time his took a portfolio of drawings and watercolours of old Vienna completed with 'painstaking care', as one of the academy staff recalled.[8] The works showed a total lack of imagination or originality and clearly did not impress. There is no record this attempt proceeded past the informal stage and as far as an official third application. Hitler remained in Vienna painting his postcards and peddling cheap watercolours until May 1913, when he moved to Munich to avoid arrest for evading his call up for military service. Upon arrival, he reported to the police authorities, giving his occupation as *Künstler* (artist).

After Hitler moved to Munich, he raised his output of sketches, watercolours and oil paintings to meet an increased demand for his work, but his clientele had little intellectual understanding of art. Unlike in Vienna, he was patronised by a number of middle- and upper-class customers such as Dr Ernst von Döbner and Dr Schell, who both commissioned work from him. However, he remained an artist of the lowest level without training, without a support group and essentially with little talent. It says much for Hitler's total reliance upon a meagre income stream from his sales that he was able to overcome any professional pique at having to change the colours of one of his paintings to keep it more in line with Döbner's furnishings. It says rather less, however, for Döbner's artistic appreciation.[9] Whatever his aspirations may have been, Hitler's approach to his art was encapsulated in a letter he wrote to an acquaintance in which he said, 'I paint what the people want to buy'.[10]

There is no doubt that Hitler's detailed paintings of rural German life, though emotionally barren, uninspired, and at times turgid, were sufficiently liked by enough customers to just about keep him from starvation. Often Hitler would make the rounds of cafes, bars and shops taking a selection of paintings. Sitting in a café, Dr Hans Schirmer remembers a 'very unassuming, quite shabby-looking young man' try unsuccessfully to sell his work and bought one of his paintings out of pity. Hitler immediately went to a nearby shop and bought a piece of bread and two sausages, which he ate immediately.[11] Struggling to make enough to eat was one thing, but disaster threatened in the early part of 1914 when the Austrian military caught up with him about his military service. After some questioning, however, they deemed him unfit to serve and passed on. Despite this, when the First World War broke out in August 1914, Hitler volunteered and was accepted into the German army. He served on the Ypres front, spending much of his time sketching battlefield scenes and his fellow soldiers.

After the war, Hitler became involved in the revolutions that wracked the country. He fought on the side of the reactionaries and thereafter equated modern art movements of the time with left-wing politics. His negative attitude can be seen from his *Drunmheit oder Verbrechen* (drunkenness or crime) speech of 3 January 1921 in which he calls the current artistic culture 'products of insanity [which are] incomprehensible to the common man' and presumably to himself. He went on to call it no more than a 'Jewish business hoax' with the aim of destroying German culture.[12] When he spoke of politics as being an art not a science, he was referring to his belief that to flourish, art, like politics, required an innate skill which cannot be taught to those who do not possess it. He used the example of Bismarck, a statesman of genius whose statecraft involved a great deal of artistic creativity, as a precedent for his own elevation from artist to politician.

Whilst serving a sentence in Landsberg prison for his part in the abortive Beer Hall Putsch of 9 November 1923, Hitler wrote his manifesto *Mein Kampf*. Despite his assertion in the book that he had become an artistic revolutionary, he devoted only two very short passages to art itself.[13] The first passage, which is a singularly negative critique of modern art, follows on directly from a discussion on syphilis and prostitution: a clear indication of how he saw the three themes as being connected. He singles out Cubism and Dadaism for special condemnation as symptoms of a 'biological degradation' that threatens the German people. He recalls the art and artists of the Bavarian Council Republics of 1919, which he helped to destroy, as bearing the stamp of political and cultural decline, and were thus the precursors of collapse into revolution. The second passage is concerned with architecture of the state that must express the aesthetic qualities of Ancient Greek and Roman cities in buildings and statuary that would become symbols of the age. The state must be prepared, he wrote, to commit all its resources to monumental buildings that reflected the political will of the people.

Very soon after he was released from Landsberg, Hitler is thought to have made sixteen sketches of huge public buildings that encapsulated the ideas he had first come up with in *Mein Kampf*. It was almost as if he was solidifying his political convictions in stone. He abandoned any further attempt to paint, and all his artistic energy now went into architectural design. For a few years he refrained from making any public statements about art and seems to have reappraised his own abilities as an artist. During his time in Vienna and Munich before the war, Hitler's world had revolved around art, but since the war and his imprisonment, politics had become a new obsession and it was now a question of how these two aspects of his life would relate to each other, and which of them would become more important. There was no question of him abandoning the artistic ambition so deeply ingrained in him, but as a public figure he would now be held up to scrutiny and any weaknesses used against him by his opponents. All his earlier painting seemed now to be an embarrassment to him, and he did not want his growing political reputation to be besmirched by evidence of any hint of failure in his background. A special documentary unit was established in Munich tasked with hunting down all his watercolours and oil paintings, and buying them back so as to erase all evidence. There was no such attempt to recover his architectural drawings, suggesting he was still of the opinion that they had significant artistic value and might actually enhance his artistic reputation. There was an intimate link growing between Hitler's ambition to recreate German culture according to his own ideas, and architecture which would be fundamental to the creation of the urban landscape of his dreams.

After 1925, Hitler supplemented his income by writing articles for the *Völkischer Beobachter* and together with royalties from *Mein Kampf*, started a personal collection of paintings. One of the first artists he bought was the nineteenth-century painter of monks and tavern-keepers, Eduard von Grützner, whom he likened to Rembrandt. In total he acquired over thirty of his works. It is no surprise that Hitler's passion for rustic art drew him to Breughel's work, and there were even a few French painters he admired, but essentially it was German and Austrian painters like Rudolf von Alt he revered the most. Among his favourites were those who had graduated from the Vienna Academy of Fine Arts such as Hans Makart, Ferdinand Waldmüller and Moritz von Schwind. Of the German artists, he was fond of Anselm Feuerbach, whose history of rejection and disappointment was so like his own experiences.

While it would become Hitler's habit to make broad suggestions about measures that might be taken against modern art and its acolytes and would leave it mostly to others to take action, this would never be the case where architecture was concerned. Right from the start he took a personal interest in all important plans for party and government building projects such as airports and army barracks. He rejected Paul Schultze-Naumburg's ideas of an architecture rooted in the solid masonry and tiled roofs of farms and country houses. While Hitler may have eulogised the art of the nineteenth century, his concept for architecture had ignored the recent past and leapfrogged millennia, seeking to incorporate the idealised forms of Ancient Greece and Rome into the monumental new state architecture of the future.

A speech by Hitler on 26 January 1928 in Munich is the first public statement about the relationship between modern art and the state of the country under the Weimar Republic. In the speech he sees the people alienated from both their culture and their political leadership and promises to address this, claiming that he will 'enfranchise [the] people politically [and] culturally'.[14] It is a measure of his political acumen that Hitler identified the way in which the minority elitist appeal of modern art, from which the general public felt disconnected, could be linked to the people's sense of alienation from a government that seemed to care little for their problems and grievances. When he bemoaned the fate of those artists, ignored by the modern art world, who are the 'decent, honest reservoir' of art and still seek to create the art of the 'true' Germany, he was speaking to all those 'true' Germans in society who felt abandoned by the state.[15]

When Hitler came to power, the *Kampfbund für deutsche Kultur* (Combat League for German Culture (KfdK)) was quick to urge him to make good his promises to promote traditional art. They also felt confident enough to take it upon themselves to enact purges of museum directors and university professors who stood in the way of their campaign against Modernism in art. The architect Schultze-Naumburg, who was also the author of *Kunst und Rasse* (Art and Race), personally petitioned Hitler to publicly denounce museums that continued to patronise modern art, but Hitler assured him that he would soon enact measures that would ensure all artists whose work proved acceptable to the Nazi regime would be well catered for, with enough commissions to keep them in work. Although the work of these artists would have little, if any, political content, its value as home decoration would be useful as a means of creating a sense of security, wellbeing and confidence in the regime. Speeches Hitler made at the annual Nuremberg rallies after 1933 regularly saw him drawing art into politics, which firstly increased state control over the arts and secondly allowed the arts to be weaponised as a means of moulding public opinion. It was at this point, when Hitler was clearly projecting himself as an expert on artistic taste and relevance, that some of his opponents, in a direct jibe at his failed pre-war artistic career, begin referring to him as a housepainter, since many of his paintings had been of various types of buildings.

Hitler certainly had his own perspective on modern art. Disgusted by 'the outlandish use of colour and a distorted perspective', he claimed that under the Third Reich, 'German art would be clear, without contortion, and without ambiguity'.[16] All the major artistic figures who were taking part in the movement at the time were censured and denigrated by the authorities. In a speech, Hitler clearly exposed his profound condemnation of Klee's 'foolish scribblings', of the 'subhuman style' of Käthe Kollwitz and Ernst Barlach, of that technical 'bungler' [Emil] Nolde, of the 'ethical nihilism' of Otto Dix and Georg Grosz.[17] At the climax of his anti-Semitism, Hitler even declared that 'Modern art was an act of aesthetic violence by the Jews against the German spirit'.[18] The alleged perversion of Modernism, including its 'suggestion of hidden obscenity', simply could not be associated with the purity and dignity of the Aryan race and therefore became another victim of the Third Reich.

Hitler himself fully understood the usefulness of art in politics. In 1935 he declared that 'art must be comprehensible to the people' in ways that science and philosophy never could be.[19] In his speech at the Nuremberg rally on 2 September 1933, Hitler spoke of the need for harmony between politics and the people, and by people, of course, he meant Aryans. Only then would the vital power of the German race find its natural aesthetic expression. This interaction of which he spoke would be brought about through his own initiative; it would be one-way traffic from the artist-politician, whose intuitive awareness of what his people needed, to the formless, passive masses whose world view would be shaped by the leader's vision. The essence of the aesthetic he would bestow upon the nation was to be found in a range of values incorporating late nineteenth-century realistic painting, the music of Richard Wagner, and the architectural style of Vienna and Paris.

Whatever Hitler thought of himself as an artist, he must have known that he lacked the spark of greatness. Painting and drawing had filled much of his time as a youth, and he had acquired a certain competence in the medium, but he never rose above mediocre. None would have dared to comment to his face and there were few who actually commended him. He kept a portfolio of his favourite works right up until his death in 1945, so his works must have had some significance for him, perhaps as the fading glimpses of an ambition that he was never able to realise. Other than those forty or fifty paintings, he had obviously decided to get rid of the rest, which began to see as an embarrassment.

Once he was famous, those people who had bought paintings from him were offered quite large sums to return them, which consequently attracted attention. He had authorised Hoffmann, his personal art dealer, to publish a number of his wartime pictures, possibly to encourage the German youth who were being called up for conscription. However, when one or two started appearing in American magazines, Hitler outlawed any public comment about his paintings and banned further publication inside Germany. Critics now took a hard look at them and passed judgement. Forgeries also began appearing. In 1936, Austrian police began scouring Vienna for any of Hitler's paintings that were still in existence. Rudolf Hess, as head of the NSDAP central party archive, was given responsibility for tracking down and confiscating any documents relating to Hitler's early life, including all his paintings.

Early in the twenty-first century a trade developed in paintings reputedly done by Hitler. In 2005 Jeffery's Auction House in the small town of Lostwithiel, in southwestern England, had sold what it claimed was a painting by Hitler of a Dutch postman. A year later they offered twenty-one watercolours and sketches attributed to Hitler, which went on to be sold for a total of £118,000. According to them, the works, depicting rural landscapes on the border of Belgium and France, were found by an elderly Belgian woman in a battered suitcase in a loft. At the time doubts were raised about the paintings' authenticity, but bidding was brisk.

In 2009, the auction house of Mullock's, Shropshire, sold fifteen of Hitler's paintings for a total of £97,672. Richard Westwood-Brookes, a historical documents expert for Mullock's, said the paintings were confirmed as being authentic by art historian Peter Jahn from Vienna. 'Due to my thorough knowledge of Hitler paintings, I consider this one as an original', the statement attached to one of the watercolours read. The paintings were supposedly found in 1945 by an unnamed officer of Britain's Manchester Regiment and had been in a private collection ever since. A number of the works were accompanied by certificates of authenticity provided by Jahn and another art historian, Hans O.A. Horváth. Over the next few years Mullock's staged a further thirteen auctions of what they claimed to be Hitler original watercolours, oil paintings, pastels and sketches, although none of these could be verified as being authentic, claimed Dutch investigative journalists Jaap van den Born and Bart F.M. Droog. These two had already questioned the authenticity of a painting owned by the Dutch Institute for War, Holocaust and Genocide Studies (NIOD), which had been authenticated by Professor Dr August Priesack. It had been known since 2002 that Priesack was a peddler of fake Hitler pictures, a fact which the NIOD seemed blithely unaware of. Even Dr Karl Springer of the Viennese police, who had been active rounding up Hitler's pictures for Hess in 1936, said they simply did not resemble any works collected and registered by the NSDAP during the years 1936–1940.

Priesack and another self-styled expert, Peter Jahn, had set themselves up as authorities on Hitler memorabilia. Little is known about their early lives apart from what they themselves have told. What is certain is that Jahn had been an Austrian art dealer who, in the years 1920–1930, had been sentenced to prison seven times for fraud and theft. From 1936–1938 he traded in alleged Hitler works and in 1938 had had a brief contact with Dr Ernst Schulte-Strathaus. From as early as 1963 he had been issuing certificates of authenticity for what turned out to be forgeries of Hitler's paintings, but at the time his stamps and seals of approval were accepted with few questions.

The Hermann Historica auction house in Munich had sold a number of paintings purporting to be by Hitler and, when they brought up for sale a watercolour that Jahn had described as an 'excellent original from the hand of Adolf Hitler', they felt the need to reassure their patrons with a statement about Jahn. It read

> Peter Jahn was an art historian commissioned by the NSDAP in 1937 through the German Embassy in Vienna to search for watercolours painted by Hitler in Vienna. Having permanent contact with

> D. Schulte-Strathaus, Dr. Dety, Dr. Lehmann, Heinrich Hoffmann and the Brown House in Munich, he purchased a considerable number of Hitler's paintings in Vienna during the Third Reich for the Historical Department of the NSDAP Central Archives and was therefore regarded as one of the leading experts on Hitler's works.

Jahn was exposed in one particular case in the 1960s when he authenticated a painting by Hitler and issued a certificate to that effect. However, the work had a stamp of a Viennese art trader at the back. As the telephone number given was R32197, this means that the stamp was in use in or after 1928, when the telephone system in Vienna was reorganised. Before 1928 no numbers began with a letter, meaning the stamp must have been put on the painting many years after Hitler's last known work was made. In March 1978, Charles Hamilton Galleries in New York had sold an alleged Hitler watercolour for $4,500 to a private collector who had been comforted by the fact that it had been verified by Jahn. Nobody had, at the time, queried how picture had been signed 'A. Hitler, München 1912', when Hitler had only moved to Munich in 1913.

Elsewhere, in 2012 the Darte auction house in Slovakia sold a painting called 'Maritime Nocturno' for €32,000. The very high price may have had something to do with a bill of sale and a signed letter by Albert Bormann, brother of Martin Bormann, that went with the picture. Two years later, on 18 November 2014, a watercolour by Hitler of the old registry office in Munich (*'Standesamt und Altes Rathaus Muenchen'*) sold for €130,000 at an auction conducted by Wiedler in Nuremberg. In the following year, fourteen paintings dated 1904 to 1922 by Hitler were sold for a total of €391,000. A watercolour of Neuschwanstein Castle by Hitler was sold for €100,000 to a buyer from China. A year previously, Weidler auction house had sold a Hitler painting to a buyer from the Middle East for around €152,000.

Chapter 3

ART IN WEIMAR GERMANY

> 'Fiercely experimental, iconoclastic and left-leaning, spiritually hostile to big business and bourgeois society and at daggers drawn with Prussian militarism and authoritarianism.'[1]

The Weimar years in Germany from 1918 to 1933 were characterised by social crises and cultural liberation. On the one hand unemployment was high, the economy was virtually destroyed by inflation, and criminality was rife, while on the other there was a blossoming and liberalisation of modernist art, music, theatre, design, dance and film. During a period when the country was struggling to create a liberal, tolerant society from the ruins of its militaristic past, it saw those same sensibilities release a wave of artistic energy, the pace and variety of which caught the attention of the world. A new approach to design developed at the *Bauhaus*, jazz and cabaret became hugely popular, and Expressionism touched every aspect of the arts from painting and sculpture to cinema, with masterpieces such as Robert Weine's *Das Cabinet des Dr Caligari* (The Cabinet of Dr Caligari, 1920) and F.W. Murnau's *Nosferatu* (1922).

Since the beginning of the twentieth century, museums, art dealers and critics had become enamoured of modern art, especially Impressionist and Post-Impressionist artists. The *Nationalgalerie* in Berlin had added works by Paul Cézanne, the *Museum Folkwang* in Essen bought paintings by Paul Gaugin and Vincent van Gogh, while others across the country covered their walls with pictures by Édouard Manet, Claude Monet, Auguste Renoir and Paul Signac, as well as the more recent works of James Ensor, Wassily Kandinsky, El Lissitzky, Henri Matisse, Piet Mondrian and Pablo Picasso. Important international exhibitions in Cologne in 1912, Dresden in 1919, and Dusseldorf and Hannover in 1928 drew in dealers from across the globe, while travelling exhibitions of contemporary German art, which differed from other European countries with its greater emphasis on modernity and topicality, were seen in Florence, London, New York, Paris, Pittsburgh and Stockholm. In Berlin, it was the Dada and New Objectivity movements that set the agenda.

Many young Weimar artists, such as Bertolt Brecht, Kurt Weill, Alban Berg, Paul Hindemith and Walter Gropius were gripped with an almost religious fervour to find new ways to express their response to war, its consequences and its aftermath. A new liberal culture that was exploding across the post-war world, not least in Berlin, dazzled them with its vigour and excitement. It was now considered acceptable to express all sorts of emotions from disgust, fear, anger, madness and lust in an individual way that could not be done through any existing style. The inner life of the individual was crying out for emancipation. Dadaism was a reaction against what Georg Grosz and John Heartfield called 'the cloud-wandering tendencies of so-called holy art'.[2] It differentiated itself from the paintings by artists of the New Objectivity movement by its preference for collages, assemblages, photomontages and graphics, but also from performance art.

A backlash against this modern art had grown steadily inside Germany, however, from within the traditional artistic community. Movements such as Expressionism, Cubism and Dadaism were condemned for being elitist and difficult for the masses to understand. It was not difficult to create in the minds of the general public, who were more attuned to chauvinistic realism in art, the idea that these modernist works were an insult to their intelligence. As early as 1911, 120 German artists had issued a manifesto, *Protest deutscher Künstler*, decrying modern art and demanding that museums buy their work in preference to works by Cézanne and van Gogh. This had little effect since museums were free to choose what to hang on their walls and modern art was what the gallery-frequenting public wanted to see. Things would only begin to change in 1931, when, in a taste of things to come, a temporary Nazi government in Thuringia ordered the removal of Expressionist paintings from the *Schloßmuseum* in Weimar. Later, the posters advertising the great 1937 exhibition of 'approved' art would rail against what they called municipal institutions that had irresponsibly squandered millions of the German people's money, while German artists were starving to death.

Under the Weimar government of the 1920s, Germany had become the leading centre of the avant-garde and a thriving laboratory of artistic and cultural innovation, despite the government being essentially indifferent to art. It is hard to think of an artist as being apolitical, but there was no sense of an artist's actual work as being either of the left or right despite what politics they espoused. It would later transpire that artists who had been feted during the Weimar period, regardless of their politics, were suspected by the Nazis of being left wing and subversive to a greater or lesser extent. The people showed great enthusiasm for contemporary art of all types, with the opening of a museum devoted to modern art in Halle with other museums in Berlin, Essen and Frankfurt setting aside special sections devoted to it. There was opposition, however, with the founding of the *Deutsche Kunstgesellschaft* (Association of German Artists) and the dynamic *Kampfbund für deutsche Kultur*, which advocated 'common action against the corruption of art' and the promotion of an 'art that was pure German'.[3]

There was an, often openly authoritarian, monopolisation of the institutions of public artistic culture in the 1920s by the modern artistic elite, which precipitated a long-running feud between modernists and conservatives. The appointment of numerous modern artists to professorships at state art academies and the extensive, virtually exclusive, acquisition of modern art by public collections after 1919 saw a growing resentment towards established members of the modern elite by artists who thought of themselves as creating the true traditional art of Germany, and who were consequently being sidelined. The art world of the Weimar Republic, out of which the art politics of the Third Reich emerged, was a battlefield with many fronts.

The Weimar Republic had become synonymous with Expressionism, which was really a European movement having adherents such as the Spaniard Pablo Picasso, Frenchman Georges Braque and Russians, such as Wassily Kandinsky, but was still regarded as a German movement by people such as Emil Nolde and Josef Goebbels. This movement explored not only what could be seen in the world around them but delved into the human mind to examine how people reacted emotionally to what they saw. The challenge for Impressionist artists, whether painters, writers or sculptors, was to express unmediated feelings. Naturally this meant that they had to capture the essence of irrational as well as rational sensations, which opened the way for the interpretation of many different personal experiences. Emerging from the horrors of the First World War, many artists had rejected old artistic norms and looked for new ways of expressing their world view in a political and economic environment riven with strife. Nothing in the traditional canon seemed adequate to express the intense emotions they now felt as a result of their wartime experience, and traditional styles lacked a sufficiently powerful language in which to communicate with their audience.

Expressionism as an art movement had, by some assessments, been around since 1891 and was associated with the new psychoanalytic theories of Sigmund Freud. Works by Vincent van Gogh, Edvard Munch and James Ensor are generally considered to be amongst the first works to inspire painters such as Ernst Ludwig Kirchner, Fritz Bleyl, Karl Schmidt-Rottluff and Erich Heckel to create a society of artists calling themselves *Die Brücke* (The Bridge) in Dresden in 1905. Their ambition was to attract other revolutionary and innovative artists to join them in a spirit of freedom in order to create a new aesthetic for a new century. The group of artists moved to Berlin in 1911, where they worked together for another two years before going their separate ways. During this time, other groups had followed where *Die Brücke* had led.

One of the early Expressionists was Paula Modersohn-Becker, who was probably the first female artist to paint a nude self-portrait. Working in Paris in 1906, she told her sister, Milly Rohland-Becker, that she had 'become somebody' and was 'living the most intensely happy period of [her] life'. She returned to Germany the following year but tragically died on 20 November 1907, at the age of 31, a few days after giving birth to a daughter Mathile (Tilly).[4]

The international New Artists Association of Munich (*Neue Kunstlervereinigung Munchen* (NKVM)) was set up in January 1909, under the leadership of Wassily Kandinsky, with the stated ambition to search for artistic forms freed from anything secondary to focus on the very essence of what it meant to be alive. Its manifesto said:

> We start from the idea that the artist is continually collecting experiences in his inner world, separate from the impressions which he receives from nature, the external world. The search for artistic forms that would express the mutual interpretation of all these experiences – for forms which must be freed from anything secondary, in order to throw the existential sharply into relief – in short, the struggle for an artistic synthesis, seems to us to be a banner which currently is again uniting an increasing number of artists.[5]

Artists who became associated with the NKVM were Georges Braque, Pablo Picasso, Georges Rouault, André Derain, Maurice de Vlaminck and Kees Van Dongen, amongst others, but soon disagreements caused a rift when Kandinsky led a breakaway movement in 1911 called *Die*

Blaue Reiter (the Blue Rider), named after one of Kandinsky's paintings. The NKVM were seen as insufficiently spiritual and unwilling to explore the relationship between vibrant colour and music. A lack of organisation that had been the downfall of the NKVM soon saw *Die Blaue Reiter* implode, before the outbreak of war in 1914 scattered the artists back to their homelands.

The Expressionist movement yearned for an *Erneuerung des Menschen* (renewal of mankind) that might release new forms of individual liberty, encourage a depth of understanding of the human mind and personal feelings, and reject the superficiality of the Naturalist and Impressionist movements.[6] Germany became the centre of Expressionist art in the early Weimar years but lost momentum due to what Kathleen Kuiper calls 'vagueness of its longing' and the 'intensely personal and inaccessible nature of its mode of presentation'.[7]

Neue Sachlichkeit (New Objectivity), also called *Magischer Realismus* (Magic Realism), was not a movement as such but a sort of shared approach to art that emerged in Germany after the First World War alongside the predominant Expressionism but was distinct from it in that it rejected its tendency toward exoticism and impassioned subjectivity. This new realism reflected a more liberal society and moral depravity and decadence in the context of the economic collapse and growing political extremism. Artists such as Max Beckmann, Otto Dix, Georg Grosz, Christian Schad, Rudolf Schlichter, Karl Hubbuch, Georg Scholz and Jeanne Mammen, who became associated with New Objectivity, looked at the modern world with sober and unsentimental eyes. They responded in common fashion to the social change around them, which they saw as alienating people and causing them to turn away from society.

Gustav Hartlaub organised an exhibition of 124 pictures in divergent styles by 32 artists at the Mannheim *Kunsthalle* in June 1925, which he called *Die Neue Sachlichkeit, Deutsche Malerei seit dem Expressionismus* literally translated as 'The New Objectivity, German Painting since Expressionism'. However, this does not convey exactly what Hartlaub meant. Both German and English words seemed to encapsulate the spirit of the time, but *Sachlichkeit* has the more complex and subtle meaning of approaching a subject with a neutral, sober and unsentimental attitude, looking at its function and utility beneath any decorative frills. It was less a style than a shared aesthetic that rejected the exoticism and passions of Expressionism that had dominated the pre-war avant-garde. If there was a binding theme, it was an awareness of the growing isolation and disconnectedness of the individual in a modern world.

The artists on display fell roughly into two different groups that had little in common apart from the figurative style: the *Novembergruppe* (November Group) of 'social commentators' such as Grosz, Dix, Schlichter and Scholz, who held their first exhibition on 4 November 1919, and the *Magischer Realismus* (Magic Realism) group that included Georg Schrimpf, Carlo Mense and Alexander Kanoldt, which had some similarities to the French Surrealists. The 1925 exhibition seems to have precipitated a new outlook for many of the artists involved. Grosz issued a pamphlet entitled *Die Kunst in Gefahr* (Art in Danger) along with Wieland Herzfelde that heralded the 'dismantling of the artist in his present form' and gave him two alternatives; merge with industry as a designer or advertising man, or become a propagandist for the revolution.[8]

Some artworks attacked political and social wrongs while others reflected on the harshness and turmoil of the historical moment, which was at odds with the way the Nazis would later consider art should reflect the life of the nation. The experience of the chaos and brutality of war was still a dominating factor in the way artists expressed their emotions. Artworks often showed street scenes populated with disabled veterans, unemployed workers, prostitutes and murder victims as emblems of a society irreparably scarred, both literally and metaphorically. Otto Dix's prints *The Match Seller* and *Card Players* depicted the long-lasting effects of war. August Sander included the unemployed and the disabled in his photographic documentation of social types, while other artists such as Georg Scholz and Karl Hubbuch created portraits that reflected the harsh realities suffered by many. The November Group of artists, including Georg Grosz and Georg Scholz, also targeted corrupt politicians, monarchists and profiteers, caricaturing their complicity in the misfortunes of the nation. Hitler's appointment as Chancellor brought New Objectivity to a premature end. Artworks were condemned as pernicious and degenerate by the Nazis and a significant portion of New Objectivity's output was lost or destroyed in the years between 1933 and 1945.

Berlin in the 1920s was believed by some to be a 'Metropolis of Vice'. Prostitution, drug-taking and the black-market flourished. Thrill-seekers from across the world came to experience its vibrant and exotic nightlife that catered for all tastes. It was also a powerhouse of Modernism in all the arts, but this was generally not appreciated by ordinary Germans. The movement was a vehicle for a small and unrepresentative section of the population, many of whom would otherwise have been marginalised or suppressed. The advocates and enthusiastic followers of this avant-garde movement came from a small unrepresentative layer of German society; left-wing or liberal, largely Jewish. Peter Gay said living in Berlin at the time was 'a precarious glory, a dance on the edge of a volcano'.[9]

Others saw things differently. Because of its themes and styles, avant-garde art inevitably provoked controversy and reaction from bourgeois traditionalists who called for a return to realistic art of the previous century. Right-wing nationalists thought that modern painting showing the horrors of war mocked German patriotism and insulted German values. Thomas Wehrling, a Weimar cultural critic, had already published an essay called 'Berlin is Becoming a Whore' in *Das Tage-Buch* in 1920. In it, he sees the moral debasement of women in what he describes as their obsession with fashion as they 'stream in herds down the *Kurfurstendamm* on Sunday mornings'.[10] The German press also often referred to Berlin as a whore and a sensual metropolis; a dangerous space where crime and death were associated with prostitution which tore at the fabric of traditional bourgeois German society. Their rage, however, failed to influence the left-wing government. Banning modern art was out of the question in a democratic Germany.

In 1920, it had been the Nazi ideologist Bettina Feistel-Rohmeder who set up the *Deutsche Kunstgesellschaft* in Dresden to promote the *Völkisch* tradition. Its purpose was to call a halt to what it called the 'rotting of art' through foreign influences and return to a purely German art that captured the true 'German essence'. The association began getting public funding from around 1926 and founded the *Deutsche Kunstkorrespondenz* (German art correspondence) and later the *Deutscher Kunstbericht* (German art report), who provided over a hundred German newspapers and magazines with propagandist art news and reviews. Feistel-Rohmeder championed the racist and nationalist *Völkisch* movement to combat cultural modernism and exaggerated the plight of 'true German' artists. With the growing influence of the National Socialists, she was able to set up an Executive Council of United German Art and Culture Associations to pave the way for a cultural renaissance. This organisation would go on to work closely with the Third Reich through the publication of its journal *Das Bild* to reinforce Nazi ideals through art by being the first to introduce the idea of purging galleries of 'degenerate' works and using them as 'kindling for the heating of public buildings'.[11]

In his 1928 book *Kunst und Rasse* (Art and Race), Schultze-Naumburg, the darling of right-wing cultural circles,[12] had argued that 'great art was the product of great races' and only racially pure artists could convey timeless ideals of classical beauty. Only they could produce 'healthy' art while racially mixed modern artists could create only 'disordered artworks and monstrous depictions of the human form'. To emphasise his point, the book contained medical photographs of diseased and deformed people juxtaposed with illustrations of modern paintings and sculpture.[13] Works such as this gave Hitler theoretical precedents with which to legitimise his own warped theories of race and culture.

Museum curators throughout Germany were confused about exactly what constituted acceptable art in the eyes of the Nazi administration. Hitler had made vague comments about modernist art, but had made no specific recommendations. Exactly which artists were modernists remained subjective. The question of whether all works by a particular artist fell into the same category was unanswered. Nobody could say for certain what qualities of an artwork rendered it open to the accusation that it was modernist. Those in the Nazi Party who thought they knew the answers were soon to be given free rein to show what was needed.

In 1929, the Nazi Wilhelm Frick was elected to the *Innenminister* (Minister of the Interior) for Thuringia when he issued an 'Ordnance against Negro Culture' and showed just what artists could expect if, and when, there was a complete Nazi takeover of power. He took advantage of Article 48 of the Weimar constitution, which allowed for emergency powers to be called upon by federal states in times of crisis. The crisis, he maintained, was here, and he issued the decree *Wider die Negerkultur für deutsches Volkstrum* (Against the Negro Culture for German Racial Heritage). The police were authorised to crack down on any stage performances of 'Negro' music, dance or theatre. Public libraries were purged of pacifist literature, and he had pictures by Barlach, Klee and Feininger removed from the *Schloßmuseum* in Weimar. Initially there was a sense that his actions were little more than pique, but when Frick took it upon himself to destroy the legacy of the *Bauhaus* art school in Dessau, the mood darkened. One of Frick's first acts was to replace Walter Gropius at the *Bauhaus* with Schultze-Naumburg, who went on to have considerable influence on the Nazi approach to modern art. He introduced the practice of comparing paintings made by the mentally ill to avant-garde works by modern artists, which would become a familiar technique used more widely by the Nazis to denigrate and condemn contemporary artists of all genres. Schultze-Naumburg's inaugural act of vandalism was to obliterate Oskar Schlemmer's murals with white paint in what he called 'the march of history'.[14]

The *Staatliches Bauhaus in Weimar* (State Bauhaus in Weimar) had been founded on 1 April 1919, when the cornerstone was laid for the school of design and architecture. Walter Gropius was made director of this new institution, a combination of the former *Grossherzoglich Sächsische Hochschule für bildende Kunst* (Grand-Ducal Saxon University of Fine Arts) and the *Weimar Kunstgewerbeschule* (Weimar School of Applied Arts). Its opening coincided with the setting up of the Weimar Republic and reflected the new democratic spirit of awakening in the political landscape. With particular attention to design and architecture, Gropius hoped to create a vision for a new model of education that would unite the divisions between the fine and the applied arts by persuading high calibre teachers such as Gerhard Marcks, Lyonel Feininger, Johannes Itten, Paul Klee, Oskar Schlemmer, Wassily Kandinsky and László Moholy-Nagy. He called for 'the conscious collaboration and cooperation' of 'a new guild of craftsmen, free of the divisive class pretensions' to 'create the new building of the future'. He called on architects, painters and sculptors to 'recognise anew and learn to grasp the composite character of building, both as a totality and in terms of its parts so that their work may once more imbue itself with the architectonic spirit, which it lost in salon art.'[15]

None of the artists recruited by Gropius had any experience of teaching, but they were assured that their role was mainly to work, create and simply to inspire the students who would attend the school. Gropius believed that the place would organise itself and there would naturally emerge a 'community of kindred spirits' in an ethos of freedom, respect and cooperation.[16] By 1921, the *Bauhaus* was already moving away from Expressionism and looking more to the Dutch de Stijl movement. The painting techniques and styles of Wassily Kandinsky and Paul Klee changed noticeably. Meanwhile, it was becoming clear that the character of an old city like Weimar, renowned for its history and full of traditional German architecture, was not a comfortable fit for the *Bauhaus*. The hometown of Goethe and Schiller was not an open-minded place and began to show signs of discomfort with the radical ideas of avant-garde artists and designers.

Within a few short years, Gropius was being pressured to move his school elsewhere and chose the town of Dessau, half-way between Weimar and Berlin, which allowed it to enter fully into the machine age and engage directly with the industrial institutions in the town. Dessau mayor, Fritz Hesse, offered to pay most of the wages of the staff on the understanding that Gropius would design and build new housing complexes for the burgeoning population coming into the town to work in the factories. He provided an open space and finances so that Gropius's architects could design and build a new, modern, futuristic school that reflected all of its ideals, but in doing so, inadvertently contributed to its eventual fate by turning away so deliberately from the past and further away from National Socialist dogmas at a time when socialist and fascist politicians were becoming ever-more intolerant of each other.

The relationship between the *Bauhaus* and the Nazis was complex and, from the Nazis' viewpoint, quite cynical and disingenuous. Their inheritance through the *Völkisch* far-right anti-modernist movement fuelled their virulent attacks on the *Bauhaus* for what they saw as its rootless cosmopolitanism, abstraction and its foreignness. The movement's modernistic ethos was essentially contrary to Nazi ideas of tradition and solidity but, in many ways, the Nazis also wanted to appeal to some in society as modern and cosmopolitan and actually appropriated many *Bauhaus* concepts of simple craftsmanship, folk designs, conservative luxury products and fashionable product design to be applied in the service of National Socialism. Many ex-students would later go on to play down their association with *Bauhaus* and apply the skills, designs and techniques they had learned there to work in the Third Reich.

Even before the *Bauhaus* had opened in Weimar in 1919, the political climate in Germany was diverging into conservative and communist camps. By 1923, the *Bauhaus* had welcomed representatives of almost all important artistic disciplines. As an example of its modernist approach to music and critical journalism, Hans Heinz Stuckenschmidt had created his Musical Cabaret of 'sensual nonsense works of the visual, literary, and sound arts'. Ernst Krenek put in an appearance with his jagged jazz opera *Jonny spielt auf* (Jonny Strikes Up), which was an enormous hit on the German operatic stage.[17] The *Bauhaus* even had its own jazz band that performed in Berlin at the *Rio Rita* or *Moka Efti*.

Films were hugely popular and several *Bauhaus* artists, such as László Moholy-Nagy, became absorbed in the medium, employing revolutionary techniques wherever they could. Three avant-garde feature films became classics of high art: *The Cabinet of Dr Caligari* (1920), *Metropolis* (1927) and *Mädchen in Uniform* (1931). Theatre in the *Bauhaus* was represented by Lothar Schreyer and Oskar Schlemmer, while Max Reinhardt, Leopold Jessner and Erwin Piscator agreed with Bertolt Brecht on the need for the theatrical arts to serve society.

The *Bauhaus*, which was state financed, became associated with the left, which made it a convenient political pawn because of its modernist approach to art and architecture. When a right-wing coalition took over from the previous left-leaning government in Thuringia, funding for the *Bauhaus* was cut in half, prompting its relocation to Dessau where it reopened on 14 October 1925. In Dessau, the political climate was more favourable right up until August 1932 when, because of its 'cultural Bolshevism', local Nazis put pressure on the Anhalt government to close it. Other political groups in the area failed to speak up for it and, facing certain closure, the school relocated to an abandoned telephone factory in Berlin, where it survived for only a few months before its staff rejected calls to align its teachings to be more in line with Nazi policy. When the latest *Bauhaus* director, Ludwig Mies van der Rohe, turned up for work on the morning of 11 April 1933, he found it cordoned off by armed police who had people inside searching for a secret printing press suspected of publishing anti-Nazi propaganda, as well as for documents linking *Bauhaus* to the Communist Party. They found none, but the building remained closed. Three months later it was given permission to reopen if it agreed to align its teaching with 'the demands of the new state' and get rid of Kandinsky. Van der Rohe, who had tried to keep the *Bauhaus* out of politics, now took it upon himself to call all the staff together, drink a champagne toast and declare the *Bauhaus* formally closed.

All the arts in Germany were affected by the economic recession of 1929 and gave Nazis like Alfred Rosenberg unexpected opportunities to clamp down on what they saw as all degenerate forms of artistic expression, such as the music of Kurt Weill and the plays of Berthold Brecht. Rosenberg, who was chief editor of the *Völkischer Beobachter* at the time, had been encouraged by Hitler to establish the *Nationalsozialistische Gesellschaft für deutsche Kultur* (National Socialist Society for German Culture (NGDK)) on 4 January 1928 to 'defend natural German values' against 'the flood of degeneracy spreading from Berlin'.[18] This was later renamed the *Kampfbund für deutsche Kultur* on 19 December of the same year. He had written the indigestible tome *Myth of the Twentieth Century* in which he claimed that the Nordic race had produced not only great German architecture but also Greek sculpture and the masterpieces of the Italian Renaissance. It was never officially endorsed by the Nazis, but it proved to be a convenient theoretical justification for the party's crusade against modern art, especially during the mid to late 1930s. Although Hitler never read the book, he welcomed its nonsensical ideas and his approval greatly enhanced Rosenberg's profile in the Nazi Party. Rosenberg railed against avant-garde artists such as Grosz, Dix, Gropius, Weill and Brecht, whose 'trend toward greater sensuality in art' he saw as a threat to German culture.[19]

Alfred Rosenberg had been born in Estonia to a Baltic German family but moved to Munich after the Russian revolution. He was virulently anti-communist and anti-Semitic, believing that the two had connived in the downfall of the Czar. He had met Hitler as early as 1919 after writing two anti-Semitic books. Hitler recognised his credentials as a racist ideologue but also welcomed him for his lack of the charisma or vision that would make him no threat to his leadership. Many in the party resented Rosenberg for his Baltic roots and remained his enemy all through the Nazi years. One of his contemporaries said of him that he had 'the gift of erecting systems of ideas on a truly noble scale from the most improbable premises'. His 'perilous superstructure of ideas [could be] successfully juggled only in the drawing-room.'[20] The writer L.F. Gittler saw Rosenberg as 'a quiet-spoken man with an academic air who spent his time [addressing] German culture clubs and editing magazines and newspapers'.

Having been sentenced to prison for his treasonable leadership of the Beer Hall Putsch in 1923, Hitler had appointed Rosenberg as acting head of the National Socialist movement until he was released. Lacking leadership qualities and quite without charisma, Rosenberg was no threat to Hitler and could be relied upon not to try to carve out a permanent leadership role for himself. When Hitler was released, Rosenberg took on minor roles and was easily intimidated by more abrasive party members, of which there were plenty. He still had power, though, even if he was not well-regarded, and he was still able to prevail occasionally over Goebbels and Göring in matters of the arts. Goebbels was known to be fond of Modernism, which put him in something of a delicate position if Hitler was ever called upon to take sides in a dispute. Göring, on the other hand, had little interest in art other than that which he could hang on his walls, so it is perhaps not surprising that Rosenberg was able to close down Rudolf Wagner-Régeny's opera *Die Bürger von Calais*, under Herbert von Karajan's musical direction, even though it had been sponsored by Göring.

With the denigration of modern art and a general clear-out of museum curators who favoured it, a group of artists representing the so-called right wing of the New Objectivity, Alexander Kanoldt, Georg Schrimpf, Franz Lenk and Franz Radziwill, put themselves forward to take the place of those dismissed and inaugurated a new movement they called 'New German Romanticism'. The hope was that they might be tolerated or even encouraged by the new regime but, again, it was not appreciated at the time how difficult that was going to be. For Schrimpf it was especially difficult because he had campaigned for the left-wing Soviet Republic in Munich in 1918, but he was still able to get a commission from none other than Hitler's deputy Rudolf Hess without ever having to join the Nazi Party. Radziwill was also known to have left-wing sympathies, but this did not prevent him from being appointed to a professorship at the Düsseldorf Art Academy. It seemed as if the Nazis were going to be tolerant of modern art, despite their early purges, but this was a false interpretation of what was going on. The underlying penchant for *Völkisch* art was still strong and was even growing within the most reactionary factions, but the lack of any coherent leadership on the issue from Hitler and the level of internal factional disputes within the Nazi Party meant that there was a policy vacuum that administrators, for the moment, were not confident about filling.

Chapter 4

ART UNDER THE NAZIS

'I will not tolerate unfinished paintings.'[1]

Adolf Hitler

In as much as all major policy decisions emanated from Hitler, it is worth looking at the extent to which he was interested in cultural affairs and the degree to which he sought to impose his will in that field. As was the case in many other areas, Hitler suggested broad principles, but it was lower-level functionaries who turned pronouncements into policy, hoping that they had correctly interpreted his often-nebulous intentions. Party functionaries with no clear hierarchical dominance would strive to overwhelm one another, often cancelling each other out in the process. Hitler would initiate basic policy and then stand back to watch the ensuing chaos, believing that the political energy created would produce dynamic results. This often made everyone but himself appear weak and unfocused. The most successful of his acolytes were those who best interpreted his intentions, which were not always consistent, and were the most ruthless in achieving the results that pleased him.

In a Nazi world there was no such thing as art for art's sake. Art could assume many forms and serve several purposes, including influencing popular attitudes toward the regime. The central task of culture would be to spread a Nazi world view, but a secondary purpose was to entertain the people and divert their attention from the more disturbing issues such as unemployment. Hitler's interest in art was most evident in his love of opera and films, the latter passion being shared by Goebbels, and it was Goebbels who called film the primary 'leadership tool of the state' in which political ideas were couched in aesthetic forms.

Max Nordau had coined the expression *Entartung* (degeneration) as early as 1892 in a book of the same name, where he explained modern art as a product of people 'so corrupted and enfeebled by modern life that they had lost the self-control needed to produce coherent works of art'.[2] He had been influenced by the criminologist Cesare Lombroso who tried to prove that certain physical characteristics were indicative of criminal tendency and that modern art was the product of perverse souls living in a corrupted society. Art, he said, should be wholesome and uplifting and should not glorify ugliness. 'The degenerates babble and stammer instead of talking…they draw and paint like children,' he wrote. People were becoming 'infected [by] a black plague of mental illness, degeneration and hysteria…they praise crime, deny morality, sanctify their drives [and] scorn science'.[3] In view of the later association of degenerate art with the Jews and foreigners, it is ironic that Nordau, himself, was a Hungarian Jew. In 1911, the German dictionary *Unverfälschte Deutsche Worte* revised its 1890 definition of *Entartung* by saying it was manifest in

> the self [being] no longer aware of its roots in the blood and soil of its people…we who are wholesome must be careful to protect ourselves from infection by these creatures who are rotten to the core.[4]

The concept of a Germanic spirit, a sort of noble, mystical, rural and moral, ancient wisdom, exemplified by the works of the composer Richard Wagner, had existed long before the rise of the Nazis. Hitler, in his early years, had been greatly influenced by the writings of the painter and architect Paul Schultze-Naumburg, which imbued in him a belief that classical Greece and the Middle Ages were the true sources of Aryan art which had culminated in the nineteenth-century genre paintings. For Schultze-Naumburg, modern 'degenerate' art was a manifestation of mental or physical disabilities and racial defilement. All those who promoted it were undermining German racial purity. For the Nazis, a chief role of culture was to disseminate the Nazi world view. The tenets of their creed would be expressed through their sponsorship of art and in the design of their buildings. One of their first acts was to instil Nazi ideology and policy in all professional and social organisations. Art and culture were fundamental to this programme and it was soon made clear that the whole modernist movement was an anathema to them and had been since the November Revolution of 1918.

Anything associated with the left-wing movements of that time, however spurious that connection might be, was damned. In its place, they championed a distinctly fascist artistic style that embodied a clear political message of anti-liberalism, anti-communism and anti-Semitism. Subjective, unconventional, and non-figurative art such as Cubists' fragmentation of reality and Fauvist's unrealistic colours were condemned. In its place was an emphasis on a kind of romantic-mystical aesthetic where realist figuration was the preferred idiom. Militarism, masculinity, racial purity, national unity and heroism would be instilled into the population to the extent that all forms of behaviour would eventually conform and become manifestations of Nazi ideology. Art showing the horrors of war was unacceptable. War scenes could only suggest courage, masculinity, and heroism. All artistic forms of fashion, architecture, theatre, film, sculpture and painting were expected to fall into line with this programme.

While other countries, even fascist Italy, had embraced modernist art forms such as Cubism and Futurism, Germany, for the most part, had resisted. Of course the modernist movement there had been of international importance, but the majority of the population, which had turned inward after the humiliations of defeat in war and the devastating inflationary crisis that had wiped out much personal wealth, had remained indifferent to it, and when the Nazis came to power and began preaching their own *Kulturpolitik* of agrarian-romantic *Blut und Boden* (blood and soil) aesthetic, they found an attentive congregation. In an almost religious context, they used mythological imagery to bind the German people to their *Heimat*, a word which might be translated as homeland, but for the Germans had a deeper, mystical meaning. Rural values were prized above all others, with family life and strictly defined traditional gender roles adding depth to the sense of wellbeing.

Since before they took political power in 1933, the National Socialists had planned to destroy Modernism in the arts throughout Germany and replace it with their own culture, one that was related to the core values of their aesthetics and preferred representational over abstract, and the natural beauty of the countryside against the ugliness of industrial cities. Once the Nazis had a firm grip, they immediately began their crusade against what they saw as the decadence of Weimar culture. One of the first victims was the 'young, handsome, and hugely popular' stage actor Hans Otto.[5] Only days after Hitler became Chancellor, Otto was dismissed from the Prussian State Theatre where he was performing in Goethe's *Faust*. He had performed in many classical plays throughout the 1920s and early 1930s but was known to be a communist sympathiser. When he refused to leave the country, he was arrested by Nazi stormtroopers in a small café on Viktoria-Luise-Platz, taken to their headquarters, beaten, and killed by being thrown out of an upstairs window. Others were targeted but suffered less. The actor and communist Wolfgang Langhoff was sent to Papenburg-Börgermoor concentration camp in 1933.

During spring 1933, 10 per cent of all pre-1933 personnel were dismissed from stage theatre companies, including one third of all directors, many of them Jews. Expressionist dramatists such as Hermann Sudermann, Arthur Schnitzler, Frank Wedekind, Walter Hasenclever, Ernst Toller and Carl Zuckmayer, whose work favoured the psychological examination of conflicted individuals, were condemned in favour of productions with the Nazi message of 'positivist dynamism in racially defined communal settings'.[6] The last Weimar-style opera, Jürgen Fehling, Otto Klemperer and Oskar Strnad's surreal interpretation of Wagner's *Tannhäuser*, was performed at the Berlin *Staatsoper* on 12 February 1933 before being closed down.

Hans Prinzhorn, who was born in Heimar in 1886, would have a huge impact on the way the Nazis went on to use art as a means of reinforcing their political message. He entered Tübingen University to study art history and philosophy but soon moved to Leipzig and then, exhibiting his 'pathological restlessness', to Munich in 1906 at the age of 19.[7] Along with friends, he formed an art association but again changed his mind and moved to Freiburg to start a medical degree. When the First World War broke out, he was drafted into the army medical corps where he met another doctor, Karl Wilmanns. Conversation turned to a particular interest of Wilmanns', which was artworks created by the mentally ill, and Prinzhorn was immediately hooked on the topic. Soon after their meeting, Prinzhorn was wounded in the Marne offensive of 1918 and had time to think about what Wilmanns had told him. The war was soon over and Wilmanns invited Prinzhorn to work at the Heidelberg clinic on the very subject they had discussed. Prinzhorn wasted no time in agreeing.

At the same time, two eminent German psychiatrists, Karl Binding and Alfred Hoche, were publishing a pamphlet that discussed certain types of psychiatric patients whom they referred to as 'incurable idiots'. The publication had the nightmarish title of *Die Freigabe der Vernichtung lebensunwerten Lebens* (Permission for the Destruction of Life Unworthy of Life) and was essentially a charter for involuntary euthanasia. Nothing came of it, but the idea would not go away and would re-enter the narrative some years later.

When Prinzhorn took up his appointment in Heidelberg, he began his research on patient art and found a small collection of artworks that Wilmanns had put together, but decided he required much more and so sent out a request to other psychiatric institutions across Germany for any paintings, drawings or sculptures that patients had created, along with a medical history of the creator of each work. Art was a common therapy for patients and Prinzhorn was not disappointed with the response. Once he had amassed a sufficient collection, which had been greatly enhanced by artworks of veterans mentally damaged in the First World War, Prinzhorn invited debate over its importance. Many in the psychiatric profession were fascinated and saw artistic merit in the artworks, but Wilhelm Weygandt, professor of psychiatry at the University of Hamburg, was scathing. While he agreed that creations of the mentally ill were valuable 'medically', he vehemently denied they had artistic merit. He called them 'congenital nonsense' and had already railed in the press against 'extreme modern art' in the public domain, which he also saw as the products of insanity. Works by Paul Klee he described as 'insane images' and those by Picasso as 'delusional'. Not that he claimed artists such as Kandinsky and van Gogh were mentally ill, rather they were merely degenerates who 'contributed substantially to lowering the dignity of mankind'.[8]

By introducing the concept of degeneracy, Prinzhorn was opening up a wider debate about what people like the composer Richard Wagner called racial hierarchy. The writer Max Nordau had enlivened the debate with his view that some authors and artists exhibited the same mental characteristics as criminals and lunatics. Artists who produced anything other than realism, he said, were clearly ill with their false colouration and distorted figures and should be committed to an asylum to prevent them infecting the population. Nordau's views were widely disseminated in Germany and gained wide approval. Here we see the first official attempt to make the connection between the modern art movement of the Weimar years and mental illness and criminality.

Prinzhorn travelled widely throughout Germany expounding his theories, and even visited Walter Gropius at the *Bauhaus*, but Gropius was sceptical and it took some persuading before he would let Prinzhorn speak to his students. In 1922 Prinzhorn published his monumental book *Bildnerei der Geisteskranken* (Artistry of the Mentally Ill). Many modern translations have it as 'Art of the Mentally Ill', but Prinzhorn chose the word *Bildnerai* carefully to express the idea of images or pictures rather than *Kunst*, which was a clear reference to art itself. The book was well received and soon became part of the German cultural landscape.[9] Prinzhorn's reputation spread beyond Germany and even saw him going on a lecture tour of US universities in 1929.

German urban society, meanwhile, had evolved to embrace Modernism in all its many forms. With unflinching zeal, *Neue Sachlichkeit* artists dominated Berlin theatres, nightclubs and galleries, much to the dismay of most of the population who did not take kindly to their capital earning the sobriquet of the world's centre of depravity. Hitler was quick to exploit this animosity in speech after speech in which he railed against Jewish-Bolshevik art and monkey-dances. Immediately, local branches were established across Germany and activists were urged to campaign against museums and galleries that supported modern art.

Amongst the many ambitious Nazis who joined the *bund* was Schultze-Naumburg, who had first encountered Hitler at a dinner party hosted by the Romanian princess Elsa Bruckmann in 1925. At the time, Schultze-Naumburg thought Hitler 'unimpressive' and quiet, until the topic of racial influences on art was introduced, after which Hitler grew animated and dominated the rest of the evening with his own take on the subject. Schultze-Naumburg, of course, had written *Kunst und Rasse,* which foretold the decline of the Nordic races through interbreeding with 'inferior' races, and whose illustrations had been supplied by none other than Wilhelm Weygandt. His central theme was that only true Aryan blood can create 'healthy' art and, of course, this was grist to Hitler's mill reinforcing his own prejudices. This further reinforced in the public's mind the idea that modern art and mental illness were intimately connected.

Schultze-Naumburg had developed his theories without engaging with supporters of modern art to get a view from their perspective. His ideas were based purely on prejudice and intolerance, devoid of any logical argument and arrived at without having been held to scrutiny. Such ideas had the strength of simplicity and would be conveniently conveyed to minds that looked for easy answers to complex questions.

After the regional elections of 1929, the Nazis were allocated two ministries in the state of Thuringia. A favourite of Hitler, Wilhelm Frick, was made Minister for both Interior and Education and, in what was one of the first Nazi experiments in manipulative democracy, inaugurated a purge of the Thuringian cultural establishment. He took on Schultze-Naumburg as a cultural adviser and the state became a testing ground for Nazi policies. Jazz music was banned as were a number of authors and film producers. Frescoes in the old *Bauhaus* building were painted over. When the Social Democrats won back temporary control of Thuringia in 1932, Frick was ousted but went on to become second-in-command to Rosenberg at the *Kampfbund für deutsche Kultur* and took Schultze-Naumburg with him. The two then went on a tour of Germany, commissioned and financed by the *Füherrat des Vereinigten Deutschen Kunst und Kultur Verbands* (Führer's Council of United German Art and Cultural Associations), holding meetings where their theories of avant-garde art as 'degenerate' were enthusiastically received by packed audiences and often ended up as riotous celebrations of Nazism. It was all part of the association's crusade to establish a wider support base for its activities and establish a leading role in the cultural bureaucracy of the Nazi Party, which it was able to do in its early days while party membership was small, but later became mired in controversy and fell foul of Goebbels' ambitions which pointed in a similar direction.

Prinzhorn was not a Nazi enthusiast but tended to overlook their excesses as somehow necessary from a purely political viewpoint. He had heard Hitler speak and found him to have a remarkable ability to 'hammer [home] a few facts and judgements and guiding principles' that were easily absorbed by his audience. His lecture tours were beginning to generate a great deal of political heat. The idea that the mentally ill could produce art that had any artistic value at all was now seen as an insult to the viewer's intelligence and fed comfortably into the Nazi narrative that the popularity of modern art, which was associated with 'madhouse art', was denying a livelihood to the many traditional artists that had previously flourished in the country and were now facing destitution. The association of 'good' art with robust mental health was feeding into Nazi eugenic theory.

In his 1939 portrait of a seemingly idyllic Aryan family, *Farm Family from Kahlenberg,* Adolf Wissel got to the very heart of the Nazis message of 'man as the dominator of nature' and woman representing 'nature itself'. Karl Alexander Flügel's 1938 painting *Harvest,* with its depiction of 'the idyllic life of country folk working in a perfect landscape' shows a bountiful land and hardworking people in an ideal agrarian setting.[10] Other paintings with similar romantic versions of the German countryside that hammer home the message with evocative titles were Werner Peiner's 1938 painting *German Soil* and Julius Paul Junghanns' *Hard Work* of 1939.

High value was placed on representations of fitness and wellbeing as the essential qualities of racial purity and Aryan superiority. Masculinity was almost synonymous with Nazism and depictions of the naked man 'steeled in battle and sport' became ideals of classical beauty and heroism in popular culture. Artists were encouraged by Adolf Ziegler, head of the *Reichskammer der Bildenden Künste* (Reich Chamber of Visual Art) to attend art courses in sporting venues to improve their nude studies of virile and sturdy models in strong or sporting poses. Their works were then displayed in exhibitions such as 'Sports of the Hellenics' and 'Olympia and the German Spirit'. Despite the regime's prudish undertones, the naked virile male, camaraderie, male bonding and youthful energy were important Nazi images. At the first great German Art Exhibition in 1934, the official symbol was a reclining nude male figure *Awakening* by Richard Klein. The human form held no fear for the Nazis, provided it was attractive, healthy and Aryan.

Militarism in art saw the warrior as a key figure embodying courage and patriotism within a Nazi philosophy that saw racial purity as a perpetual struggle against inferior races. Naturally the figure of Hitler emphasised the nation's debt to him, which was most emphatically formalised in Conrad Hommel's full-length portrait of *The Leader and Commander in Chief of the Army* in powerful pose. While traditional religious sentiment was not encouraged, the styles, methods, iconography and symbols employed in historical religious works were eagerly purloined to create a quasi-religious aesthetic. Hans Schmitz-Wieden's triptych *Workers, Soldiers, Farmer* is a clear example. To ensure the message was widely disseminated, the Nazis created museums and galleries and published a number of art magazines such as *Die Kunst im Deutschen Reich* (Art in the German Empire) and miniaturisations of famous paintings appeared on stamps, cigarette cards and postcards. Art thus became pure propaganda, while politics progressed through aesthetic to eventual terror. Nazi art was successful in realising its aim of communicating the Nazi ethos of pure race and country, with an idealised, mystical past and glorious future for a nation with military and moral strength devoid of degenerate influences of communism and Judaism.

Attacks on modern art were not new in Germany; it was the Nazi's seizure of power in January 1933 that released a systematic torrent of reaction against it. They almost immediately banned all pornographic literature and curbed prostitution in an effort to bring to an end what it saw as the moral chaos of the Weimar Republic. This was welcomed by many organisations such as the *Deutsch Evangelische Sittheckeits Bewegung* (Evangelical Morality Movement), who saw a clear connection between immorality and modern art. Modern artists and museum directors who purchased or exhibited modern art had already been barred from professional activity after the establishment of the *Reichskulturkammer* (Reich Culture Chamber (RKK)) by Goebbels, Hitler's *Reichminister für Volksaufklärung und Propaganda* (Reich Minister for Public Enlightenment and Propaganda), who was made responsible for 'all duties relating to the spiritual influence of the nation, to the promoting of the state, culture and the economy'.[11] Goebbels and his deputy Walther Funk had acquired jurisdiction over

> the whole field of spiritual indoctrination of the nation...and enlightenment of the public at home and abroad.[12]

The *Gleichshaltung*, a thorough restructuring of the way the government would control the arts and media, was now under way. Even the SS had its own art section, the *Ahnenerbe* (Ancestral Heritage), which funded worldwide research looking for evidence of early and glorious Germanic cultures. Goebbels' ministry would become vast, with nine separate departments in the rambling headquarters in the Wilhelmstraße.

As a long-time supporter of Hitler, Rosenberg had expected to take control of cultural affairs in 1933 but was sorely disappointed to see Goebbels get the Propaganda Ministry. He also had to suffer seeing Göring retain control of the Prussian theatre, and watch as Bernhard Rust was made the Minister of Education. Robert Ley, meanwhile, became leader of the *Deutsche Musikerverband*, the largest professional musicians' union in Germany. It seemed as if Rosenberg was willing to accept all manner of humiliation from Hitler in order to keep whatever status he had managed to hang onto.

At a public meeting of the *Kampfbund für deutsche Kultur* in March 1933, Rosenberg described the cultural revolution that would open pathways to a new awareness, saying, 'all expressions of life spring from a specific blood...a specific race'.[13] Only days previously an exhibition of Oskar Schlemmer's paintings and sculptures in Stuttgart had been closed down after a mere twelve days. The press had called for the exhibits to be 'left on the junk heap where they could rot away unhindered'.[14] Days later, along with others, Schlemmer was denounced by faculty members of the *Vereinigte Statschulen* as 'destructive Jewish-Marxist elements'.[15] At the same time, in Erlangen, as a precursor to the 1937 *Entartete* exhibition, an exhibition was opened to demonstrate the extent of the 'cultural collapse' under Modernism. Thirty-two paintings by contemporary artists were exhibited alongside paintings by children and the mentally ill in the *Schreckskammern des Kunst* (Chamber of Horrors of Art), with notices showing how much had been paid for them and accusations they had been foisted on the museums they had been drawn from by unscrupulous Jewish art dealers.

Once Hitler was ensconced in power, one of his first speeches showed his clear intention to 'bestow once more upon the Volk a genuine German culture [evoking] deep reverence for the accomplishments of the past' which would be accomplished through a 'moral purging' of society. A stripping of modernist works from public museums was begun. At this stage, rather than a reflection of Nazi aesthetics, the confiscation of these works was more of a convenient way of appealing to the masses with an anti-elitist message meant to emphasise that the Nazis were on the side of the common man against the forces of oppression.

Hitler's twin obsessions were the preservation of German racial purity and a crusade against modernism in the arts. It was common for Hitler to make statements in general terms about cultural matters and leave his acolytes to fill in the details. This often created a dilemma since it usually required a certain amount of guesswork. There is some truth in the suggestion that this was a deliberate ploy on Hitler's part since he, himself, had no fixed ideas beyond the brief he had given, and allowed his battling underlings to thrash out the pros and cons. This led to administrative chaos and inconsistency for a while as infighting erupted between competing factions, resulting in variations in the implementation of policies depending upon which was in the ascendancy at the time.

Having got the ball rolling, Hitler would then wait to see what each of his advisers would come up with before picking and choosing those aspects of policy that fitted into his own aesthetic and then making decisions that would have the force of directive. Supporters of *Völkisch* art were quick to come together to press their case and take advantage of the new cultural climate, but it was the state itself, in the figure of Joseph Goebbels, that now led the fight against Modernism.[16]

Goebbels was extremely well educated and considered to have intellectual qualities. He had tried and failed, in his earlier days, to write a novel in which his protagonist eulogised van Gogh for his 'marvellous, spare characterisation'.[17] The paintings of the German-Danish Expressionist Emil Nolde, with their 'wonderful colours', were a particular favourite of his and so it was natural that when Albert Speer was commissioned to decorate Goebbels' flat, he borrowed a few of Nolde's pictures from the *Nationalgalerie*. Both he and Goebbels had hoped to impress Hitler when he visited, given that Nolde was known to be an ardent anti-Semite and a member of the Nazi Party, but when he saw the pictures, the Führer was not pleased. Neither Speer nor Goebbels were apparently aware that Hitler hated Nolde for his New Testament themes and what he called 'the violent distortions and colours in his work'.[18] Goebbels upbraided Speer for his poor judgement and told him that the pictures were 'simply impossible'.[19] It was abundantly clear from this point that Goebbels' Propaganda Ministry was going to have a hard time deciding exactly which artistic styles were to be acceptable in the new modern society of Hitler's imagination. It was not even a question of what did or did not fall into the category of Expressionism. What Goebbels, Speer or anyone else thought was irrelevant; Hitler's opinion was all that counted. Ironically it was Goebbels' early championing of Modernism that had persuaded Hitler he was the man to guide him through the modernist maze and find within it those elements of eternal values that fitted into his vision for the future, but it had got off to a bad start. If Goebbels was expecting much help, he would be disappointed. Both Rosenberg and Schultze-Naumburg had a poor opinion of him, as did many of the arch conservatives who had inveigled themselves into Hitler's inner circle. Goebbels was not yet ready to abandon modern art entirely, however. Right up until 1937 he had a Barlach statue prominently displayed in his office.

It was not only Goebbels and Speer who were confused. Max Sauerlandt, director of the Hamburg *Kunsthalle,* even tried to pass Expressionists off as exemplars of Nordic Germanic art. National Socialist students in Berlin praised Dr Ludwig Justi's modern collections at the *Nationalgalerie* but when Schultze-Naumburg showed Hitler photographs of some of the exhibits, the Führer angrily demanded that Justi be sacked and his avant-garde exhibition closed down for 'reorganisation'. Justi's successor, Alois Schardt, was immediately attacked by Rosenberg, Frick and Schultze-Naumburg. He tried to defend himself by saying that 'dynamic consciousness had been returned to Germany by the Romantics and Expressionists whose styles he linked to ancient Germanic folk forms'. If he thought that would get him of the hook he was soon disabused of that notion when he, too, was fired and fled to the US.[20] On 13 May 1933, the Prussian Academy of Arts asked for the resignations of ten of its members. While Dix, Kollwitz, Max Liebermann and Mies van der Rohe complied, Nolde refused, hoping that his Nazi credentials would protect him. Even after many of his works had been destroyed, Nolde continued to petition Goebbels for the return of the ones that survived.

Munich had a special place in Hitler's Germany, and it was here that a new *Haus der Deutschen Kunst* (House of German Art) would be built. Hitler hoped that this 'new temple in honour of the goddess of art' would turn Munich into the capital of German art.[21] King Ludwig I had begun the transformation of the city during the nineteenth century in a bid to rival Paris and Vienna. Drawing on inspiration from classical Greece and renaissance Italy, he championed an extensive building programme in the Ludwigstraße Boulevard and the Königplatz Square, encouraging the city to become an international artistic centre.

On 15 October 1933, the stone-laying ceremony took place for a new *Haus der Deutschen Kunst* building. Hitler's ambition was to endow the ceremony with a deeply symbolic meaning marking the beginning of a renaissance of authentically German art, free from Jewish interference and influences. After a parade of SA and SS paramilitary units had marched past the location, Hitler delivered a speech which included a warning that the artistic community would have only four years to adjust to the new cultural policies of the regime. He saw art as playing an important role in nation building and was assiduous in his efforts to equate what he saw as true German art with national identity. The crux of his message was that he seemed to reject the idea that the past was any guide to the future and suggested that a whole new aesthetic approach was required, but did not give any clues as to what that might be like except to say that 'We must not permit incompetents and charlatans [to] enlist under the banner of the new state'.[22] The drama of the occasion was somewhat diminished when Hitler's ceremonial hammer broke as he struck the cornerstone.

This unfortunate incident was followed by another that did not quite strike the intended note. A parade had been organised to round off the ceremony, but it proved to be something of an anti-climax. Parades were a common spectacle and had been widely used by the Nazis to take their message to a wider audience, but the one planned to follow the stone-laying ceremony was the first of a new kind and proved to be a step too far for its organisers. The parade, entitled *Glanzeiten Deutscher Kultur* (Glory Ages of German Culture), had been intended to celebrate a cultural continuity between previous German 'golden ages' and the new era of national rebirth under the Nazis. The men who had been chosen to organise the parade had enviable credentials. Overall control was in the hands of the local Nazi Party chief Adolph Wagner, with Karl Wenzl in charge of propaganda. The artistic director, Josef Wackerle, was a professor at Munich's Academy of Visual Arts. Overall organisation was in the hands of Professor Conrad Hommel, while two other professors Leo Paersetti and Julius Hess designed the costumes. Yet another professor, Georg Buchner, decorated the route with banners and flags. Despite this fine array of academic prowess, the parade itself lacked coherence and the symbolism employed was simply too complex or obscure to be appreciated or even comprehended by the people lining the route.

The concept was for the fifteen main groupings of costumed people and floats to represent a different theme or epoch of German history, but whether by intention or mismanagement, there was no clear chronological sequence which completely failed to convey the narrative of a logical progression towards Nazi rule. It started off well enough with a float depicting the *Hoheitsadler*, a Romanesque eagle designed by Hitler himself to represent the Nazi Party and the state, a symbol of the German spirit.

Then came floats celebrating Greek art, portrayed as a period of German art history, which featured the Ancient Greek goddess Pallas

Athena, associated with wisdom, warfare and handicraft. Athena was featured not only on the floats but also, to emphasise the connection between Germany and Greece, in the form of a giant medallion suspended between two pylons that marked the beginning of the parade route on the Ludwigstraße. A profile of Athena with a torch, set against a background of columns, would become the official symbol of all future *Tage der deutschen Kunst* (Days of German Art) parades. Her presence clearly sent a message to the crowds that the Greeks were also German and that their art belonged to the Nordic race. Floats featured gothic and rococo art, but the spectacle fell apart at the mid-point, after which the floats became jumbled and confused with sagas and fairy tales, usually associated with the medieval coming almost at the end along with more floats about Ancient Greece that were clearly out of place. All in all, it was a celebration of the kind of stiff, stylised solemn art, a 'vaguely kitschy imitation of culture' that Hitler, with his petit bourgeois tendencies, freely associated with high art.[23]

It is notable that while Hitler's speech was widely covered and lavishly praised in the press, little was written about the parade. The US academic Joshua Hagen wrote

> The 1933 parade reflected a party and leadership that remained unsure how to exercise power, how to articulate their cultural policies, and even what those policies were.[24]

They would get another chance four years later when the *Haus der Deutschen Kunst* was opened and a bigger, better parade was planned.

At the Nuremberg rally in 1933, Hitler had also failed to give moral support to the KfdK and Rosenberg's New Expressionist movement, which was central to Rosenberg's crusade against the avant-garde, but Hitler's Munich speech, his first public pronouncement on art since the Nazis had taken over the government, did little to clarify his views. It was Goebbels' job to define that goal. To achieve this, art had to be comprehensible to the people and have enduring appeal with its positive message celebrating the good, the beautiful and the healthy. Germany, which for more than a decade had been a cultural powerhouse with artists of international reputation, was now a country that left people like Barlach feeling as if they were 'sitting on a volcano'.[25] Despite its *Völkisch* aesthetic that should have given it a head start, with little political nous, the KfdK was no match for Goebbels' RKK that creamed off many of its most competent activists as well as its best ideas. It was unfortunate for them that, at the time, Hitler was waging an internal struggle against reactionary elements in the Nazi Party, and it was convenient for him to downplay any suggestion that reactionary *Völkisch* art was central to the programme of cultural rebirth.

Goebbels had initially welcomed a 'new modernity…in art and intellectual matters'.[26] He admired Expressionist artists such as Barlach and Nolde, whose chaotic Gothic spirit he equated with the restless spirit of Nazi youth and in them saw something of the true German soul, but he was firmly opposed in this by Alfred Rosenberg, in his role as guardian of German culture, who saw the *Völkisch* tradition as the pinnacle of intellectual and ideological achievement in art. Rosenberg described modern paintings as 'monstrosities'[27] and called Nolde's paintings 'negroid, bereft of piety, raw and without true inner power of form'.[28] He had founded the militant *Kampfbund für deutsche Kultur* in 1928, the forerunner of Goebbel's Ministry for Enlightenment and Propaganda, to proclaim the superiority of German culture, even though his own artistic output was limited to 'tame and tedious little landscape paintings'.[29]

Adolf Ziegler was another, like Goebbels, who had the unenviable task of trying to interpret the mood of a nation in transition. Ziegler was a technically gifted, but mediocre, painter, popular with the Nazis, whose prim, Neoclassical work relied heavily on realistic interpretation of pure Aryan types. In 1925, he had been chosen by Hitler to paint his niece Geli Raubal and, in 1933, was made Professor at the Munich Academy of Fine Arts, which essentially elevated him to the position of official painter of the Third Reich. As head of the *Reichskammer der Bildenden Künste*, Hitler had instructed him to make a collection of artworks ready to adorn the walls and chambers of the enormous *Haus der Deutschen Kunst* when it was completed. Ziegler had been given no clear guidelines as to what was acceptable but assumed that it should include a wide range of styles, including contemporary works, and so he invited artists from across the country to submit works in an open competition. He eventually received 15,000 entries from which, still without clear guidelines, he chose 1,000 that would go on display at the grand opening scheduled for 1937.

His dilemma would not be helped by the wave of purges that the *Kampfbund für deutsche Kultur* had launched against those museums with collections of modern art. Various organisations took it upon themselves to join the moral crusade against subversive art which they defined in their own individual ways according to what they thought might impress their Führer. Paul Klee was hounded out of the Düsseldorf Academy and fled to Switzerland. Otto Dix was ousted from the Dresden Academy and Max Beckmann from the one at

Frankfurt. Accused of being Jewish, Oskar Schlemmer was removed from the *Vereinigte Staatsschulen für freie und angewandte Kunst* (United State School for Fine and Applied Art) in Berlin.

At the Mannheim *Kunsthalle* in 1934, Gustav Hartlaub had put on his *New Objectivity* exhibition and two years later, *Paths and Directions of Abstract Painting in Europe*. The museum had probably become the major centre in Germany for the acquisition of Expressionist and modern art. This brought the wrath of the Nazi propaganda newspaper *Hakenkreuzbanner* down upon his head. There were public protests against his purchase of Marc Chagall's *Rabbiner* (Rabbi). Too much of the collection was not 'genuine German art' wrote Otto Gebele von Waldstein. Hartlaub was the first of many museum directors to be unceremoniously removed and Gebele, who took his place, wasted no time in rearranging many of the works into what he called *Kulturbolschewistsche Bilder* (Bolshevik art), thus creating the first art exhibition of works specifically chosen because they were thought to have no artistic value. Not everyone saw things that way, however. The *Nationalsozialistischer Deutscher Studentenbund* (National Socialist Student's Association) put on an exhibition in Berlin which included works by Barlach and Nolde and was intended to show that Expressionism was a true German art form. For three days it welcomed large crowds but on the fourth, Frick shut it down and student leaders were expelled from the union. It would become notoriously difficult to define was Nazi art actually was, but it was getting easier to work out what it was not.

Other students were less tolerant of dissent. On 10 May 1933, as an expression of what the *Nationalsozialistischer Deutscher Studentenbund* and the *Deutsche Studentenschaft* (German Student Union) called 'the rage of the people', thousands of books were burned. Book burning has a long and undistinguished history. The Chinese did it in 221 BCE and the Christian Church had destroyed heretical writing too, but more recently, students under the guidance of Theodor Körner, who would become a Nazi folk hero, burned books at the Wartburg Festival in October 1817.[30] Already Nazis in the Reichstag had tried to introduce a law making 'cultural treachery' a crime and then in August 1932, the *Völkischer Beobachter* had printed a list of what it called 'decadent writers' who would be silenced as soon as the Nazis came to power. Goebbels and Rosenberg had been instrumental in drawing up a list of books to be burned, which was distributed to all universities, although it should be noted that not all universities took part. Public and university libraries were raided for books on the blacklist and private individuals were encouraged to purge their collections of Sigmund

Freud, Karl Marx, Heinrich Mann, Carl von Ossietzky and Erich Maria Remarque, amongst others, to add to the pyre.

Detailed plans were printed in all national newspapers to coordinate the action of *Säuberungsaktion* (act of purification). Careful attention, the note said, was to be given to the selection of speakers at the burning events. Lawyers were especially favoured choices. Wearing their academic robes, university faculty members such as Professor Ernst Bertram in Cologne, Professor Hans Naumann in Bonn, and Rector Leo von Zumbusch in Munich gave their blessing. Energised by their book-burning, right-wing students now became more involved politically and protested at the appointment of 'Jewish-Marxist' lecturers in their universities.

At around this time, debate amongst psychiatrists, under pressure from the Nazi regime, had begun to focus on the extent to which the German state could continue to bear the financial 'burden' of the mentally ill. Sterilisation, which was legal in the US was touted as one measure, but even more drastic ones were discussed. Hitler was keen to 'cleanse' society of these unwanted members but, having made his views clear, typically left it to others to realise his ambition. It fell to the ever-reliable Frick, who threw himself into the task with energy. He appointed Schultze-Naumburg to his special committee of 'experts' that also included SS leader Heinrich Himmler. Frick was unambiguous when he called the 'hopelessly genetically diseased' a drain on the economy. The first piece of legislation was the 'Law for the prevention of Genetically Diseased Offspring' which included provision for forced sterilisation. When the law was passed on 1 January 1934, there were almost 400,000 referrals from the medical profession.

It would take the intervention of Hitler to bring Goebbels and Rosenberg into line in a way that favoured neither man, although he was latterly known to have had quite a low opinion of Rosenberg. In a speech at the Nazi Party rally in September 1934, Hitler attacked both modernist 'saboteurs of art' and 'backward-looking' Teutonic factions living in some 'laughable Germanic dream world' who did not have 'the slightest idea of what the national Socialist revolution was all about'.[31]

There is a strong argument that says Hitler made no specific recommendations and appeared confused about modern art because he lacked the intellectual and empathetic sensibilities to make a judgement about something that was essentially subjective. He had no sense of what another person's emotional state might be and lacked the imagination to see the world through any eyes but his own. He warned of the dangers of modern art but cautioned against excessive nostalgia, allowing for his own particular perspective, which was essentially racially motivated, to become the accepted face of Nazi art. Goebbels was quick to latch on to the change of mood and abandoned his earlier enthusiasm for Modernism. Rosenberg had used his editorship of the *Völkischer Beobachter* to undermine Goebbels' RKK at every opportunity, but had been replaced by Wilhelm Weiss, who was much less inclined to risk upsetting Goebbels. Rosenberg was effectively demoted when the *Kampfbund für deutsche Kultur* was merged with Robert Ley's *Kraft durch Freude* (Strength through Joy) movement to form the *Nationalsozialistischen Kulturgemeinde* (National Socialist Culture Community). He received a fancy title, Commissioner for the Entire Intellectual and Ideological Training and Education of the Party, but was still lower in the pecking order than Goebbels who had a cabinet ministry with vastly superior resources. A deeply frustrated Rosenberg, who considered himself to be the true intellectual of the culture wars, retaliated by uncovering examples of decadence throughout the Reich and bringing them to the attention of Hitler with the sole purpose of embarrassing Goebbels.

After Justi's departure from the *Nationalgalerie*, Eberhard Hanfstängl, a cousin of Hitler's favourite Ernst Hanfstängl, took over the curatorship. He was no champion of Modernism but continued to exhibit and acquire contemporary works as well as others by Caspar David Friedrich, who was known to be a particular favourite of Hitler. Preoccupied with architectural projects that had been the real reason for his trip to central Berlin, Hitler only winced when he saw the modernist exhibits, but a year later, when he visited the Images of Decadent Art exhibition in Dresden, he was to associate it with Hanfstaengl's display and railed against both, calling exhibits 'dirt for dirt's sake' painted by 'facile daubers of paint' in a 'contemptible' style, which was an insult to the masters of the past.[32]

As soon as the 1936 Summer Olympic Games were over, Goebbels, now settling into his role as propaganda czar, set about closing down access to the contemporary art displays in the *Nationalgalerie* in Berlin, the *Museum Folkwang* in Essen and the *Kunshalle* in Hamburg. The period of relative liberalism in the arts was at an end now that foreign athletes and visitors had left. This would be made manifest by the overt Nazi style of displays in the German pavilion at the Paris International Exposition the following year. The cultural war that was gaining momentum appealed to Hitler as a useful way of rousing the people's hostility towards Jews and Bolsheviks. Most people had little or no love for modern art, which to them was either incomprehensible, idiotic or childlike, and it was not difficult to mobilise this antipathy into a political reaction against it. In early 1937, Goebbels had authorised the *Deutscher Kunstbericht* (German art report), which included a five-point manifesto written by German artists who felt they had been marginalised and undervalued by the modern art movement. They issued a document in which they demanded all works of a cosmopolitan or Bolshevist nature should be removed from German museums and collections and, after being exhibited to the public, burned, and any museum director who 'wasted' public money buying 'un-German' art should be fired. Goebbels knew exactly how to make use of this, but the timing was not yet right. Many traditional artists, encouraged by Goebbels, now began pouring out paintings in the 'blood and soil' aesthetic, making idealised portraits of Nazi officials.

Also in 1937, Albert Speer and Richard Klein, an artist of high standing with the Nazis, founded an official national magazine devoted to contemporary art. To adorn the cover, Klein created a new symbol of Nazi art. It comprised a burning torch (Promethean creativity), the helmeted head of Athena (continuity of Aryan culture) and the imperial eagle bearing a swastika wrapped in an oak wreath (the anti-Semitic state). This was so enthusiastically received that Klein went on to design other symbols in a similar vein to propagandise Nazism among the German workers.

For artists who wanted to make a living for themselves in Germany, the message was clear and exhibiting in what became an annual event was the only way to sell their works. It became customary for public buildings and government offices to be decorated only by works that had been purchased at these exhibitions. Modernism was out. The history of German art was being re-written as a victory for mediocre genre painting over the avant-garde. After Hitler's intervention during the selection process, all the artworks now conveyed the necessary characteristics of happy family life, motherhood, heroism and bucolic splendour with realistic portrayal of people. One foreign observer would scathingly remark that the exhibition appealed to all feelings except the aesthetic. It seems to have been beyond Ziegler to make a clear distinction as far as sculpture was concerned, however. Some sculptors such as Rudolf Belling had works exhibited in both the approved and degenerate art exhibitions. Georg Kolbe and Gerhard Marcks, whose earlier work had been confiscated from museums as unacceptable, now had others which were approved.

Ever since the Nazis had come to power in January 1933, their habit of 'thinking with blood' had sealed the fate of the entire modern movement in Germany.[33] Its supposed association with the left-wing revolutions of 1918–1919 and the fact that it was closely linked with

Jews as patrons was enough to condemn it. Modernism was also very much an intellectual movement from which the vast majority of the population felt alienated, and to a great extent insulted, which made it an easy target. Over the following few years, artists whose work had been condemned had been forced to find other ways to earn a living without drawing attention to themselves. Willi Baumeister continued to work 'in utter isolation'. Not even his children were allowed to know. Schlemmer took a job with a firm that specialised in painting commercial murals in Stuttgart, which eventually saw him painting camouflage on factories and military buildings. Some, like Klee, Grosz and Kandinsky, left the country.

Chapter 5

THE GOOD THE BAD AND THE UGLY

> 'When, four years ago, the ceremonial cornerstone laying for this building took place, we were all aware that it was imperative to lay not only the cornerstone for a new building, but also the foundation for a new and genuinely German art.'
>
> Adolf Hitler at the opening of the *Große Deutsche Kunstausstellung*, 18 July 1937

On 18 July 2017, an exhibition was put on at the *Haus der Deutschen Kunst* in Munich to mark the eightieth anniversary of one of the most shameful acts of art censorship in modern history, when works branded as 'undesirable' by the Nazi state were removed from the country's museums and galleries. During the purge, some 21,000 objects were systematically taken from both public and private collections to be burned or sold abroad, but not before the German people would be educated about the difference between 'great' and 'degenerate' art and encouraged to appreciate why the purge was essential to purify German culture.

This had required two simultaneous exhibitions, both held in Munich, the *Große Deutsche Kunstausstellung* (Great German Art Exhibition), which opened on 18 July 1937 in the *Haus der Deutschen Kunst*, and the *Ausstellung Entartete Kunst* (Degenerate Art Exhibition) a few metres away in the *Deutsches Archäologisches Institut* (Institute of Archaeology) at the Hofgarten a day later. The *Haus der Deutschen Kunst* was a monumental building of imposing height with the cold symmetry of a long row of columns stretching down the street. With customary wit and irreverence, the Bavarians called it the *Bratwurstelgalerie* because the columns resembled a long row of sausages hanging in a butcher's shop. While the interior layout of the building was typically sterile with its marble columns, potted plants and busts of Hitler, it did have an air of semi-ecclesiastical grandeur with spectacular lighting that suppressed conversation to a whisper.[1] The building had been commissioned to herald a new Nazi aesthetic, but the lack of clear direction from Hitler about exactly what was and what was not considered to be 'Nazi art' resulted in a building with a flat roof and plain, functional construction free of ornament; characteristics of *Bauhaus* design that Hitler had so derided.

The *Große Deutsche Kunstausstellung* had on display works in the classical style, often presenting idealised pastoral scenes, while the *Ausstellung Entartete Kunst* contained 650–700 works that were considered to be incompatible with Nazi ideology or propaganda, many of which were made by Jewish artists and were claimed to be offensive to women, soldiers and farmers, and insulting toward religion (see Appendix 1 for artists and art movements in the exhibition). 'Degenerate' artworks were placed alongside drawings by mentally disabled people and photographs of physically handicapped individuals, a ploy designed to highlight their 'diseased', 'Jewish-Bolshevist' and 'inferior' character with its implicit warning of cultural decline. It is hard to know what the Nazis made of the fact that, according to newspapers at the time, five times as many people visited *Entartete Kunst* as saw the *Große Deutsche Kunstausstellung*.

At that time, the art critic, Bruno E. Werner, in the *Deutsche Allgemeine Zeitung* commented that most of the painting showed a very close relation to those that had been produced by the Munich school forty years earlier.[2] The subject matter was farmers, farmers' wives, woodcutters, shepherds and interiors lovingly depicting many charming facets of country life. The large number of landscapes in the old traditions were accompanied by portraits of government and party leaders. Every painting projected either spiritual elevation or challenging heroism. All gave the impression of an intact life from which the stresses and problems of modern existence were entirely absent, and there were no pictures showing urban or industrial life at all.

In one picture, Hitler was portrayed as a mounted knight clad in silver armour and carrying a fluttering flag. Both male and female nudes were on display but in ways that celebrated delight in the healthy human body. The *Berliner Illustriere Zeitung* thought Adolf Wissel's *Peasant Group* was redolent with intimate secrets of the German countenance and saw Adolf Ziegler's *Terpsichore* as grasping modern painting with 'the purity of classical antiquity in its conception of the human body', while Elk Eber's *The Last Hand-Grenade* gave sublime expression to his vision of the suffering of war.[3] The *Frankfurter Zeitung* expressed what had been obvious to German artists for a number of years when it said,

> It may well be that many an artist will no longer have the courage to create anything new after the opening of the House of German Art at Munich.[4]

The satirical periodical *Simplicissimus* would later bemoan the fact that people would no longer have to worry about deciding what was good or bad in art: they would be told in no uncertain terms.

In direct contrast to what had been written about the *Große Deutsche Kunstausstellung* at the opening of the *Entartete Kunst,* its organiser Adolf Ziegler said:

> Our patience with all those who have not been able to fall in line with National Socialist reconstructions during the last four years is at an end…The people trust, as in all things, the judgment of one man, our Führer. He knows which way German art must go in order to fulfil its task as the expression of German character...What you are seeing here are the crippled products of madness, impertinence, and lack of talent... I would need several freight trains clear our galleries of this rubbish... This will happen soon.[5]

The *Entartete* exhibition travelled to a dozen major cities across Germany and was seen by an estimated 3 million people. In a clear attempt to inflame public opinion against Modernism, at each venue artworks were hung chaotically and accompanied by text deriding them. Modern art was depicted as a movement of aesthetic violence perpetrated by Jews against the German people, even though very few of the artists who made significant contributions to German art at the time were Jewish. The Munich exhibitions were not the only ones that year. Goebbels went on to organise his own *Große antibolschewistiche Ausstellung* (Great anti-Bolshevist Exhibition) in Nuremberg in September 1937, before taking it to several other cities. Then there was the NSDAP-sponsored exhibition *Der ewige Jude* (The Eternal Jew), which toured the country over Christmas and the New Year.

The terms Classicism and Neoclassicism will be use frequently in the context of Nazi aesthetics, so it is worth defining them before we go any further. Classicism refers to art produced at the peak period of classical civilisations and derives its popularity from contemporaneous discoveries of Greek and Roman archaeological sites. Art of antiquity is understood to have been a search for artistic perfection, whereas Neoclassicism is more an appreciation of and fascination with antiquity within a contemporary context. It is art inspired by antiquity and draws its inspiration from classical forms and motifs but has greater relevance to modern sensibilities and is closely linked with modern philosophical concepts. It rejects ostentation and concentrates on symmetry, harmony in composition, and focus on proportion.

The National Socialists based their standards for art on the idealised Neoclassical figures and sentimental landscapes that had been so popular in the nineteenth century, and which Hitler personally admired as racially pure. It was art that could be easily understood, but there was a deeper purpose to this aesthetic. It aimed to bring the nation together under a moral code that everyone should adhere to in which there must be beauty without sensuality. Anything new was suspect and the public was guided towards accepting only simple representations of people and landscapes in a traditional style. This was the art that would save the nation from the modernist desecrations that were the work of a decadent Weimar age before the Nazis came to power. Respectability, chastity, family life and harmony were to be the new moral values of the age, alongside a retelling of history as a battle to uphold unchanging traditions. Together the old and new would bind the nation together in its quest for order in an ever-more challenging world. In essence, the message the Nazis were giving out was: 'live in the past and leave us to take care of the future'.

The opening of the *Große Deutsche Kunstausstellung* was to be an occasion for Hitler to make one of his most important statements about German culture. Eager to ensure that all plans were being followed, he visited Munich with Goebbels on a swelteringly hot day in early June 1937. The exhibition was not Hitler's only project in his favourite city. There were many architectural schemes he had personally planned with Paul Ludwig Troost that were in the process of realisation, but the building at the southern end of Munich's Englisher Garten that would house the exhibition was of prime interest. Ziegler awaited the visit with trepidation. The artworks he had selected from the many he had been presented with were ready for inspection, but choices had been made with little understanding of what Hitler actually considered to be great German art and debate had raged since the first stone had been laid over what exactly would be put on show to celebrate Nazi culture. Sculptures were a particular problem for him given that here the artist's motives were much more difficult to work out. As it turned out, works of sculpture by the same artist featured in both the 'good' and 'bad' exhibitions. Hitler's ploy of facing Rosenberg and Schultze-Naumburg against Goebbels with Ziegler in between was typical of his style of management. It had not been difficult for Ziegler to weed out artworks that were obviously not going to be acceptable, but that was only half the battle. There were many that had been argued over during the selection process and still defied simplistic categorisation. It was impossible to know just how Hitler would react when he saw them. Goebbels feared the worst and wrote in his diary that the painting side of the exhibition was going to be 'a real catastrophe', but it is hard to see how Ziegler could have done better. Goebbels had outlawed artistic criticism on the grounds that the people should be allowed to make up their own minds whether a particular piece of art was good or not. Of course, this was completely cynical since it was the primary purpose of the exhibition to do that very thing for them.

When Hitler entered the building, artworks selected for inclusion were marked while a secondary display of possible candidates were piled up in the centre of each room. His reaction was swift and merciless. He flared into a rant at Ziegler, asking how he could allow people to think that so many of the works were expressions of Hitler's own aesthetic. He stalked through the rooms jabbing his finger at anything that offended him and authorised the inclusion of others that Ziegler had rejected. There was no way Ziegler could survive such a humiliation and he was consequently replaced by Heinrich Hoffmann, who had previously acted as Hitler's personal art dealer and knew perfectly well that his patron was not attracted to paintings where 'you can't tell whether they're upside down or inside out'.[6] Leaving the city the next day, Hitler considered postponing the whole event for a year while a new set of exhibits was chosen, but his doubts were assuaged early in July when he again went to Munich to see how Hoffmann was getting on. He was not disappointed. The exhibition had been stripped of all works that Hitler had found confusing or ugly and consisted now of only those that glorified the Nazi vision, including several of Hitler in heroic pose. 'The Führer is very happy', Goebbels wrote in his diary this time.

When Goebbels introduced Hitler to a crowd of 30,000 people at the opening of the *Große Deutsche Kunstausstellung* in 1937, he eulogised him as the 'master builder' who combined statesmanship with artistic skill.[7] The Bavarian Minister of the Interior followed up by calling Hitler 'the greatest of living artists'. When Hitler spoke, he announced that he would 'wage a merciless war against the last remaining elements of cultural disintegration.' He spoke of how the exhibition of artistic creativity which, of itself,

> Does not create a new age [rather] it is the general life of peoples which fashions itself anew, and therefore often seeks to express itself anew, and goes in search for new forms of expression.

It is not the artist or the intellectuals who shapes and leads the nation, he said, it is the party that has ended the era of narcissistic self-indulgent individualism in art in which the nation had become cut off from the spiritual life of the community. A new artistic age was dawning, promising social and political regeneration.[8]

A clear distinction was made between 'clean and healthy art' on display at the *Große Deutsche Kunstausstellung* and the 'filthy, subversive and abominable' works across the road at the *Ausstellung Entartete Kunst*. During his ninety-minute tirade, Hitler railed against 'degenerate half-wits who see blue fields, a green sky, and sulphurous clouds'. What the nation needed, he said, was artists who sought out

> the true and genuine quality of the national being and a sincere and upright expression of the inwardly-divined law of life.[9]

As Hitler warmed to his theme, Paul Ortwin Rave, curator of the Berlin *Nationalgalerie*, described him as

> drumming with his fists [and] foaming with rage, dribbling from his mouth so that even his entourage stared at him in horror.[10]

Ominously, he went on to warn that

> all those mutually supporting and thereby sustaining cliques of chatterers, dilletantes and art forgers will be picked up and liquidated.[11]

This exhibition of German art was expected to become an annual event celebrated with concerts, banquets and parades under the banner of *Zweitausend Jähre Deutsche Kultur* (Two Thousand Years of German Culture). The four years since the *Glanzeiten Deutscher Kultur* parade had given Adolph Wagner plenty of time to learn from his mistakes and re-evaluate the way he promoted the cultural programme to the public. This time it was described in the event programme as a chance to

> experience German history, experience its greatness and tremendous past, and see how proudly the German future is being built. [The parade] is a glowing tribute to the historical achievements of our Volk [and a] journey into the great future of eternal Germany.

The *Völkische Beobachter* called it 'a grand demonstration of German culture'.[12]

Every facet of the 1937 parade was on a grander scale and organised in a more coherent presentation of Nazi doctrines. It stretched for nearly 4 kilometres and took two hours to pass. While overt Nazi content was minimal in the 1933 parade, this one left no doubt about what was on show. Leading the way were riders carrying flags and banners of the Nazi Party. There were floats presenting tableaux from periods of Germanic history all the way back to the Vikings, emphasising German accomplishments through the ages. Germanic gods and goddesses with the eagle Hresvelda were accompanied by hundreds of men and women dressed in different period costumes. Next came the floats and costumed followers reflecting Nazi ideological doctrine of racial purity and military might. Two thirds of all participants depicted warriors. Bringing up the rear were floats celebrating the achievements of the previous four years of Nazi rule, culminating in a large eagle and models of recent monumental buildings celebrating Nazi architecture. Ironically, given the circumstances, there was next to no inclusion of floats celebrating German art, which might have reflected the fact the organisers still had no clear guidance from above as to what would be acceptable to Hitler. The Prinzregentenstraße was lined with 160 pylons, each nearly 30 metres high, depicting the eagle and swastika symbol. All the way from the railway station to the city centre, flags were flown at 20-metre intervals on flagpoles nearly 25 metres high.

The spectacle attracted hundreds of thousands of people. It was a deliberate attempt to draw observers in and feel part of the spectacle, but the narrow streets were ill-suited to generating that kind of mass reaction since, unlike the Nuremberg parade grounds, it was not possible for sufficient numbers to be massed together in any one place where the atmosphere could be electrified. However, the press responded with predictable enthusiasm. The *Völkischer Beobachter* newspaper reported that, 'Today we sat as spectators in the theatre of our own time and saw greatness'.[13] The *Berliner Boersen-Zeitung und Boersen-Courier* called the exhibition 'a new day for German art' and the *Deutsche Allgemeine Zeitung* hailed 'a liberation of German art from the tyranny of sadism'.[14]

Peter Guenther was 17 years old when he visited the *Große Deutsche Kunstausstellung* just a few days after it had been opened in Munich. His three-day visit was to have a profound effect upon him, and he later wrote about it. He had grown up with a keen interest in both traditional and modern art, and was fairly well qualified to make judgements about what he saw on that day. Before seeing the exhibition, he had read a transcript of Hitler's speech in the newspapers, which had confused him because there was nothing in it that gave him any real indication of what the official opinion of modern art was and how he was expected to distinguish it from that which was unacceptable to the regime.

The entrance hall he found uninteresting, adorned as it was with all the usual Nazi regalia, but the quiet church-like atmosphere had surprised him. His first impression was how bland the Breker and Thorak sculptures were. Despite their gigantist style that tried to capture the Greek aesthetic, they left Guenther with a negative impression and seemed to him to lack the grandeur and balance that were the hallmark of the Greeks. They held no appeal for him compared to much smaller unpretentious works.

Many of the paintings struck Guenther as being almost indistinguishable from photographs. He was surprised by the extent to which these were admired for their realism. One of Hitler and Paul von Hindenburg was reputed to have taken three years to complete. He was aware of none questioning why so much effort should go into such a work when it differed so little from a photographic image that could have been produced in a considerably shorter time. When it came to pastoral scenes, Guenther, who was familiar with country life, was quite unimpressed with paintings by artists such as Julius Paul Junghanns and Fritz Mackensen that depicted farming families as living in an heroic paradise, knowing just how far from the reality of farming life that was. The whole exhibition was a great disappointment to the young Guenther.[15]

When Hitler had raged at the preview of the *Große Deutsche Kunstausstellung* in early June, Goebbels saw an opportunity to make his mark while the Führer's anger was still warm. He turned to the already tried and tested idea of holding an exhibition in Berlin of degenerate art simultaneously with the Munich exhibition. He manoeuvred Hitler into agreement by wisely leaving the door open for him to contribute his own suggestion and allowed him to claim the idea for himself. The embellishment added by Hitler was little more than a decision to stage the exhibition not in Berlin but Munich, where this Jewish-Bolshevik degenerate art, which was a threat to the very morals of the people, could be viewed alongside great uplifting and life-affirming German art. Afterwards, Goebbels, in self-congratulatory mood, recorded in his diary that the Führer had shown 'great confidence' in him. It was a clear attempt by Goebbels to upstage Rosenberg.[16]

It is hard to say if it was a punishment or a chance for Ziegler to redeem himself, but he was given authority to travel around the country and identified works for this exhibition according to their propensity to 'insult German feeling, or destroy or confuse natural form, or simply reveal an absense [*sic*] of adequate manual and artistic skill'.[17] To help him, Ziegler had Count Klaus von Baudissin, who was ever eager to please the Nazis, the venomous art critic Wolfgang Willrich, Hans Schweitzer, Robert Scholz and Walter Hansen to help him decide what fitted into Hitler's definition of *Verfallskunst* (decay art). They took as their guiding principle anything that struck them as works embodying 'weakness of character', 'mental disease' and 'racial impurity'. Essentially, just to be on the safe side, anything painted after 1910 that looked remotely like Expressionism or Dadaism was suspect and removed. German artists such as Kirchner, Pechstein and Beckmann were singled out, but foreign painters such as Picasso, Henri Matisse, Edvard Munch and Marc Chagall did not escape the cull. It would be a hectic two weeks as Goebbels had asked that for each selected artwork there should be accompanying documentation showing how much had been paid for it and who had authorised the purchase. They visited all major museums in the country and had 700 works shipped to Munich, where they were hastily arranged in the gloomy atmosphere of the *Deutsches Archäologisches Institut*. At the same time they had a further 16,000 works illegally sent to Berlin and stored in a warehouse in Köpernickerstraße. They were later removed to *Schloss Schönhausen,* where Goebbels selected those that could be sold abroad to raise foreign currency for the government. Owing to the lack of preparation time, the exhibition had been arranged in a chaotic assemblage of works: some were crowded together, others not hung but just propped up against a wall. Some paintings without frames were tacked to the walls and packed tightly together. Where artists names were given they were often incorrectly ascribed. At intervals in all the rooms were notices saying *Bezahlt von den Steuergroschen des arbeitenden deutschen Volkes* (paid for by the taxes of the German working people).

While respectability was the watchword of 'normal' art, the enemies of respectability were those creatures of instinct, unable to control their passions, who created and traded in degenerate art. It was not a new idea. Indeed, it had been around in some guise since the French Revolution, when governments saddled their enemies with accusations of immorality and sexual perversion capable of all manner of extreme acts. Avant-garde artists, in particular, were charged with acting against public morality by creating a chamber of horrors in the name of art. For a nation that was being urged to ossify into a permanent state of passivity and calm, the modern world of speed, nervousness, immorality and crime, especially in the cities, was a threat to the very foundations of the state. For the propagandist Johann von Leers, modern art was all a 'Jewish conspiracy' designed to undermine society and contaminate the people's brains with frenzy and lust. There were whole sections of society, von Leers said, who had become 'infected' with these perversions. Specifically, it was the mentally ill, Jews, homosexuals and habitual criminals who had become unbalanced by a sort of nervousness that the Nazis now equated with serious illness. All who were deemed to have departed from the norm were 'degenerate' and could be identified by physical deformity, feebleness and exhaustion. Such people posed a threat to others.

The term 'degenerate' had been used since the 1890s to denigrate artists who had apparently lost or never had the ability to observe correctly and could only produce work that was a reflection of their tortured minds. Degenerates were associated with fear and ugliness. In his contribution to the written guide for the *Ausstellung Entartete Kunst*, Hitler had asked, 'What do these people create? Misshapen cripples and cretins, women who can arouse only revulsion.' [18] It was as if the Nazis were now promoting themselves as a new moral arbiter to take the place of Protestantism that held sway over so many in the countryside.

One of the most difficult issues addressed by the new moralists was the question of nudity. The Nazi's love of Classical Greek and Roman art meant that artists, especially sculptors, were required to depict the ideal male figure naked, and the naked virile male became a prominent Nazi image. Greek male statuary had long been seen as 'the paradigm of beaty for all time', but now the challenge was to create a finished work that was devoid of any hint of sensuality. The lithe and supple muscularity of Greek statues had embodied all the virtues of strength, harmony, dynamism and order that the Nazis so clearly wanted to claim for themselves. Nudity, however, was entirely against the Nazi moral code. The solution was to create the male form depicting all the required virtues but portrayed in an aggressive or martial posture in which the body became almost an abstract symbol of Aryan beauty. Artistic depictions of women in public places were less controversial, with strong, healthy but passive figures mostly fully clothed or at least with sufficient modesty to appear demure. In his private salons, however, even Hitler had paintings of full-bosomed nude women.

The whole purpose of the *Ausstellung Entartete Kunst* was to show all that was indecent and ugly in art, and by extension, society. It inevitably created a sense of unease in all who came to see it and, with all the negative propaganda that accompanied the artworks, had the effect of engendering a reliance on the state to protect respectable members of society and preserve moral values, especially of the young. It was opened on the day after the *Große Deutsche Kunstausstellung* had opened and introduced in a speech by Ziegler, who compared the appalling artworks on show with the true works of German art in the magnificent exhibition across the road. 'All around us,' he told the assembled dignitaries, 'you see the monstrous offspring of insanity, impudence, ineptitude, and sheer degeneracy. What this exhibition offers inspires horror and disgust in us all.'[19] To emphasise the worthlessness of the exhibition, the German people would not be insulted by being charged an entrance fee to see it and, to make clear just how offensive the artworks were, entry was prohibited to those under 20 years of age.

The German press was ever willing to add their weight to the scorn. The *Deutsche Allgemeine Zeitung* condemned 'Trainloads of dirt' that had been 'emptied into the museum's halls', while the *Münsterischer Anzeiger* said that 'basements have opened up to disgorge their refuse'. The *National-Zeitung* of Essen missed the point altogether by saying that 'Expressionist colours literally screamed at the visitors, instilling horror with the wackiness of the lines and with the decadence of expression', which, of course, was exactly what the artists had intended.[20]

Having two days of his holiday to spare after his visit to the *Große Deutsche Kunstausstellung,* Peter Guenther next day visited the *Ausstellung Entartete Kunst.* He saw what director of the *Nationalgalerie,* Paul Ortwin Rave, described as:

> Pictures huddled together in these long galleries with the worst possible lighting...The pictures were hung as though by idiots or children, just as they came, as close together as possible, obstructed by pieces of sculpture...and provided with provocative descriptions and obscene jibes.[21]

Guenther described his experiences. The first thing he saw at the top of the stairs at the entrance to the first room was the frightening *Kruzifixus* (Crucified Christ) by Ludwig Gies, which he felt lacked impact because of how it was displayed. A note condemned how it had hung as travesty of a First World War memorial in Lübeck Cathedral. Entering the first room, Guenther was overwhelmed by the brilliant colours of the Nolde paintings, including the nine panels of his *Leben Christi* (Life of Christ) in which he had attempted to break away from the sweetness and sentimentality of so much Christian art. People around him muttered 'blasphemy', which would have pleased Goebbels if he had heard it, but the young Guenther could not understand why Barlach's small, quiet, deeply moving bronze *Christus und Johannes* (Christ and John) was even in the exhibition since, to his mind, it could hardly have offended anybody.

The following rooms he found chaotic and claustrophobic, with paintings far too close together and interfering texts with quotations from speeches by Hitler and Goebbels. He heard visitors criticising a painting by Kandinsky as 'stupid' because it had no recognisable objects. Expressionist artists were ridiculed because they apparently could not draw properly. It was increasingly clear, said Guenther, that most people had come to see the exhibition with the intention of disliking everything in it. The atmosphere in the rooms made him afraid; he knew how dangerous it was to question official viewpoints.

On his second visit, Guenther found himself listening to a man who seemed well-spoken and educated arguing that abstract works were created by dangerous foreigners and Jews to undermine German culture. Many who were seeing modern art for the first time were simply not allowed to make up their own minds about it. However, Guenther was heartened to see some visitors lingering since the exhibition was less crowded and he even heard murmurs of appreciation, but he could not throw off the feeling of sadness that so many works he admired had been treated with such disdain.[22]

The *Ausstellung Entartete Kunst* proved to be such a great success that it had to be extended until November, and then other major cities competed openly to acquire it, with thirteen eventually succeeding. The popularity of the exhibition poses significant questions about motives for holding it in the first place, given that it included works that should be denigrated and not admired. It must be assumed that the authorities were convinced the message they were putting out with the exhibition was positive from their perspective. It was not so much the works themselves as the message that went with them. The quotations and comments accompanying many of the works equating Modernism with anti-social and revolutionary sentiments was an essential component of the battle to denounce intellectualism and reinforce the Nazi ethos of traditional values and pastoralism.

The *Entartete* included only a portion of the 'decadent' art that had been purged from the country's museums, and it soon became apparent that the instigators of this clean-up operation were representatives of certain art dealers who saw an opportunity to get their hands on modern masterpieces either cheaply or at no cost at all. Bettina Fetstel-Rohmedcr was one of those who had railed at modern art even before 1933, but she was only one writer among many who did so. There was still a sizeable group of experts willing to defend Expressionism, however, and even within the Nazi leadership there was no consensus over what was acceptable. Rosenberg was one of the most violent opponents of modern art, although he had few administrative powers in this capacity as opposed to Bernhard Rust, who was responsible for the Berlin *Akademie der Kunste* (Academy of Arts), the art colleges, and the museums. Nordic Expressionism was vigorously defended by a number of art historians, but the issue had been effectively decided by Hitler's speech to a conference on culture at the 1933 Nuremberg party congress. What he called representatives of decadence would not be allowed to become the standard bearers of the future. Policy hardened in 1935 when wholesale purges of 'degenerate art' were carried out, but many of these works were not destroyed and simply sold by the museums.

Count Klaus von Baudissin, director of the Museum Folkwang in Essen, began selling works of art from his museum in 1934 to institutions such as the Guggenheim Museum in New York, which acquired Kandinsky's *Improvisation 28* for 9,000 Reichsmarks.[23] Baudissin wrote that 'the high price attained could benefit a type of art for which we really care'. This resulted in an increased demand from art dealers, who saw an opportunity to acquire works of art held in German museums. Early in 1937 works by Dix, Marc, Mueller, Nolde and Max Pechstein were sold from the Dusseldorf collections to *Kunsthandlung Bammann*, while works by Dix, Oskar Kokoschka, Paula Modersohn-Becker and Nolde went to the art dealer Ferdinand Möller.

Works of art that had been impounded in two separate purges were shipped to Berlin, after which Rust, who had claimed formal jurisdiction over museums and art academies, called directors of German museums to a conference in Berlin on 2 August 1937, where he instructed them to record and store any other works in their collections by artists whose works had been exhibited at the *Entartete*. Elsewhere, museums, galleries and collections, whether owned by the Reich, the individual regions, or the local communities, were ordered to do likewise by Goebbels, who thought Rust was getting too much control. It was Goebbels who created the various confiscation commissions from this point onwards.

The confiscation commissions went far beyond the list of *Ententarte* artists so that between August and October of 1937, German museums were deprived of their entire holdings of modern art. Walter Hoffmann, general secretary of the *Reichskammer der bildenden Kunste*, was made responsible for their safekeeping and stored them in an empty grain warehouse on Kopenicker Straßsse, owned by the *Berliner Hafen und Lagerhaus*. Hitler visited the warehouse on 13 January 1938, after which Goebbels noted in his diary that Hitler despised every item he saw there.

Expropriation as a policy was now decided on, and the Law effecting the Confiscation of Products of Degenerate Art was passed on 31 May 1938. A *Verwertungskommission* (disposal commission) was then set up under Goebbels's nominal chairmanship. It consisted of Franz Hofmann, assistant department head at the *Propagandaministerium* (Reich Ministry of Public Enlightenment and Propaganda); Rolf Hetsch; the Berlin art dealer Karl Haberstock; Hitler's man Heinrich Hoffmann; a consultant from the *Reichskammer der bildenden Kunste* Carl Meder; the head of the department of fine arts at the Rosenberg bureau, Robert Scholz; the *Reichsbeauftragter fur kunstlerische Formgebung* (Reich commissioner for artistic design), Hans Schweitzer; antiquities dealer Max Taeuber; and Adolf Ziegler. Before they could start, however, Göring selected thirteen paintings (four van Goghs, four Munchs, three Marcs, a Cezanne and a Signac), which he instructed his personal art dealer Josef (Sepp) Angerer to sell on his behalf. This he did, and with the proceeds bought Old Masters and tapestries for Göring to hang on the walls at Carinhall. Despite a ban on members of the commission dealing privately, some such as Haberstock did so, selling a work by Gaugin, exchanging it for a Rubens and keeping the proceeds.

Hofmann began preparations for the sales campaign by first moving the collection to the *Schloss Schönhausen* in the Pankow district of Berlin and appointing Rolf Hetsch to oversee the operation. It was 'probably the most spectacular collection of early twentieth century art ever assembled in one place'.[24] All were in place by 17 September, by which time several offers had already been received from foreign dealers, amongst them the Galerie Zak in Paris and the Colnaghi Gallery in London. The latter wrote to Hitler offering to purchase the whole collection, hoping to impress him by saying that they were the only English firm of any size to eschew degenerate art, which they claim to have found vulgar and repugnant. Hitler declined the offer.

By November, after all the Munch paintings had been sent to be auctioned in Norway by Harald Halvorsen, it was agreed to set up an auction in Lucerne to be conducted by Theodor Fischer, the only non-Jewish Swiss auctioneer who had both international contacts and extensive experience in public auctions. It was a unique opportunity for Fischer to handle so much high-quality art with such impeccable provenance. He had worked in Berlin for a number of years and was very familiar with the artists on offer and their work. It was made clear to Fischer that all proceeds from sales would be placed in a foreign currency account and made available to the Reich. The money would be handled by the Bank of Switzerland and deposited in an account in London. He agreed on a commission of 15 per cent, except for six major works, four van Goghs, a Gaugin and four Picassos, where it would be reduced to 6 per cent. Reserve prices were agreed with Hofmann.

The Fischer auction of 108 paintings and 17 sculptures was held on 30 June, but it was not a total success. Despite the works on offer, many collectors boycotted the auction fearing that the proceeds would go towards Germany's war effort. When US dealer Alfred Frankfurter asked where the sale money was going, Fischer told him, disingenuously, that all proceeds would go to German museums for new purchases. Rumours that it was going to the Reich, he said, had been started by a French consortium hoping to dissuade US buyers and so keep the prices down. Despite his assurances, the international response was less than he might have hoped for.[25]

The auction began at 3.00 pm in a salon of the Grand Hotel National overlooking Lake Lucerne. The room was packed with 350 guests, including Swiss collectors Emil Buhrle and Gertrud Dubi-Muller; Alfred Frankfurter; the painter's son and international art dealer Pierre Matisse; Joseph Pulitzer Jr, of Saint Louis; the American film director and art collector Josef von Sternberg; Curt Valentin; and Karl Nierendorf. Also present were representatives from museums in Antwerp, Basel, Bern, Brussels and Liege. The auction was conducted in German, English and French and bidding was in Swiss francs. Many bidders were unknown to Fischer and others were acting on behalf of clients who wished to remain anonymous. A van Gogh self-portrait that had been taken from the *Neue Staatsgallerie* in Munich attracted the most attention and was eventually bought by Frankfurter for 175,000 Swiss francs. He immediately hurried out with it, loaded it into the boot of his car and drove off. The Belgian contingent, Dr Jean Buissert of the *Musee des Beaux-Arts*, Liege, and Professor Dr L. van Puyvelde, director of the *Musees Royaux des Beaux-Art*s in Brussels bought fifteen paintings between them. Prior to the auction, Buchholz had contacted Georg Schmidt, director of the *Kunstmuseum Basel*, to negotiate a sale of works not in the auction and Schmidt augmented these with a further eight paintings at the auction. Prices were fairly modest compared to London and New York action houses for works of similar reputation. Total sales were some 500,000 Swiss francs, which Fischer deposited in a British bank account marked EK. He complained to Hofmann that forty works had not been sold because 'the Jewboys boycotted the auction'.[26]

The works that had remained in the Kopenicker Straße warehouse had to be removed to make way for grain storage, but rather than find a suitable place to take them, on 20 March 1939 some 5,000 of them were burned in the courtyard of Berlin's fire station on Rosenberg's orders. A plaque on the wall of 225–25 Köpenicker Straße commemorates the event, with an inscription declaring that over 1,000 oil paintings and sculptures and around 4,000 watercolours, drawings and graphic sheets were destroyed. A considerable number, however, had been rescued before the fire by four dealers, Bernhard Böhmer, Karl Buchholz, Hildebrand Gurlitt and Ferdinand Möller. Gurlitt had already been hounded out of two positions. In 1930 he had been dismissed from the *König Albert Museum* in Zwickau for his championing of modern artists and then suffered a similar fate in 1933 when he was forced out of the *Kunstverein* in Hamburg by local Nazis. However, his knowledge of modern art and his international contacts proved decisive, and his Jewish grandmother was overlooked when Goebbels realised that his expertise was required to get the best prices for the remaining works that would be sold privately to buyers who did not want to be identified.

It was expressly forbidden to sell any works to German dealers, but it was impossible to prevent this and many were simply kept by members of the *Verwertungskommission*. When war was declared on 3 September 1939, many works remained unsold and new ways were devised in order to continue selling to American, Norwegian, Swiss and Dutch customers in particular. Foreign currency everywhere was hoarded, so to get around this works were simply exchanged for nineteenth-century art. In one spectacular deal, a fairly uninspiring painting by Carl Gustav Carus, *Heimkehr der Monche ins Kloster* (Monks returning to the monastery) was acquired by the Germans in exchange for a staggering forty-eight works of art: six works by Karl Hofer, five by Heckel, four by Lyonel Feininger, four by Mueller, three by Maurice de Vlaminck, two each by Dix, Gross and Nolde, one each by Grosz, Kokoschka, Rudolf Levy, Heinrich Nauen, Ernst Wilhelm Ney, Schlemmer and Paul Adolf Seehaus, together with ten Becker sculptures. Many works found their way into the collections of US patrons of modern German art such as William R. Valentiner, Alfred H. Barr Jr, Hilla von Rebay, Emmy (Galka) Scheyer, and I.B. Neumann.

Chapter 6

ARTIST OUTCASTS OF THE THIRD REICH

'We should never judge artists by their political views.'[1]

Adolf Hitler

Ludwig Mies van der Rohe

In 1921, Mies van der Rohe made a dramatic modernist debut to what would become a glittering architectural career when he submitted a revolutionary futuristic entry for a competition to design the Friedrichstraße skyscraper in Berlin's major commercial street. His angular, glass-walled pinnacle did not win, and in fact no tower was ever built, but his design would come to be recognised as the most innovative and historically significant of all entries in the competition. He followed up the next year with a taller curved version named the Glass Skyscraper, which was never built either but confirmed his reputation as a modernist and got him other commissions. After his successful administration of the 1927 *Werkbund* exhibition in Stuttgart, Mies was commissioned to design the German Pavilion, the world's first truly open-plan house, for the 1929 International Exhibition in Barcelona.

He tried to ignore the rising tide of Nazism to concentrate on his work, but when he succeeded Meyer as director of the *Bauhaus* in 1932, he could no longer hide from the truth of what was taking place all around him. With the closure of the *Bauhaus* in 1933 it seemed as if Mies' modernistic style of white walls, steel and glass, and flat roofs would have to give way to Rosenberg's *Völkisch* right-wing sentimental and more 'German' architecture. However, Hitler had himself not quite made up his mind about modern architecture, despite his diatribes against other modernistic movements such as Expressionism. He would remain ambivalent throughout the 1930s, as shown by his selection of Mies' sleek *Bauhaus*-inspired designs for autobahn service stations. At first Goebbels was able to persuade Hitler that the progressive, symbolic power of industrial Modernism was just what the regime needed, and Hitler even spoke of 'a functionalism of crystalline clarity' in design and the need to be 'logical and above all to be truthful', which was not at all an anti-modern message.

Mies and Gropius believed that their use of modern technology, which spoke of a bright revolutionary new order, would appeal to the Nazi mentality. When Mies said, 'Architecture is the will of the epoch translated into space', he might have been excused for believing that he reflected Nazi sentiments.[2] He and Gropius won contracts from leaders such as Göring, which encouraged Mies to sign a motion of support for Hitler, while at the same time joining Goebbels's *Reichskulturkammer*. It looked to have worked when he was shortlisted to build the state's new Reichsbank, with a fiercely modern, abstract design, and Goebbels even pressed him to design the *Deutsches Volk Deutsches Arbeit* exhibition in April 1934. Things were not so bad, although success had been achieved at the cost of compromise. A number of surviving Mies and Gropius designs are decorated with swastikas. His design for the Reichsbank, which incorporated much steel and glass, however, was firmly rejected by Hitler, who favoured a traditional Heinrich Wolff design that had not even made it onto the shortlist.

Then Hitler came under the spell of another young architect, Albert Speer, who quickly became a court favourite. Speer had studied under Heinrich Tessenow, a leading proponent of simple, traditional architecture. After joining the Nazi Party in 1931, Speer was commissioned to redecorate their district headquarters in Berlin's Grunewald offices. Goebbels, quick to see which way the wind was blowing, abandoned his championing of Mies and hired Speer as chief architect for the Propaganda Ministry and then designer for the Nazi rallies at Tempelhof Field. Hitler gave Speer a sketchbook filled with architectural ideas he had developed over the years, and it was this that Speer would use to design and build the cities of the future for him. Hitler had found his man and when Speer came up with plans for ever larger, more extravagant stage sets for the Nuremberg rally complex and the Cathedral of Light, Hitler was intoxicated with enthusiasm and forgot all about Mies. When Troost died in 1934, Hitler chose to work with municipal authorities to execute his architectural plans, but soon became frustrated at having to work through official channels and employed Speer to deal with that sort of irritating detail. Speer then began to create a space for himself within the Nazi Party and vied with Hermann Giesler to become Hitler's favourite architect.

Having failed to get the Reichsbank commission, Mies struggled to find work. He was forced to soften his style but not enough to make much of a difference. He had suddenly become yesterday's man. He had to wait and hope that things would change, but they only got worse. He continued to refuse to speak out against the Nazis and, at last, chose to leave Germany and go to the US in 1937, where he found artistic tastes much more to his liking and patrons falling over themselves to give him lucrative commissions.

Ernst Barlach

His first teacher in art school had advised Barlach to 'give up art since he would never create anything worthwhile'. Undaunted, he went to Paris to study briefly at the Académie Julian, but soon became frustrated at having to reproduce 'miserable monotonous' representations of the human form. He travelled to Kharkov in Russia to visit his brother and hoping to uncover in the land of Tolstoy, 'words for those religious depths of my nature that have been striving to enter my work since I was a child'. It was here on the steppes that he found the 'short, squat, round-headed, flat-faced beggars, monks, pilgrims and peasant women' who were to become his principle subject matter for the following three decades. He told the publisher Reinhold Piper that he had found a 'complete unity of inward and outward being [a] symbolic quality [of what] human beings are'.[3]

After Barlach's trip to Russia in 1906, the themes for his work were transformed from the allegorical and sentimental to representations of the archai that would become his trademark. In his painting and sculpture, the human torso is reduced in size in relation to hands and face through which the subject's emotions are expressed. To Piper, he wrote in 1911, 'my artistic language is the human figure or the object through or in which man lives, suffers, rejoices, feels, thinks'.[4] Returning from Russia and despite his preference for depicting country life, he joined the Berlin Secession, a modernist art movement that had been set up in 1898 to challenge restrictions on modern artists that had been imposed by Kaiser Wilhelm II. He also signed a contract with the prominent German-Jewish art dealer Paul Cassirer, whose despotic behaviour towards his artists verged on what Nolde called 'artistic slavery', which now marked him out as a member of the cosmopolitan elite.

Barlach was one of the artists most admired by the young Nazi students and activists, as well as a few prominent art historians of the day who saw his work as essentially both Germanic and revolutionary, which fitted in well with the Nazi concept of a national rebirth. However, evidence testifies to Barlach's antipathy toward mass politics and social conformity, and his work would later render him vulnerable to attacks from right-wing groups. Rosenberg derided his 'solitary, ruminating individuals…contradicted every National Socialist ideal of German men and women, who find themselves by serving country and Führer'.[5] Mecklenburg's Gauleiter Heinrich Hildebrandt called him 'foreign to the German essence' by refusing to depict his subjects as tough, self-confident battlers for the Nazi cause. His 'Slavic' figuration was increasingly seen as diametrically opposed to Nordic ideals.

His association with Cassirer and the Berlin Secession was instrumental in him being identified with Jewish art and for many, it was no great leap to see his sculptures, which celebrated the individual, as contrary to Nazi ideology which favoured the collective even though that ideology itself was inchoate and often subject to modifications. It was probably his war memorials, publicly commissioned and completed between 1927 and 1931, that put the nails in his professional coffin. In the eyes of the Nazis, he had made the cardinal error of conveying to the viewer that war was tragic and terrible rather than 'a happy hunting excursion'.[6] Whilst elevating him to the artistic elite, his unconventional monuments, neither traditionally heroic nor simplistically abstract, failed to resonate with the ideological and aesthetic ideas of many in the centre and far right. All were removed from public view and in some cases destroyed.

After Hitler's accession to the Chancellorship, Barlach's sculptures were dismantled and confiscated, as were many of his drawings. 'My little boat is sinking fast,' he wrote to Piper. 'I pull my hat down over my eyes.'[7] He was thrown out of the Prussian Academy of Arts, but still had private patrons and benefitted from the often-contradictory signals that emanated from the central leadership of the Nazi Party. This confusion over what was acceptable caused Barlach much distress but, in his more optimistic moods, he felt confident enough to believe that Nazi excesses would subside, and he signed a 'Declaration for Adolf Hitler!' It was not enough. Goebbels, who was losing the battle with Rosenberg over Expressionism, now saw that he could no longer continue to support him and, despite still admiring Barlach, felt compelled to describe his work as 'poison'. It was not until the *Ausstellung Entartete Kunst* of 1937, in which a single work of his was shown, that clarity reigned and Barlach eventually recognised the truth of what was happening to the arts in Germany. He made every effort, thereafter, to keep out of the limelight and made no further attempt to challenge Nazi ideology, which left him free to carry on working until he died, a broken man, on 24 October 1938, still searching for his 'true self in dark unconscious depths'.[8]

Emil Nolde

Hans Emil Hansen was born in Nolde, Schleswig to a Danish-German peasant family. Having been turned down by the same Munich Academy of Arts that would reject Hitler eight years later, Nolde went to study at the Académie Julian in Paris. From there he returned to Germany, calling himself Emil Nolde, to join up with the Berlin Secession and start painting bright intense pictures. Soon he had argued bitterly with both the Secession leader Max Liebermann and the art dealer Paul Cassirer, both Jews, which drove him to join the Nazi Party at some time in the early 1920s.

Nolde fought hard to carve out a place for himself in the Nazi movement. He had many admirers, including one of Hitler's closest allies during the 1920s, Erna Hanfstängl, sister of Ernst. A member of an influential art-publishing family, she displayed Nolde's pictures at her private art gallery on Munich's Karlsplatz in the hope of impressing visiting Nazi dignitaries. She also placed several Nolde watercolours in the Munich apartment of her brother Ernst, who was another personal friend of Hitler. The idea was that Hitler would see them, like them, and then take Nolde on as a court painter, but Hitler did not care for them. Rosenberg had orchestrated a whispering campaign against him. When Rosenberg's acolyte, Schultze-Naumberg had gone on a lecture tour to denigrate Expressionism, it was pictures by Barlach and Nolde he had shown alongside images of clinically deformed patients to make a case for a connection between the two.

Nolde had become the epitome of Expressionism, which still had a few admirers in the Nazi Party, even men like Goebbels, who thought of it as an honourable part of the National Socialist movement and was what Gottfried Benn called 'the last great artistic renaissance'.[9] As late as 1937, to celebrate his seventieth birthday, an exhibition of Nolde's work was still being shown in places such as the Ferdinand Möller Gallery in Berlin. At the same time, however, 1,052 of his works had been confiscated from public displays.

Otto Dix

Otto Dix was born in Unternhaus, Germany on 2 December 1891 and, as a young man joined the Dresden School of Arts where he studied painting. When he went to war in 1914, he recalled that he saw it as an experience to 'see everything with my own eyes [and] experience all the ghastly, bottomless depths for life for myself'.[10] Dix was wounded several times during the war and almost died when a shrapnel splinter hit him in the neck. His experiences on the front line had a dramatic impact on his art, and he later recalled that 'War is so bestial: hunger, lice, mud, those insane noises'.[11] After the war, Dix said that he had recurring nightmares and his paintings and drawings became increasingly political as he tried to recreate his experiences through his art. His anger at the way war wounded were treated in Weimar Germany was most glaringly illustrated in *The Skat Players*, which depicted card-playing cripples, scarcely human with arms, legs, jaws, ears and noses shot away.

Dix was an Expressionist who had crossed over to *Neue Sachlichkeit* with its sharply focused verisimilitude, which resembled photography in its detail. Dix exhibited alongside Grosz, Heartfield and Raoul Hausmann in the *Erste Internationale Dada-Messe* in Otto Burchard's Berlin gallery in 1920, but his deeply disturbing graphic depictions, some of Western art's most haunting portrayals of the violence and destruction, created such a public outcry that museums were forbidden to purchase or display them. Although very much a left-wing sympathiser, Dix refused to join the German Communist Party when urged to do so by his artist friends, saying that he preferred to stay out of 'stupid politics'.[12]

In 1927, he was given a professorship at the Dresden School of Arts and Crafts and began a programme of recording life in Weimar society in his paintings, but then returned to the subject of war because he could see that people were starting to forget its horrors and suffering and thought only in terms of heroism and duty. In his painting *Trench Warfare*, he employed the religious triptych style that had been popular in medieval times to make altarpieces. Trouble was brewing for Dix, however, after the Nazis in Saxony called his paintings 'vulgarities of the lowest taste'.[13]

When most of his artistic friends fled Germany, Dix, who had never been openly critical of Hitler, thought he would be safe, but he might have known what was in store for him when, in April 1933, he had been forced out of his teaching role and then, a year later, was excluded from exhibitions. He had still been able to make a living by selling paintings to sympathetic individuals and institutions, but when Goebbels started his crusade against 'degenerate art' in 1936, 260 of Dix's works were confiscated for mocking the German idea of heroism by depicting soldiers as idiots, sexual degenerates and drunkards. Dix's refusal to join the NSDAP on the grounds that he was apolitical had to be reversed when membership was required as an essential prerequisite to joining the *Reichskammer der bildenden Kuenste*. In order to be allowed to continue painting, he was made to promise to paint only inoffensive landscapes or portraits.

In autumn 1939, Dix was arrested and charged with involvement in the Georg Esler plot on Hitler's life that had taken place in Munich that November, but he was released when it became obvious that Elser had acted alone. During the Second World War, he joined the army and was eventually taken prisoner by the French in 1945. He died on 25 July 1969.

Georg Grosz

Georg Ehrenfried Grosz was born in Berlin on 26 July 1893 into a strict Lutheran family. In 1909 he became a student at the Dresden Academy of Fine Arts then moved to the Berlin College of Arts and Crafts two years later. Conscripted to serve in the war, he found 'horror, mutilation and senseless destruction' as the country descended into 'a mass delirium'. He dreamed that the international socialist movement would one day put an end to all wars.[14] He expressed his disgust through his art, drawing soldiers' crab-like limbs of steel and a hospital orderly emptying a bucket full of pieces of human flesh down a pit. In 1918 he painted *Fit for Active Service* in which a well-fed doctor inspecting a skeleton with an ear trumpet pronounced it fit for duty. After he was discharged from the army with shellshock (PTSD), he joined the short-lived revolutionary *Spartakusbund* and then the KPD, led by Rosa Luxemburg and Karl Liebknecht, who were both murdered in January 1919.

Grosz became involved with Expressionism, New Objectivity, and Dada and began working with Heartfield in the new medium of photomontage rearranging selected details of photographs to form a new and convincing unity. In 1922 Grosz travelled to the Soviet Union where he had a meeting with Lenin which left him unimpressed with communism and, on his return to Germany, he left the Germn Communist Party but remained a committed socialist revolutionary. All around in Weimar Germany he saw a breakdown of morality in which 'a wave of vice, pornography and prostitution enveloped the whole country...The streets became ravines of manslaughter and cocaine traffic.'[15]

His art became a protest against what he saw as a world that was ugly, sick and hypocritical. Along with Otto Dix, Grosz was credited with developing what became known as the New Realism. His book *Ecce Homo*, a vicious, angry satire of post-war German life, was banned by the government and Grosz was put on trial in 1928 for offending public taste with his blasphemous cartoon of Christ nailed to the cross and wearing combat boots and a gas mask. In his defence he said that an artist 'cannot stand aside [from injustice and brutality]' and must become political. Following a deposition from the German Quakers, Grosz was acquitted.

Grosz had drawn a picture *Hitler, the Saviour* in 1923 at the time of the abortive Beer Hall Putsch but waited until 1930 to publish it when Hitler was becoming much more of a threat to the political system. In the picture, Hitler is seen with 'a smug and belligerent expression' and a 'dangerous, downward curve [of his] mouth', not at all what might be expected on the face of a hero of 'the great German myth'.[16]

In the same year, Grosz illustrated a children's book by Bertolt Brecht in which three soldiers, called Hunger, Disaster and Disease denounce a war made by the rich in which the rich grow richer still. Grosz saw the rise of the Nazis as a dying of humanist ideals and a growth in contempt for human life. One night in the early 1930s, he found an iron pipe at his front door with a note attached. 'This is for you, you old Jew-Pig, if you keep going with what you're doing.'[17] In January 1933, he became one of over 2,500 artists and writers to leave Nazi Germany when he took his family and emigrated to the United States.

Helmutt Herzfeld/John Heartfield

Helmut Hezfeld was born in Berlin on 19 June 1891. After working as an assistant to the painter Hermann Bouffier for two years, he joined the School of Applied Arts in Berlin and then went on to study under Ernst Neumann at the *Bauhaus* Arts and Crafts School. He avoided military service and was taken up with the ideas of the *Spartakusbund*, after which he decided to devote his art to politics and become 'a soldier of peace'.[18] In protest at Germany's involvement in the war, Herzfeld, changed his name to John Heartfield. With Grosz, he developed the artistic style of photomontage using collage and bold typography.

In 1918 the two men joined the KPD and over the next fifteen years, Heartfield produced designs and posters for the organisation but, to earn a living, he worked as a theatre set designer for Max Reinhardt and became editor of the satirical magazine, *Der Knöppel*. Through his photomontage work he began to challenge the government over its foreign policy and neglect of social issues. He gained an international reputation through *The Face of Fascism* in which the skull-like face of Mussolini is portrayed alongside his corrupt backers and his dead victims, but contemporary art critics ignored him and his works had no commercial value for bourgeois art collectors.

In 1929 he started work for the most widely distributed socialist pictorial paper in Germany, the *Arbeiter-Illustrierte-Zeitung* (AIG) concentrating his invective against 'Prussian militarism and the large-scale industries and industrialists who supplied it with arms'.[19] He would soon come to the unwanted attention of the Nazis with his montage of Hitler appearing as a puppet manipulated by Fritz Thyssen, the owner of the massive United Steelworks company. In another work printed just before the November 1932 General Election, Hitler is shown receiving a large sum of money from a man who obviously represents big business.

When the Reichstag was burned down on 27 February 1933 and Hitler swore to have all communist leaders hanged, Heartfield created *Executioner of the Third Reich* portraying Hermann Göring as a human bloodhound with his axe standing in front of the burning Parliament. Hitler ordered the arrests of all those artists that had criticised him during his rise to power, but when the police went to Heartfield's flat they found he had fled to Prague. He continued to contribute to AIG, but it was now very dangerous and difficult to smuggle the magazine back into Germany. Hitler demanded that the Czech government ban the publication of AIG and when Hitler occupied Czechoslovakia, Heartfield fled to London where he was later interned as an enemy alien. He returned to Berlin after the war and died there in 1968.

Käthe Kollwitz

Käthe Schmidt was born in Königsberg on 8 July 1867. This 'quiet, shy and nervous child' was taught by her father to have sympathy for the plight of the working-class. She, like her two sisters, showed great artistic promise and her father arranged for Käthe to have lessons with Rudolf Mauer, a local copper engraver. Later, when she was 16 years old, Käthe tried to enter the Königsberg Academy of Art but was denied because of her gender and so studied under Emil Neide instead. A year later, Käthe and her sister Lise went to Berlin where they met the poet and dramatist Gerhart Hauptmann, who described Käthe as

> fresh as a rose in dew, a charming, clever girl, who, because of her extreme modesty, did not speak freely about her calling as an artist but let it be known by her sure, sensitive manner.[20]

In Berlin, Käthe enrolled in the Berlin School for Women Artists, studying under Karl Stauffer-Bern, and later went to the Munich Women's Art School where she exhibited her work for the first time, which 'filled [her] with thoughts of glory and happiness that [she] could not sleep all night.'[21] Her skill at drawing with pen, pencil, chalk and charcoal, however, was not matched by any great talent for painting for which she lacked feeling for the subtleties of colour.

She had met an orphan Karl Kollwitz in her younger days and they had remained close. When Karl qualified as a doctor in 1891, they married and went to live in a working-class district of Berlin, where Karl treated patients under the first European system of health insurance while Käthe set up a small studio. Despite now having a child, Käthe, somewhat controversially because she was a woman, took part in a joint exhibition of Berlin artists where here talent was recognised by the critic Julius Elias, who predicted a 'rich artistic future' for her.[22]

Kollwitz spent the next five years producing a series of lithographs illustrating the Weaver's uprising of Silesia, which won the gold medal of the Dresden Museum after it had been rejected previously because of Käthe's left-wing politics. She now began work on depicting the harsh living conditions of the Berlin working-class, especially women, who despite their circumstances had 'a broad freedom of movement [and] gesture [and] a grandness of manner' and whose 'native rugged simplicity' set them above middle-class people.[23]

Kollwitz now went to teach at the Berlin School for Women Artists where she had previously studied, but the work did not suit her. She was shy among strangers and preferred to work alone in a small, single room rather than suffer the embarrassment of sharing, what she termed her 'meagre knowledge'.[24] Despite her self-doubt she was soon considered to be one of the most important graphic artists working in Europe.

When her son, Peter, was killed at Dixmuide on 23 October 1914, Kollwitz searched for ways to express her grief through her art. To commemorate her fiftieth birthday, she was given a retrospective exhibition in Berlin about which she commented, 'When people assert that my one subject is always the lot of the unfortunate [I reply that] sorrow isn't confined to social misery' but she had found it difficult to work with a positive outlook. She asked herself how one can experience joy with so much suffering in the world. When the Sparticist Uprising foundered and Karl Liebknecht was murdered in 1919, she had the family's permission to make drawings of him in his coffin.

In 1919, Kollwitz was the first woman to be elected to full professorship at the Prussian Academy of Arts and given large, fully equipped studio in which she began a series of lithographs that dealt with the impact of war on women, but she struggled to find the right medium to work in. 'I am disillusioned with all the hate that is in the world' she said, 'the world has seen enough murder, lies, and corruption.'[25]

After September 1930, when the Nazi Party had become the second largest party in Germany, Kollwitz was filled with foreboding having seen workers' rallies broken up with extreme violence. She helped to organise a public manifesto calling for unity between the parties of the left to combat to rise of fascism. In response, Hitler demanded her resignation from the Prussian Academy of Arts and Academy directors ask her to leave. To save the academy from being broken up, Kollwitz, at the age of 67, complied but continued to criticise Hitler in an interview with the Soviet journal *Izvestia*. She was arrested by the Gestapo, who threatened to have her sent to a concentration camp, although it was an empty threat. When Goebbels launched his crusade against degenerate art, Kollwitz had thirty-one of her works taken from public display and confiscated. When her sculpture *Tower of Mothers* was also seized, she was devastated by the lack of protest. Her husband was banned from practicing as a doctor and died in 1940. Kollwitz was given a chance to leave Germany, but chose to stay. Her grandson, also called Peter, was killed at Stalingrad but, despite a deep and damaging blow, Peter's father, Hans, said she 'did not grieve openly, scarcely wept [and] she tried to give us strength to bear it'.[26]

Forced to flee from Berlin in 1943 because of the bombing, Kollwitz wrote to her adopted son Georg Gregor,

> Oh, Georg, how good it all was...the fullness and richness of our lives overwhelms me again and again with feelings of gratitude. Let us tell you once more how we all have loved you.[27]

When bombs destroyed the family home at 25 Weißenburger Straße in Berlin and all her personal effects were lost, she wrote in her journal

> Every war already carries within it the war which will answer it. Every war is answered by a new war, until everything, everything is smashed.

She died on 22 April 1945 as her biographer Martha Kearns put it, 'without worldly possessions, but rich in her own person'.

Chapter 7

ARTISTIC CHAMPIONS OF THE THIRD REICH

'My artists should live like princes and not have to inhabit attic rooms.'
Adolf Hitler

Arno Breker

Arno Breker studied at the Düsseldorf Academy of Arts and later went on to study and live in Paris, where he met artists such as Jean Cocteau and Pablo Picasso, and established a fine reputation for himself. The French classicist sculptor Aristide Maillot called Breker the German Michelangelo. He returned to live in Germany in 1932, having won a prize from the Prussian Ministry of Culture. Unfortunately, his work was not sufficiently *Völkisch* for Alfred Rosenberg, who railed against him in pages of the *Völkischer Beobachter* for his close association with the modernist Paul Klee, but Hitler approved of his work and so Rosenberg was obliged to mute his criticism. It was soon clear to Breker, however, that there were two distinct and opposite artistic movements vying for supremacy in Germany and with the rise to power of the Nazis he would, at some point, have to make a choice over which one he aligned with.

He had already been impressed with the politics of fascist Italy and had even been commissioned to restore Michelangelo's marble sculpture *Rondanini Pietà,* which introduced him to the monumental imperial style.[1] It was no surprise then that he now began to be drawn to Hitler's style of leadership and began to align his aesthetic along the lines adopted by the Nazis. In George Kolbe's opinion, there had been a noticeable change in Breker's artistic viewpoint, causing him to discard earlier French influences and fall under the influence of the Nazis.

He became what the art expert Victor Dirksen called 'a state sculptor' but it was hard to know if it was expediency or political sympathy that caused his change of heart.[2] What is clear is that he abandoned any modernist influences and from here on focused entirely on Classicism. He spoke of 'massive figures built upon timeless Hellenic precedents [that] would define the aesthetic idiom both domestically and abroad',[3] but he was not averse to incorporating into his work 'frequent political allegory to suit the taste of the regime'.[4] His work belonged to a nineteenth-century tradition of 'decent and respectable' male nudity as a symbol of a young healthy nation imbued with moral strength and purity.[5] It portrayed not sexual passion but a sublimated chaste virility showing male bonding in activities such as sport. The power of Aryan masculinity is channelled into a sense of dominant guardianship of the state. Sculptures by Breker and his fellow German sculptor Josef Thorak depict 'musclemen of iron with grim expressions' as examples of the new style of monumentalism which characterised the Nazi cultural programme. This programme, in turn, was an essential component of the Nazi political message which Alfred Rosenberg, reflecting the ideological framework in which such art works were interpreted, described as 'the force and willpower' of the age.[6] Breker's works came to occupy a position of particular propagandistic importance in the cultural programme of the Nazis.

When Breker won second prize in the sculpture competition held for the 1936 Olympics, Speer took note and commissioned him to create works for the *Zeppelinfield* in Nuremberg and the Arch of Triumph in Berlin. The first Führer commissions were at the end of 1937 for two monumental bronze sculptures, which Breker called *Torch Bearer* and *Sword Bearer*. Breker himself discussed his motivations in the design of such sculptures:

> I have chosen the two pillars upon which each state is built, the man of the spirit represented by the torch, and the defender of the Reich by the man with the sword.[7]

Hitler called these images cast in stone with profiles, torsos and legs of the race's greatest specimens 'amongst the most beautiful ever created in Germany' and had them moved to take up permanent residence on the front I of the New *Reichskanzlei* (Reich Chancellery) where he took it upon himself to rename the figures 'The Party' and 'Wehrmacht'.[8]

An essential feature of Breker's *Torch Bearer* was the torch itself calling on the myth of Prometheus, the Titan god of fire. For the Nazis this symbolised the light they were bringing to lead the people out of darkness. It had been Goethe who, in his poem about Prometheus, had celebrated the courage of a man who had become the master of his own destiny after rebelling against the gods. It is hardly a coincidence that such an emphasis had been placed on the Olympic torch when its long journey from Olympia had been made such a feature of the 1936 games. The Nazi penchant for torchlit parades fits neatly into the symbolism of Prometheus also. The people were left to make the obvious connection.

Breker had modified his style to produce stilted and brutish caricatures of virility: steel-like bodies that owed everything to size and exaggeration and were simply perversions of the classical ideal.[9] No other artist in the Third Reich would go on to play such an important role in the politico-cultural life of Nazi Germany, or receive so many prestigious commissions, and Breker would become a wealthy man as a result. Many of his later wartime sculptures were a celebration of warfare itself, as in *Readiness*, a 1939-sculpture with a clearly military propagandistic message of a man, with his sword half-drawn, ready for battle, a symbolic call to arms for the German people. In the famous photographs of Hitler in Paris in 1940, with the Eiffel Tower in the background, it is Speer and Breker who stand on either side of him.

Josef Thorak

The Austrian sculptor Josef Thorak was another protégé of Albert Speer who had made a living in the 1920s by designing cemetery monuments for soldiers killed in the war. During this time, he had become friendly with Hjalmar Schacht, who would later become president of the Reichsbank under the Nazis. His reputation grew amongst members of the Nazi Party and in the early 1930s he won commissions to sculpt a bust of Goebbels and the death mask of Paul von Hindenburg. He would later be called on to create monumental statues to decorate Nazi buildings and provide beautiful, imposing nude sculptures of Greco-Roman-like athletes for the Olympic stadium in Berlin. Perhaps his most famous sculpture was *Comradeship*, which stood outside the German pavilion at the Paris World's Fair in 1937. The work depicted two muscular and enormous nude males clasping hands and posing in mutual defiance. Like Breker, Thorak became a very wealthy man under the Nazis, but his art went out of fashion somewhat after 1940 before surprisingly coming back into style again later in the war.

Breker and Thorak owed their style to the art historian Johann Winckelmann, who had written the *History of the Art of Antiquity* after visiting Rome in 1759, where he studied classical statuary. In his book he described the statues he saw as 'images of calm, confident masculinity, the embodiment of virtues both physical and moral'. Illustrations showed athletes immortalised in stone as the aesthetic ideal of strong, harmoniously proportioned men demonstrating an air of serene composure, even in the midst of strenuous effort.[10]

Heinrich Hoffmann

Heinrich Hoffmann's father had been Court Photographer to His Majesty the King of Bavaria. Although a fairly meaningless title, it gave the young Heinrich a sense of the growing importance of photography. In 1905 he had gone to England to work in a photographic studio and later became an official German aerial war photographer during the First World War. In Munich, after the war, he started an image agency called *Photobericht Hoffmann*, selling postcards and photographic booklets about the Munich revolution of 1919–1920. He also published a book of that time called *Ein Jahr bayerische Revolution im Bilde* (A Year of the Bavarian Revolution in Pictures). In 1920 he was one of the first to join the NSDAP (membership number 57) and became a close friend of Hitler, whom he had inadvertently come across in 1914 although neither had been aware of it at the time. He had taken a picture of crowds at Odeonsplaz in Munich on the day war was declared. Fifteen years later Hitler had seen a print in Hoffmann's studio and, having gone over it with a magnifying glass, was able to pick himself out as a young man of 25, with a wispy, undefined face. However, after years of examining the photograph, in 2010 the historian Gerd Krumeich, a noted German expert on the First World War, came to the conclusion that Hoffmann had either doctored the image or had mendaciously convinced Hitler of its authenticity.

Hoffmann had been on the lookout for subjects he could photograph and sell prints of. He believed that no pictures of Hitler existed, and he set out to get one. He followed Hitler around and saw him entering his publisher's building in Munich so waited to catch him as he came out. When he did, however, Hitler was grabbed by two men and dragged into a car. As the car drove away, Hitler saw Hoffmann with his camera and saluted him ironically. Some weeks later, Hoffmann met Hitler while he was taking pictures at the wedding of a Nazi Party member, Hermann Esser. Hitler approached Hoffmann, thinking he recognised him. The circumstances of their first encounter were then confirmed, but Hitler declined to let Hoffmann take his photograph. Fearful of attack, Hitler would not let anyone take his picture despite many times avowing that 'I am convinced nothing will happen to me, because I believe that destiny has assigned a task to me. But if the time ever comes,' he told Hoffmann, 'when I can [allow it] you will be the photographer.'[11] About two years later, he came to Hoffmann's studio for his first portrait study.

Hoffmann's photographs were an important part of Hitler's propaganda campaign to promote himself to the Nazi Party as a leader. In 1926, Hoffmann took photographs of the party's rally in Weimar, showing the march-past of 5,000 stormtroopers, saluted by Hitler for the first time with his arm straight out in front in the fascist salute. These images were distributed by the thousands throughout Germany.

According to Hitler's biographer Alan Bullock, Hoffmann came from the same lower middle-class background as Hitler and was a vulgar, jolly, earthy Bavarian with a weakness for drinking parties and hearty jokes. He was present at the Beer Hall Putsch and recorded it for posterity. Hoffmann's daughter Henriette was reputed to be one of only two women whom Hitler could 'sit next to without feeling irritated' and become 'free of all weariness and listlessness'.[12] The other, of course, was his niece Geli Raubal.

Hoffmann's biographer, Louis S. Snyder, considers that much of Hitler's early popularity was due to Hoffmann's superb photography. He had become the *Reichsbildberichterstatter* and was the only man permitted to take and distribute official pictures of the Führer. The world saw Hitler through Hoffmann's lens. He took some 10,000 images of him and compiled a number of best-selling picture books. These were sold under the titles *The Face of the Führer, Hitler as No One Knows Him, Hitler in His Everyday Life, Hitler in His Mountains, Hitler in His Homeland, Hitler in Bohemia* and *Hitler in Italy*. This ensured that he became a very wealthy man. When Hoffmann's image of Hitler was used on postage stamps, the Führer received a royalty on each one sold, and this became the most important legitimate source of his personal wealth.

When he was interviewed by Bernard Taper for *The New Yorker* magazine in 1950, Hoffmann said that Hitler was not an easy person to photograph. Hoffmann had not felt confident enough to tell him how to pose and Hitler would choose his own position, hand on hip or arms folded, head stiff and chin drawn in, then would announce, 'I am ready. Take my photograph.'[13] Hitler had confidence in Hoffmann and if he objected to a photographic proof, he knew that Hoffmann would not print it. One of Hoffmann's studio assistants was Eva Braun, who would later become Hitler's mistress. They met in Hoffmann's shop in 1929 when Eva was a girl of about 18. She had been fascinated by what she had heard of Hitler, and sometime later Hitler said to Hoffmann, 'The little girl is in love with me, Hoffmann. What can I do?' He started inviting Eva and her sister to Berchtesgaden and giving her presents. Eva was pretty but not beautiful, vivacious and affectionate, but by no means intellectual. She made few demands on him and for several years after she first met Hitler, she continued to work for Hoffmann but would often take two or three weeks off when Hitler was at his headquarters at Berchtesgaden to visit him.

Albert Speer

When he was released from twenty years of imprisonment for war crimes, Speer wrote extensively about his architectural work alongside Hitler. Much of what he said has been about his subordination to a murderous regime should be viewed with circumspection and his relationship with Hitler especially is described from his singular viewpoint. However, what he said is a matter of record even if his objectivity remains questionable. He readily admits that he was mesmerised by Hitler's personality and architectural ambition, but goes to great lengths to distance himself from the worst Nazi crimes. He says that he had been an artist and a technician rather than a politician.[14] It has been pointed out many times, however, that his various positions of power as Minister of Armaments within the Nazi Party put him at the centre of the war machine and he could have had no doubts about the genocide that was being committed in his name. It is only Speer's contribution to Nazi architecture that is considered here.

Speer made clear that when Hitler took him on as a young architect, he was given what he described as an astonishingly free rein with most of his projects once the general concept had been agreed, which usually meant Hitler specifying the scale and decoration and leaving style to him. For Speer this usually meant indulging his admiration for Greek architecture, but it is widely held that Hitler preferred Roman and so it is hard to know exactly to what extent Speer did have such a free hand. Commenting on Speer's assertion that he was not influenced by Nazi ideology in his architecture, the architectural theorist Léon Krier agrees that this was the case. He saw Speer's work as influenced solely by the traditions of Neoclassicism. Others major figures such as Wolfgang Schäche argue that the very scale of Speer's designs was evidence of political oppression in the fascist tradition and separate it from the Neoclassical tradition. Speer, of course, said that the scale was determined by Hitler and he had no choice but comply with his wishes. Others have called the debate futile. 'Stones speak no language', said Hartmut Frank, 'fascism is a problem not of stones but of men'. While architects may well be political, Frank goes on to say, 'architecture is not'.[15]

Further arguments demand that we look at the architecture of the time being practised in other democratic countries like France, Great Britain and the United States and acknowledge that it is not so different from much of the German product of the time. Many buildings in the United States, such as the Federal Reserve Board in Washington, exhibit the same scale, thick walls and antique motifs, lack of ornamentation and appear equally durable and dominating. Indeed, almost all public buildings of the US Public Works Administration exhibited many similarities to buildings designed by Speer and were what US government officials called 'temples of democracy'. This is not surprising, writes Barbara Lane, since during depressed times with public unrest, all governments will try to project an image of stability to calm nerves and discourage agitation.[16] This line of argument, however, does not take into account Speer's penchant for additional spectacle through the use of flags, banners and, most spectacular of all, the 'cathedral of light', which all helped to serves the Nazi agenda of power and dominance rather than stability. When Tessenow, Speer's old tutor and mentor, saw Speer's plans he dismissed them as 'showy, nothing more' but, of course that was the whole idea.[17]

We must not forget also that many of Hitler's speeches and Nazi publications drew attention to the architecture of the time as being representative of Nazi ideology. This message was so ubiquitous that few could have failed to sense these huge buildings as the expression of a dominating regime, especially given all the other controlling mechanisms of the state. Speer later claimed that it had been he, rather than Hitler, who had the vision for the monumental buildings, but there is no evidence in the work he is known for of any truly monumentalist features. Of those buildings he designed, such as the new *Reichskanzlei* in Berlin, the majority could not be described as gigantic. Many had classical features such as repetitive vertical elements, but overall his designs show clear modernist influences in their simple geometric forms and lack of ornamentation. Hitler seemed willing to accommodate Speer's penchant for modernity, but he was still insistent on traditional concepts, believing, perhaps, that a combination of both expressed his aesthetic vision.

Speer had been influenced early in his architectural education by archaeologists such as Daniel Krencher and Walter Andrae. It had been Andrae, especially, whose influence he had absorbed long before he had come under the Nazi spell and it was Andrae who had worked on the excavations at Assur, where Assyrian remains were being recovered. Ruins of the Temple of Tukulti-Ninurta had prompted Andrae to make a drawing of what he thought the original building would have looked like, and Speer would later imitate features of that design in the *Luitpoldhalle* in Nuremberg. The irony here is that the Assyrians were a Semitic people and it is clear that some of the buildings Speer

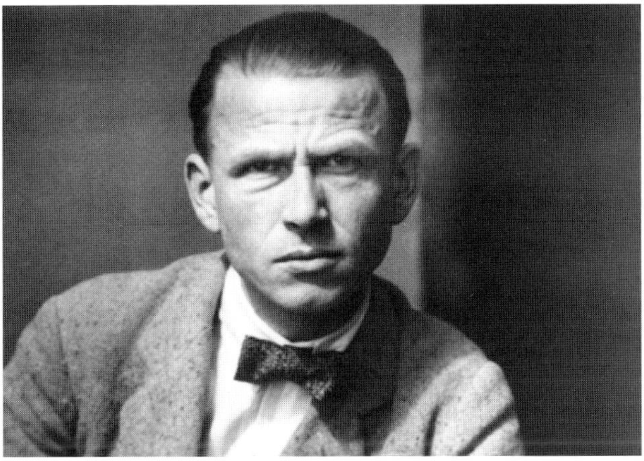

Otto Dix, one of the artists whose work Hitler called 'Entarte' or degenerate.

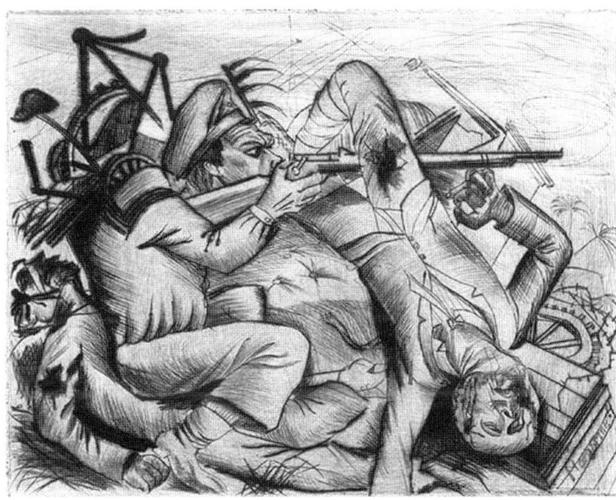

Otto Dix's *Die Barrikade* (The Barricade) depicting the horrors of war. A work described by Hitler as 'an act of aesthetic violence by the Jews against the German spirit'.

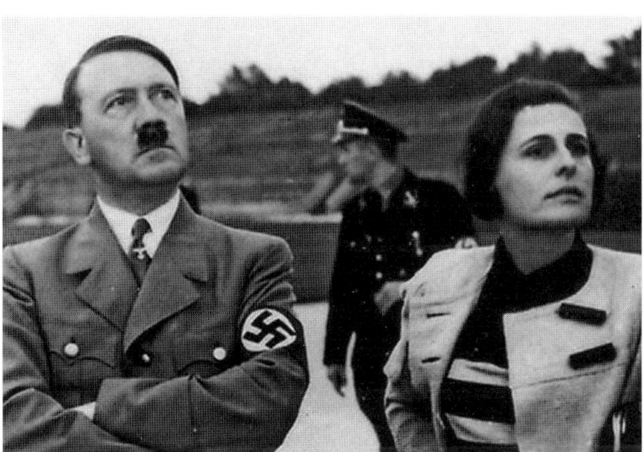

Adolf Hitler with Leni Riefenstahl, who became the first-choice film maker for the Nazis.

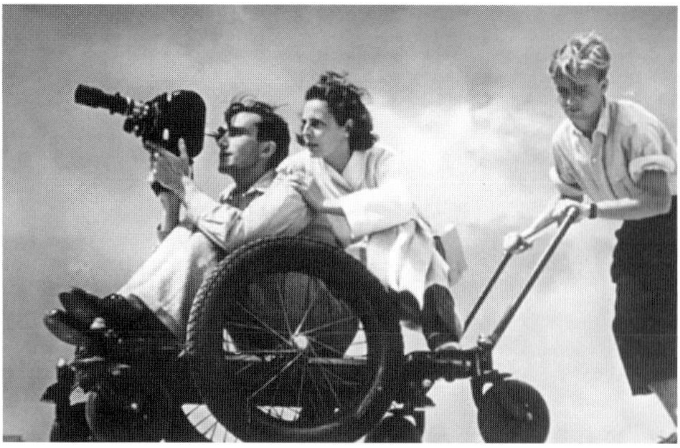

Leni Riefenstahl showing off her flair for improvisation in the filming of *Olympia* in 1938.

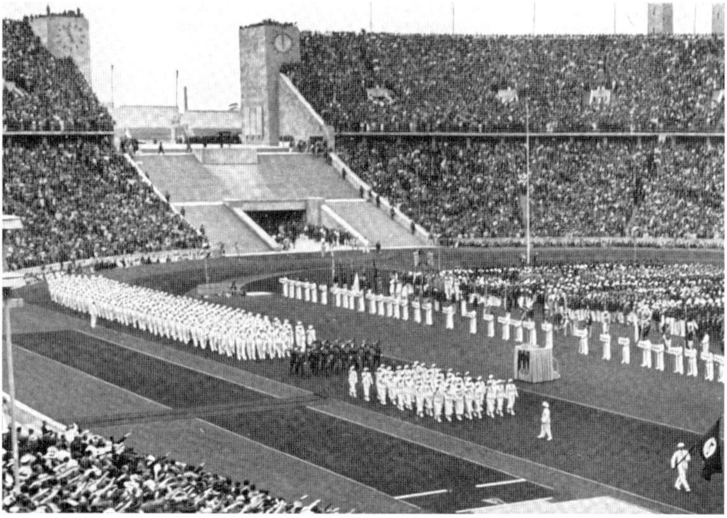

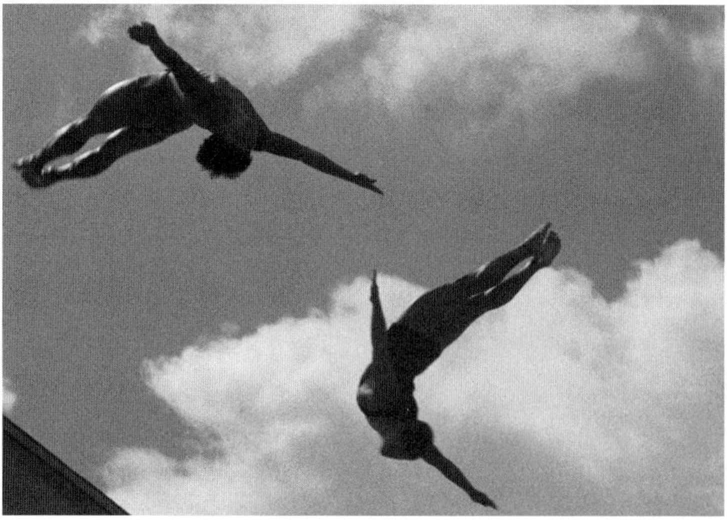

Both images: Scenes from *Olympia* depicting Nazi power and fascist aesthetics.

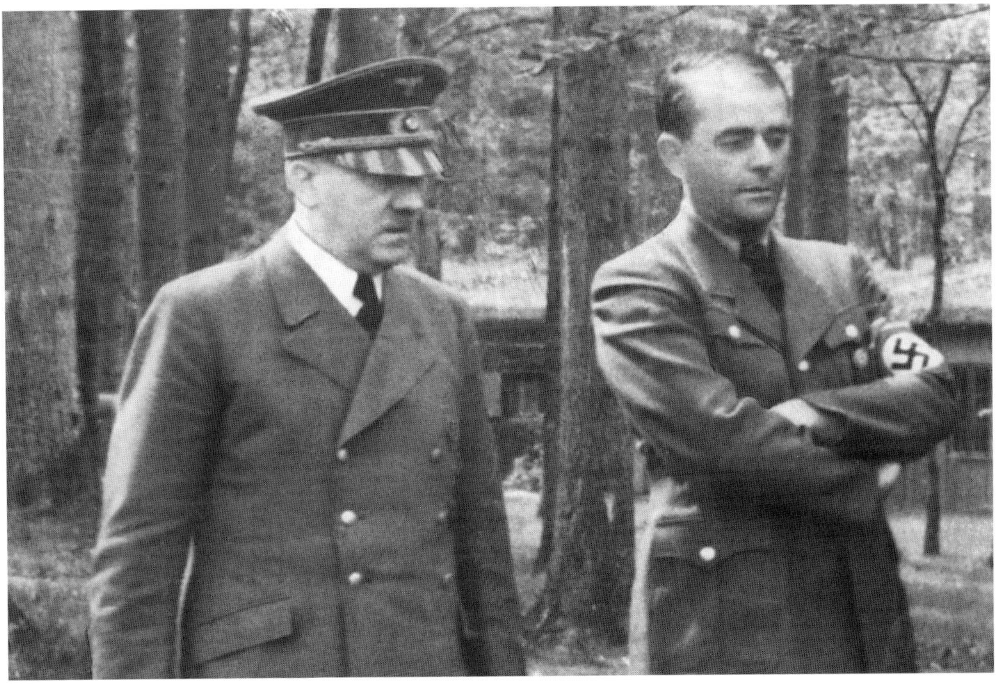

Adolf Hitler and his principal architect Albert Speer.

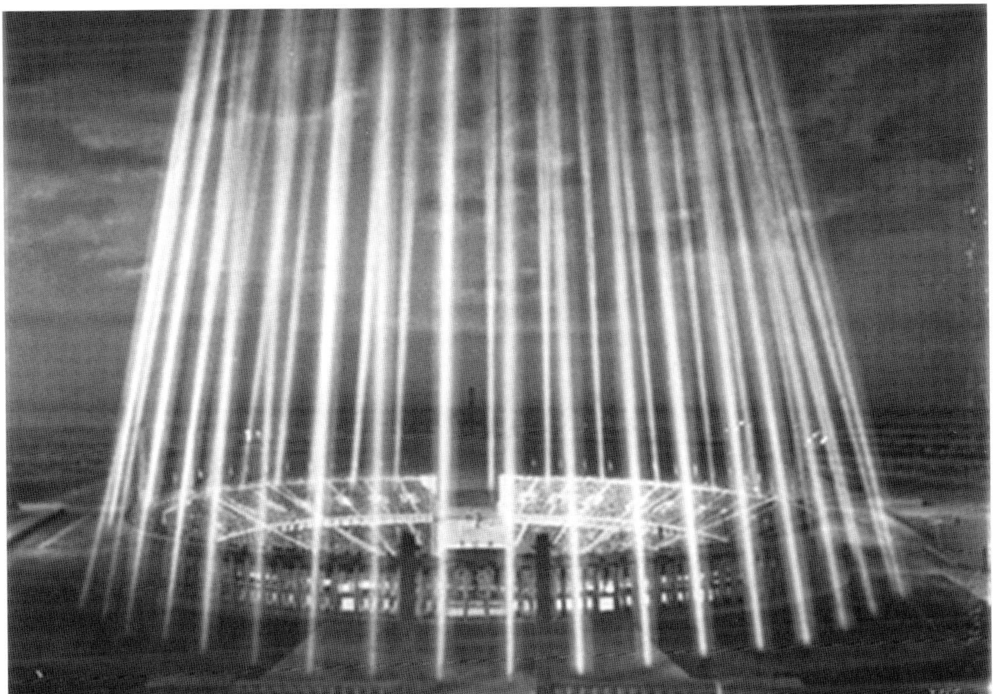

Speer's dramatic 'Cathedral of Light' at the 1936 Olympics in Berlin.

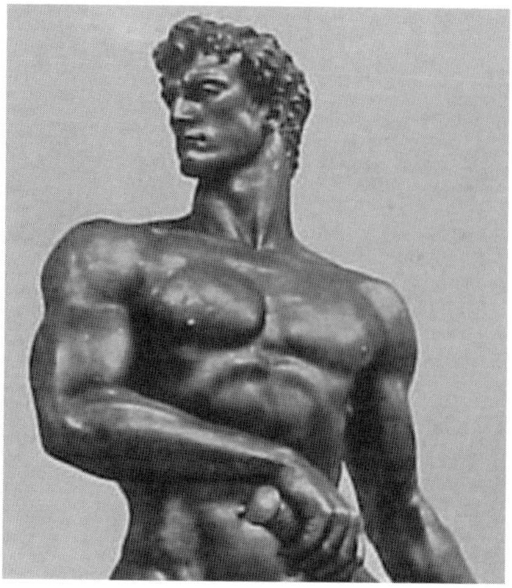

Arno Breker's *Bereitschaft*, described by Nazi propagandist Alfred Rosenberg as 'the force and willpower' of the age.

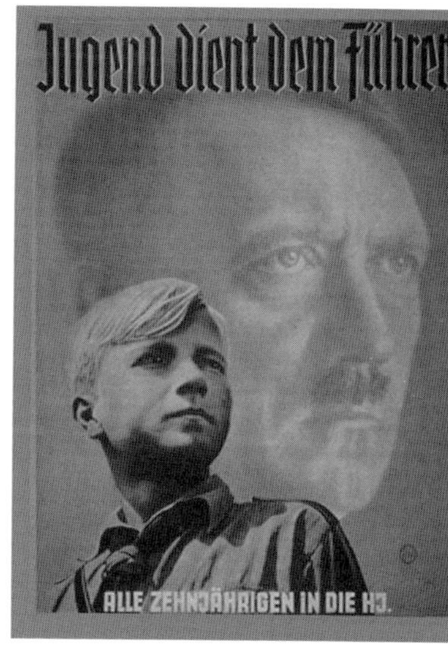

Recruitment poster encouraging German youth to enrol in the *Hitlerjugend* movement.

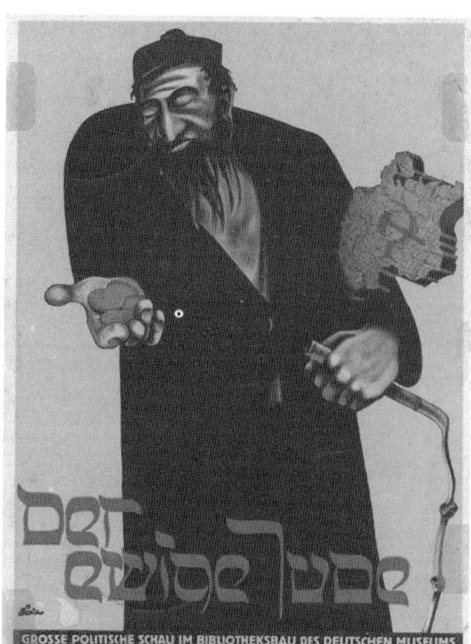

Poster advertising the propaganda film *Der ewige Jude* (The Eternal Jew), with its crude, vile characterisations.

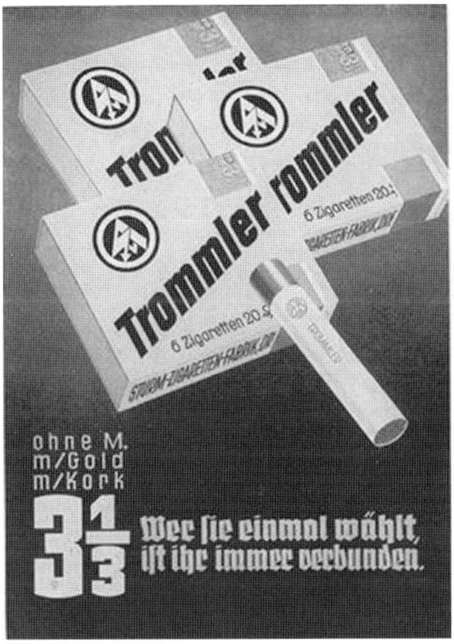

Sturmabteilung-sponsored cigarette packets carrying Nazi symbols and political slogans.

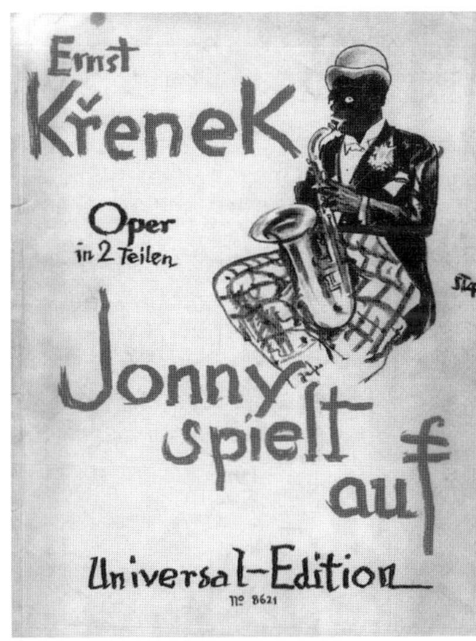

Poster advertising the popular opera *Jonny spielt auf* (Jonny Strikes Up), which featured an African-American jazz musician.

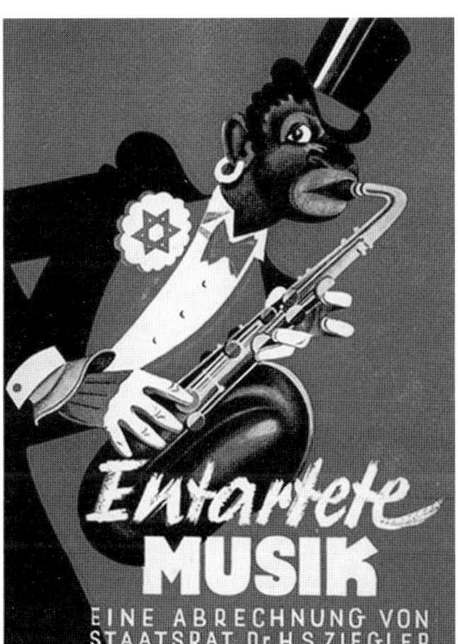

Promotional poster for the *Entartete Musik* (degenerate music) exhibition of 1938, with its caricature of the *Jonny spielt auf* poster.

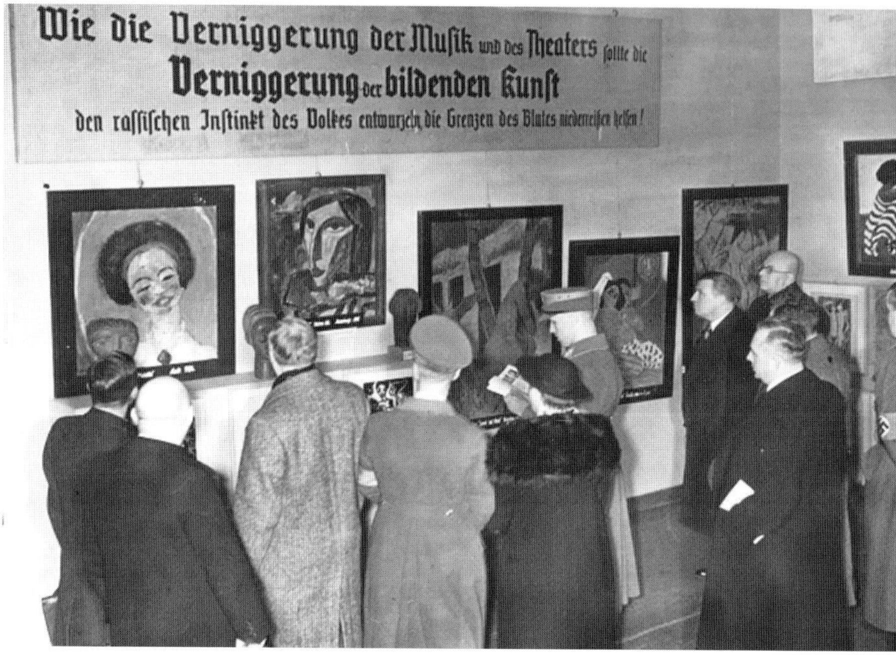

Visitors to the 1937 *Entartete Kunst* exhibition showing a lot more interest than the promoters would have liked.

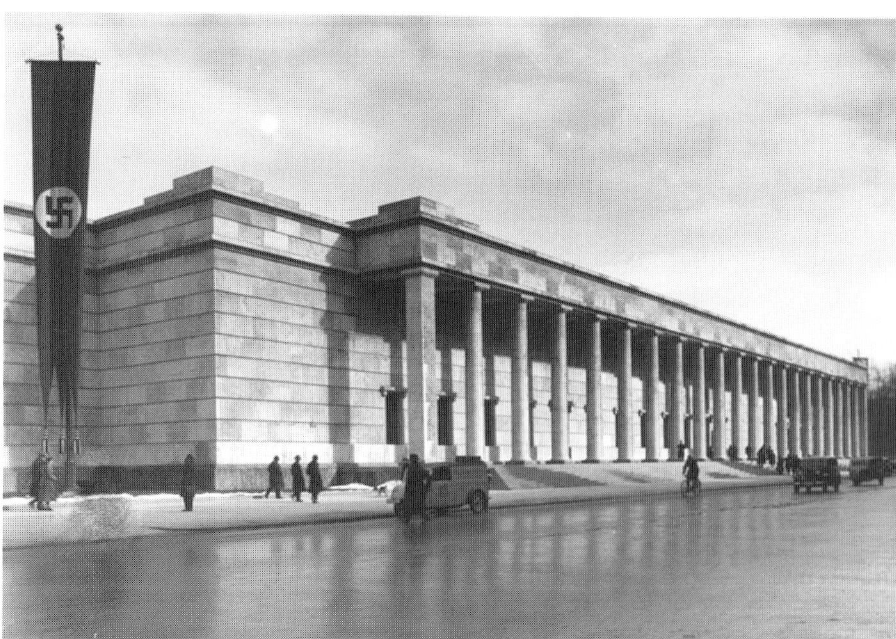

Das Haus der Deutschen Kunst was built especially to house the *Entartete Kunst* exhibition.

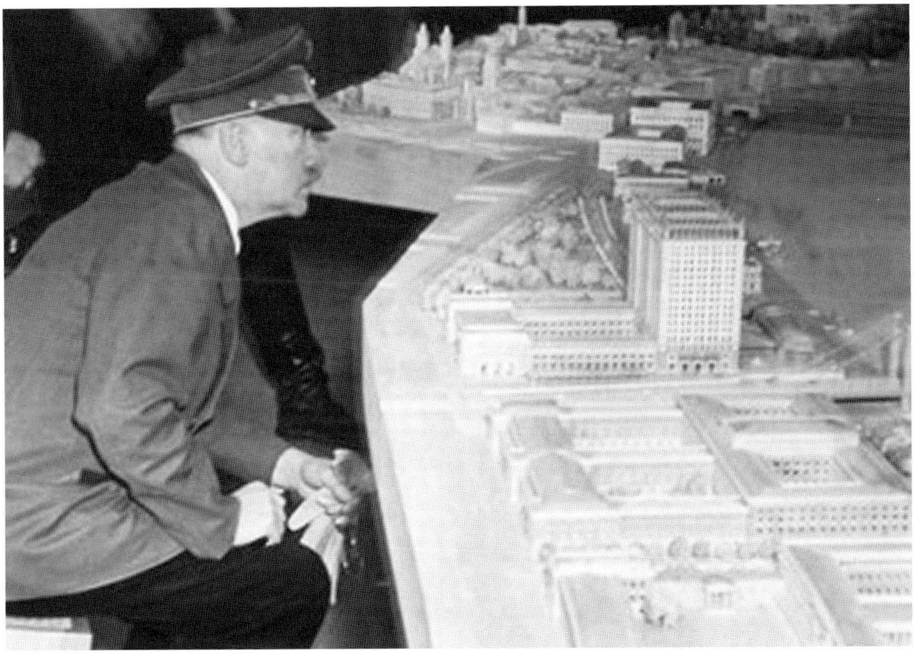

Adolf Hitler spent many hours peering over the model of Linz. His ambition was to rebuild the city as the centre of *Kultur* in the new Reich.

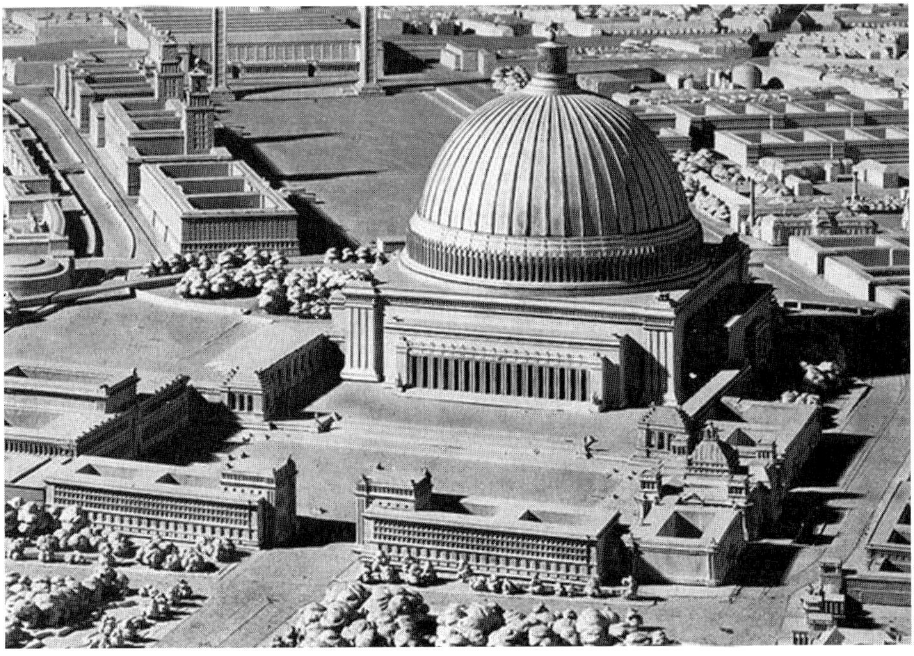

A model of the *Große Halle* (Great Hall) planned for Linz. It would be the world's largest building.

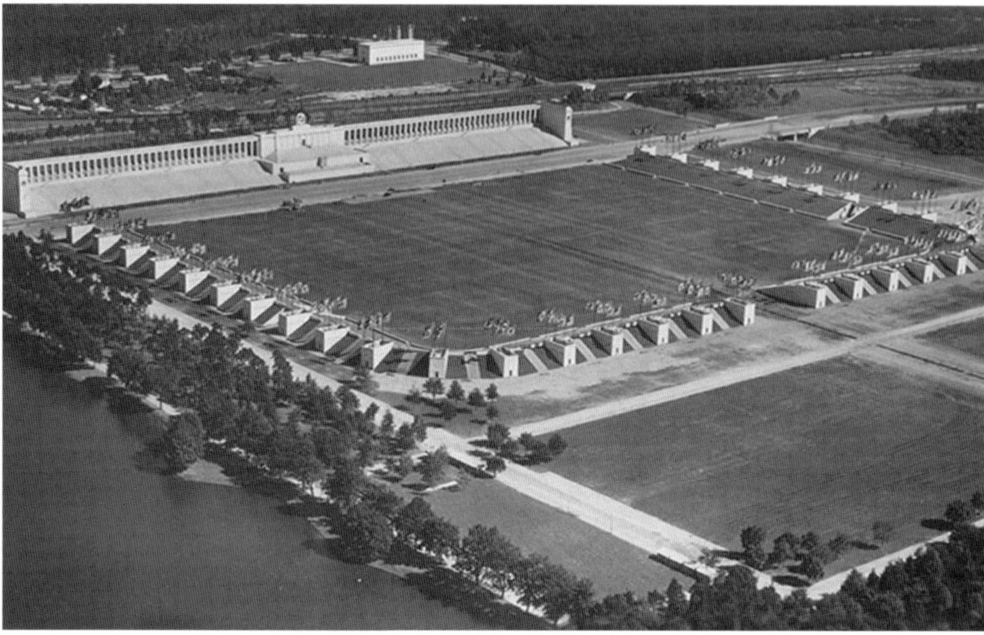

The Zeppelin Field Nazi Party rally ground.

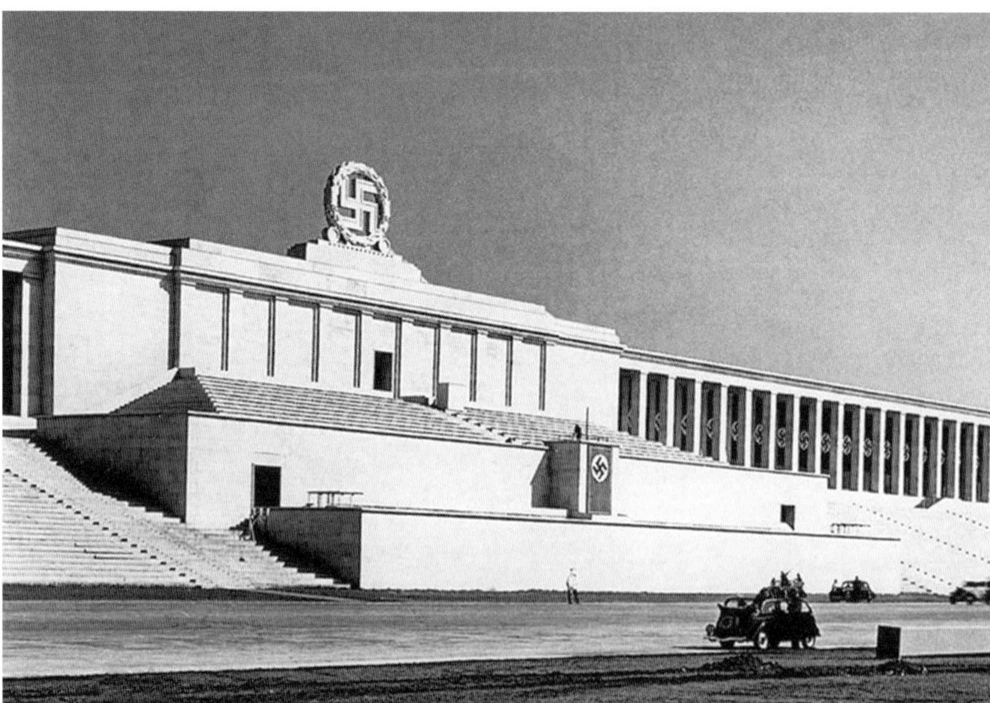

The Zeppelin Field Nazi Party rally ground.

designed for the Nazis were, to some extent, influenced by a race that was anathema to the regime. Speer admitted, years after the war, that he could have been influenced by Semitic aesthetics, but that may well have been part of his drive for rehabilitation when trying to distance himself from the Nazis.

When he had been picked up by Hitler and it became clear just how much he had impressed the Führer, it is no surprise that Speer saw a unique opportunity to realise his architectural ambitions. It was only states or patrons of immense wealth that would allow him to become involved with major projects, and Speer was clearly driven to achieve greatness in his field. As an added bonus, Hitler acquired dictatorial power, some of which were delegated to Speer, which avoided having to deal with the democratic process of spending time convincing various planning authorities to accept his plans.

Leni Riefenstahl

Helene Amalie Bertha Riefenstahl was born in Berlin on 22 August 1902. She was a strong-featured attractive child with all the characteristics that would later see her take to the screen as an accomplished actor, but before that she trained as a ballet dancer. It was while dancing on stage that she first came to the attention of the film producer Arnold Fanck who was famous for his stunning filming of alpine landscapes. Leni acted in several of his films shot on location, becoming an accomplished climber and skier in the process. Not without mishap, however, as she fractured an ankle on her first outing on skis, but it never discouraged her or subsequently slowed her down.

The first film they made together was *Der Helige Berg* (The Holy Mountain), which came out in 1926. It involved a good deal of dancing for her, but it was not long before the lure of the silver screen had driven all thoughts of a dancing career from her mind. All this filming in the mountains gave Riefenstahl a deep love of the heroic ideal. These tough fit mountain climbers fascinated her and she, even then, began to dream of making films that captured the way she felt about them. Just like Fanck's films they would capture all the majesty of the scenery and show how German life was deeply bonded to its environment. She would go on to make a total of six films for Fanck.

Riefenstahl had now turned into what David Gunston called 'a highly attractive, vigorous and determined girl' and still only 17. She could ski and climb with the best of them, but she did not lose her 'essential femininity'.[18] With each film she made she grew in confidence and became something of a star. A review in *Close Up* magazine called her 'unexpectedly fresh, unexpectedly charming [she had] a flowing free rhythm, breath-catching beauty [which was] not blatant or manufactured but sensed with authenticity'.[19] Then, with the advent of talkies, came the acid test for silent screen performers, but she passed with flying colours proving to have a voice of 'pleasant well-modulate timbre [which] recorded satisfactorily'. However, acting was not that important to her. Although she was a famous actor with a burgeoning reputation, she was becoming increasingly possessed with a desire to produce and direct her own films. It was what she called her 'passion'.

In 1931, she set up her own film production company and began work on a film, *Das Blaue Licht* (The Blue Light) in the spectacularly beautiful scenery of the Sarntal valley in the Italian Dolomites. As well as directing the film, she also starred in it, but the film was a disappointment. Critics slammed it for its 'phony romanticism' and Riefenstahl hit back at critics with anti-Semitic venom by saying

> As long as the Jews are film critics, I'll never have a success. But watch out, when Hitler takes the rudder, everything will change.[20]

Its weak story line was not helped by poor sound recording, but the scenery gave it 'powerful atmospheric impact' and is still seen by many as a film of 'extraordinary beauty'.[21]

Riefenstahl first saw Hitler at a rally in the Berlin Sportspalast on 27 February 1932. Her account of how she reacted at that time is significant in light of how she filmed him later. Upon hearing Hitler speak she would say that 'It was like being struck by lightning…I felt quite paralysed', which is the sort of reaction one associates with evangelical religious fervour. Much of Hitler's reputation as an orator stems from Riefenstahl's images of him, which undoubtedly were hugely influenced by her own emotional responses. She was moved to write to Hitler and was surprised to receive a reply within days from his adjutant Wilhelm Brückner.

Hitler had seen her in *Das Blaue Licht* and invited her to meet him at the North Sea fishing village of Horumersiel near Wilhelmhaven. She was already under his spell, urging all her friends to read *Mein Kampf*. 'You'll see,' she told them 'This is the coming man.' When they met, she found Hitler 'unexpectedly modest…like a completely normal person'.[22] He told her that he had been impressed both with the film and with her role in it. Then a few weeks later, Hitler's friend Ernst Hanfstängl was trying to find female company for Hitler that would 'tame him and make him more human and approachable' and took Riefenstahl to the Goebbels' apartment for dinner, where Hitler was also a guest. Both Hitler and Goebbels were big film enthusiasts so there would have been much to talk about. They obviously all got on well because after dinner they went to Riefenstahl's studio, where Hitler and Riefenstahl were politely left together to get to know each other. Hanfstängl recalls that Riefenstahl was 'giving him the works' by dancing in front of him and generally flirting with him.[23] Hitler was extremely nervous and avoided eye contact, choosing to look at her books rather than her. Nevertheless, Hanfstängl, and Goebbels and his wife made their excuses and left. When asked two days later what had happened after that, Riefenstahl shrugged her shoulders in a hopeless gesture.[24] She had made her mark, however, and when Hitler came to power the following year, Riefenstahl became his first-choice film maker for the Nazi Party, and they spent a great deal of time together at all of Hitler's various houses. Although there is no evidence that she became his mistress, indeed Hanfstängl was of the opinion that Hitler was impotent or homosexual, Riefenstahl did not discourage the rumour. Her perceived closeness to the Führer was something she would exploit to gain a great deal of cooperation when making films for the Reich. Hitler grew very fond of Riefenstahl and called her his 'perfect German woman'. They were seen together more and more at social functions and were frequent guests at the Goebbels' apartment. 'He respected me as an artist, nothing more,' Riefenstahl would later write.[25]

Goebbels and Riefenstahl had a mutual dislike for each other, but she became a close friend of his wife, Magda. Riefenstahl was now closely involved with Goebbels' Short and Propaganda film section of his ministry and so could not avoid contact with him, despite his persistent unwanted sexual advances towards her. Thanks to Goebbels, the unspoken but persistent rumour that Riefenstahl was actually Jewish would be kept simmering away in the background. They were seen walking arm in arm at times especially during the 1938 Venice Film Festival but even then she confided to a newspaper that 'the cripple Goebbels' was 'a big enemy of mine'.[26] Goebbels had suggested in 1933 that she make a film of Hitler after coming to the conclusion that, despite personal animosities, she was the only German film-maker who understood what the Nazis were all about. Riefenstahl imagined a film in which she would show 'the bond between the Führer and the people'.[27] The problem for Goebbels was that Arnold Raether and Eberhard Fangauf, who had been responsible for filming party rallies since 1927, had been appointed to head the film division of his Propaganda Ministry, but it was Hitler personally who finally chose Riefenstahl to film the 1933 rally.

There was potential for a serious turf war between Goebbels' people and Riefenstahl when they arrived at Nuremberg days before filming, but Riefenstahl had the good fortune to meet Speer who had been commissioned as 'chief designer' of the rally. Speer's contribution to Riefenstahl's film of the event, *Der Sieg des Glaubens* (Victory of the Faith), which is discussed in greater detail in Chapter 11, cannot be overstated. It was he who organised the mass marches and torchlit parades. It was his grandiose motifs that dominated the arena. He created the camera positions for her. By placing Hitler on a high platform, it made the choice of filming him from below an obvious one, reminiscent of the way that Fanck had filmed the climbers in his alpine epics. Together they worked out frames, angles and lighting.

Riefenstahl's presence at the rally was deeply resented by Raether and Fangauf, who tried to undermine her with rumours of her alleged Jewishness and her alleged promiscuity. She was only there because of sexual favours to Nazi bigwigs, even Hitler himself, they whispered, but Speer, who was rapidly becoming a force to be reckoned with in the party, protected her even against Hess. She was clearly indebted to Speer but would later argue bitterly against his assertions that many of the ideas about camera angles and backgrounds had been prompted by him.

It was common for Reifenstahl to suffer a nervous collapse after shooting a major film. The strength and stamina that possessed her when she was in the mountains seemed to desert her on such occasions. Even Hitler worried that she took her work too seriously and gave too much but she 'wore her breakdowns as a badge of honour' casting her work in a heroic mould.[28]

Benno von Arent

Benno von Arent was Hitler's favourite theatrical stage designer. In 1936 he appointed him to the position of *Reichsbühnenbildner* (Reich Stage Designer) with a brief to create scenery for operas and great state events. Hitler called him 'the bridge to a more beautiful world'.[29] He relished time spent with von Arent mulling over stage sets and funded many of his productions with his own money. It was not uncommon for Hitler to give von Arent sketches he had made of designs for all the scenes of productions such as *Der Ring des Nibelungen* or *Die Meistersinger von Nürnberg* and *Lohengrin* for performances at the German Opera in Berlin. Their common passion was for Wagnerian opera and what Speer called vulgar 'smashing effects', including giant choruses, parades, huge casts and spectacular costumes.

Chapter 8

THE OBSESSION WITH ANTIQUITY

> 'Never has mankind been nearer to antiquity in appearance and sensibility than today.'[1]
>
> Adolph Hitler at the inauguration of the *Ehrentempel*, Munich 1935

Alfred Rosenberg, repeating sacred National Socialist doctrine, claimed that the Greeks were a northern people, and Hitler had linked Greeks, Romans and Germans fighting the same millenarian battle to transform a nation. Appealing to historical precedent to justify political power in the present is a common practice of totalitarian regimes. It is odd, however, that the Nazis turned to Greece and Rome instead of a German past. They could have lauded the Prussian model of discipline, militarism and organisation, except that it was the Junkers who had led the country to defeat in 1918 and it was one of Hitler's greatest challenges to counter Prussian military opposition to the Nazi Party. That still left Friedrich the Great, the Holy Roman Empire and the Teutonic Knights' heroic drive for 'Lebensraum', but it was not only military power that the Nazis wanted; they craved acceptance as a cultured people and sought to perpetuate the myth, to their own people at least, that Germany had been the birthplace of European civilisation.

A few nineteenth-century German linguists and historians had come up with the Aryan myth that the Dorians of Sparta had come from the North, giving them an excuse to rewrite history and claim that the ancient Greeks and Romans had been part of the Nordic race. It was essential that the Nazis were masters not only of the present and the future but also the past in order to establish absolute domination. In her book *The Origins of Totalitarianism,* Hannah Arendt explains how totalitarianisms of both left and right tried to create an 'entirely fictitious world' and satisfy the public need for 'a completely consistent, comprehensible, and predictable world'.[2]

It was the racial anthropologist, the

> high priest of the Nordic race, pope of scientific racism, and thin-skinned ideologue of the most rigorous Nordicism.

Hans Friedrich Karl Günther, supported by eugenicists Eugen Fischer, Erwin Baur and Fritz Lenz, who first promulgated the Nordic theory of the origins of European civilization.[3] By employing a facile synthesis of ideas and sparing the reader the bothersome details of complex debates, subtle arguments or sophisticated hypotheses, they argued that this had been achieved through blood kinship, a common racial inheritance, and a shared cultural heritage.[4] By 1933, Günther's ideas, cobbled together from the xenophobic and nationalist literature of the late nineteenth century, had become the official doctrine of the Nazis and were most enthusiastically received by the *Völkisch* movement. Nordicism became the official state history of the race under the Third Reich. The Reich Interior Minister, Frick, issued a directive on 20 July 1933 to all schools in which he emphasised to pupils that the Greeks were their closest racial brethren which, he claimed, explained Germany's intimate understanding of Greek art. Teachers and instructors were advised to read Günther's books and impress upon their pupils the importance of what he called 'Roman racial kinship', but it was not all that easy to change the teaching of history in this way. There was resistance from publishers who were not eager to commission new textbooks until their current stocks of existing texts had been used up. It would not be until 1938 that wholesale revision of the curriculum was accomplished, but when it was, the message came through loud and clear.

Flying in the face of all Western tradition, the Nazis adopted an anti-intellectual approach to education, rejecting the pursuit of knowledge for its own sake. Teachers were instructed to abandon objectivity and value judgements and embrace dramatisation as the new format for historical education. Instruction, they claimed, should not focus on development of the individual either as a starting point or even an ultimate goal. Man was not a fully autonomous, self-sufficient unit in society but an inseparable unit within a group. It was no longer the role of teachers to educate the individual but to shape the individual according to the needs of the state. Eminent professors and scholars of the ancient classical world were unquestioningly obedient towards this complete makeover of the curricula and revolutionary reform of the schools by rejecting 'liberal ideology and its anaemic, hypocritical objectivity once and for all'.[5] The study of antiquity should be accepted as a paradigm of proper values for the youth of the new Germany. Even the motto proudly displayed above the entrance to all schools in Germany was in Latin '*Mens sana in corpore sano*' (healthy mind in a healthy body), which helped to link the aesthetic perfection of the body to the beauty of the mind.

The profound effect of Dr Leopold Pötsch's teachings while Hitler was a student in Linz had left him with an enduring sense of what he felt was a mystical understanding of the past. Spellbound by the master's eloquence, Hitler had been transported.[6] He wanted to emulate Pötsch and bring to others a sense of emotional attachment to the past through art and that would be achieved through the education of young minds. History must be taught not as a litany of facts but as a narrative in which all important events in the past were merely heralds of what would be a glorious future. As he wrote in *Mein Kampf*:

> The study of history is not to forget its lessons when occasion arises for its practical application, or to decide that the present situation is different after all, and that therefore its old eternal truths are no longer applicable; no, the purpose of studying history is precisely its lesson for the present. The man who cannot do this must not conceive of himself as a political leader.[7]

On 15 March 1934 Alfred Rosenberg proclaimed that the new German education system would follow the Greek method that abjured the seductive and sentimental 'humanisation of mankind' as 'a desiccated and overly cerebral rationalism' that was 'completely contradictory to all the laws of race'.[8] The Nazis, however, had to be selective of exactly which aspects of the classical tradition to follow. It was necessary to separate out the Indo-Germanic influences on Classical Greece from the Semitic impact of Orientalised Hellenism, 'the twilight of racial decadence [and] a vehicle of an anti-Nordic spiritual heritage', which had caused the dissolution of the Nordic peoples of antiquity and 'still remained a destructive poison'.[9] Ancient history, as taught in schools, would now reassume its rightful place in the new Germany and encompass the full historical and cultural measure of the Nordic race. Through comparison with the other Nordic peoples of antiquity such as the Hittites, the Persians, the Greeks and the Romans, the German people would see how the Nordic race had achieved a global reach.

The German people were encouraged to believe that all European civilisation stemmed from the Nordic-Germanic race and that even

Greek and Roman civilisations had been created by offshoots of that family tree that had migrated south from their ancestral home. 'That the Greeks were of Nordic origin is abundantly clear from their sculptures,' as *Rasse und Volk*, a Nazi Party ideological pamphlet put it.

> The figures of the gods that they carved out of stone show, in the body, the shape of the skull, the expressions on their faces, all the traits of their Nordic descent.[10]

This rewriting of Germany's racial past was aimed not only at intellectuals and educational professionals but at the entire German people, allowing them to claim all the prestige, glory and grandeur associated with these ancient Mediterranean civilisations. Rosenberg said,

> The march of world history has radiated from the north over the entire planet, determining in vast successive waves the spiritual face of the world.

The Dorians had appeared in Greece some 4,000 years ago and displaced barbarian tribes, after which Greek civilisation blossomed into the 'most brilliant…in the history of mankind'.[11]

This symbolic purloining of European culture was also later employed to justify not only intellectual dominion but territorial and military occupation of territories to which the Germanic race was simply returning to reclaim possession of what was already rightfully its own. What was purported to be a definitive history of the swastika symbol had it that the *Hakenkreuz* had migrated south with waves of Nordic peoples at a time before the birth of Greek civilisation. Large numbers of vases with the *Hakenkreuz* had been recovered during the excavations of the Dipylon cemetery in Athens, as well as at Troy and Mycenae.

The first power to unify all of Europe had been the Romans, who, according to the narrative, were Indo-Germanic countrymen who had created a strong, peaceful and centrally organised empire. A German nationalism in search of its own truth had cynically abandoned all respect for evidence-based theories. The study of history now became an ideology of the present couched in terms of a past reimagined to justify contemporary political needs. Günther employed a variety of arguments, not least the works of Homer, which were basically myths couched in a narrative having spurious relation to fact. Günther then turned to the art of ancient Greece and Rome, particularly statuary and busts, and found what he called distinct physiognomic similarities to modern Aryans. Wilhelm Sieglin, a professor of anthropology at the University of Berlin, added his own theory. Based on an exhaustive reading of ancient texts, he argued that all Greek heroes and Roman patricians had been tall and blond like Germans and Swedes. Hitler was known to refer to Sieglin's ideas when expounding his racial theories.[12]

The real flaw in the Nazis' case for Nordic origins of Greek and Roman civilisation, of course, was why had Germany not been the birthplace of European civilisation? What had happened to the culture that had supposedly spawned the Dorian migration? Where are the ancient monuments that speak of Nordic culture in northern Europe? Hitler had addressed this question in *Mein Kampf* when he wrote,

> It is an unbelievable offense to represent the Germanic peoples of the pre-Christian era as barbarians.

It was only the harshness of their northern homeland that denied them the circumstances in which their creative forces could develop. Schultze-Naumburg offered some explanation of why there were no existing examples of past Germanic cultural greatness: it was simply that ancient Germanic cultures had built their civilisation in wood and iron, both of which soon decay, rather than the stone of classical Greece and Rome that had survived the ravages of time.

Hitler's ideas about German culture were not shared by the SS secret police chief Heinrich Himmler, however. Himmler, obsessed with theories of an historic German past that included the occult, pseudoscience and legend, was willing to accept all sorts of nonsense as irrefutable fact and sent an entire regiment of SS archaeologists into the forests of Germany to look for evidence for Gustaf Kossinna's *Kultutkreis* theories of prehistoric Germanic civilizations.[13] Anywhere that ancient German artefacts had been uncovered, argued Kossinna, must have been German territory in the past and rightly belonged to the Reich. This included areas in Poland, Czechoslovakia, modern Ukraine and Russia. Himmler disdained science and logic in favour of magic. It was so much easier to create a narrative of prehistory constructed around runic writing and mystic rites of old Teutonic legends rather than have to worry about facts. Inside his hermetically sealed, fabricated world, Himmler's stubborn refusal to live in the light of reality led him to despise the artifacts of classical antiquity that proclaimed the grandeur of their culture to detriment of the Germans' own ancient heritage. The fabled Ultima Thule of a lost Nordic culture that the ancient Greek explorer Pytheas had written about 2,500 years ago was, for Himmler, the cradle of the German race.

On 1 July 1935, Himmler founded the *Deutsches Ahnenerbe e. V.*, the German Ancestral Heritage Society to promote his ideas. The task of his *Ahnenerbe* was to create a body of *Germanekunde* (Germanic studies) to rival the classicists who were dominating the agenda. Hitler was no fan of Gustaf Kossinna, however. He mocked Himmler's enthusiasm for 'crude, retrograde folklore' which had nothing to do with National Socialism. Everything that Himmler's archaeologists succeeded in bringing to light and writing about in their journal *Germanien*, which had been set up together with the Society for the Friends of German Prehistory in March 1936, left the Führer wholly unimpressed. The artifacts discovered provided overwhelming proof, in his eyes, of the incurable backwardness of a culture that he wanted nothing to do with. Himmler's '*Völkisch kitsch*', resurrecting the cults, customs and traditions of a distant past was quite wrong. Any civilisation that failed to leave behind indisputable proof of its greatness did not deserve to be called great, he said, which put Schultze-Naumburg's ideas to bed also. For Hitler, there was no doubt that it was ancient Greece and Rome, after their founding by Nordic peoples, that had been the creators of all European culture and who had left behind such a wealth of evidence for its greatness.

Eventually Himmler fell into line and created a new department within the *Ahnenerbe* to study Greco-Roman antiquity for signs of Indo-Germanic symbols or heritage. He still maintained an obsession with the occult, but realised just how central the links to ancient Greece and Rome were becoming to the Nazi cultural narrative. He ordered a review and study of all past and future archaeological discoveries and called for proof that the Roman and Greek cultures were indebted to Aryan and Indo-Germanic peoples who came from ancient German lands on the North Sea. The organisation set up archaeological research expeditions to look for evidence. In practice, however, lack of funds left it without the means to do much real research, which actually saved a great deal of money and effort since there was nothing to be found.

Once it had been decided to go ahead with the Berlin Olympics, there was a significant effort to exploit the event from a propaganda perspective by promoting German-Greek kinship, already well established as a subject of historical research, and which was frequently alluded to in arts and culture. Early in the planning stage, a row erupted over the naming of the new stadium to host the games. Predictably, Frick wanted to call it the *Deutsche Kampfbahn* (German combat arena), but Goebbels thought that rather too bombastic and chauvinistic for an international audience and suggested instead *Olympiastadion*. Neither man would give way and it was left to Hitler to side with Goebbels.

An exhibition opened on 29 July 1936 in Berlin entitled *Sport den Hellenen* that spared no effort in hammering home the link between ancient Greece and Germany through various channels, not least of which was the official poster advertising the games, which depicted a Greek athlete crowned in laurels towering over the Brandenburg Gate. Then when the games finally began there were numerous cultural activities, many with Greek themes, for guests to enjoy. One of the most spectacular was the reception hosted by Hermann Göring for the various national delegations at the foot of the Pergamon Altar in Berlin's Altes Museum, featuring steps to the altar filled with young girls in antique-style outfits and young boys decked out as archers. Bernhard Rust declared in a speech to the assembled guests that 'The modern Olympic Games have rediscovered their deepest roots'.[14]

Chapter 9

PROPAGANDA THROUGH ARCHITECTURE

> 'National Socialism offered a myth. Its narration, by the state and its institutions—and especially its artistic and academic organizations—was presented as reality. Its lies were passed off as truth: Nazi discourse did not adapt to describe an external, objective reality; rather, this discourse was shaped, internally and self-referentially, to fit the preconceived notions underlying the discourse itself.'[1]

By embracing three distinct, and sometimes contradictory forms, Nazi architecture was essentially pluralistic, but overall, Hitler believed in the slogan 'form follows function', implying that the purpose of a building should be obvious from its appearance. Formal buildings of state were to be of stripped Neoclassical design based on Greek and Roman style without ornamentation, which projected monumentality, solidity and a sense of permanence. In this way architecture served its propaganda role of urging the nation to bind together in uniformity of opinion and action. At the same time, in contrast to this, a vernacular style of traditional rural (alpine) architecture was encouraged for smaller-scale developments, fulfilling the role of evoking *Völkisch* sentiments, but this tended to lose some of its relevance in propaganda terms when Hitler became obsessed with his monumental projects. A third style was somewhat confused, however, where infrastructure projects, such as autobahns, were completed in a utilitarian style of functionality and simplicity reminiscent of *Bauhaus* design, which had been closed down for its modernist approach to architecture.

Given that he was so important in developing the Nazi style of architecture, it is worth looking in some detail at Hitler's architectural competence. The Library of Congress in Washington contains over 3,000 items from Hitler's private library, many of which relate to architecture. Christa Schroeder, one of Hitler's personal secretaries, wrote that she saw 'important architects and experts being absolutely dumbfounded by [Hitler's] ability' to hold long discourses on architecture which he would not allow political matters to interrupt.[2] During discussions of ancient architecture he would be very comfortable debating the characteristics of Mycenae, Babylon and Athens, as well as the later buildings of Frederick II (the Great) and Bernini. Speer found that he demonstrated a profound knowledge of design and followed closely the work being done on multiple projects. His sketches, even when executed quickly, demonstrated 'a good sense of architectural dynamism and proportions'.[3]

The fact that there were no specific directives coming from either Hitler or Goebbels imposing an official style to be adopted in Germany's cultural renaissance allowed acute tensions to develop between two distinct factions in the decade 1928–1938. In the realm of architecture, it was the concept of large-scale urban renewal with civic buildings of unmistakably modern appearance that won Hitler's tacit approval against the vernacular *Völkisch* lobby led by Rosenberg and Frick. Hitler's preoccupation with architectural renovation did not so much stem from any particular architectural aesthetic, but rather from his concern over the way that civic spaces under the Weimar Republic had allowed state buildings to be swamped by private dwellings and commercial buildings, resulting in what he saw as a chaotic modern-built environment ensuing from a complete lack of vision. He craved monuments dominating the skyline to symbolise the age and last not for the moment, but for eternity, to reflect the greatness of the nation and its people.

Hitler's cultural ambition for Germany was to create a nation of heroes in a classical mould for which he called on the myths, statuary and architecture of ancient Greece and Rome. When we think of Hitler and art, it is his obsession with architecture that stands out as the significant feature and it was through architecture, primarily, that he expressed his ambition for a new German aesthetic. His reasoning was convoluted and not particularly sound, but it was the effect that was important not the method. Fascist ideology tends towards ritualisation built around a core of truth and carefully constructed myth drawing on a distant past for inspiration. Hitler had little in the way of ancient German culture beyond a vague fabricated concept of rural idyll and heroic struggle, and that was a problem for him because within that narrative there was no monumantal or architectural tradition that he could draw on for inspiration. It was necessary, therefore, to fabricate a false concept of lineage from the Dorian peoples of the Classical age to modern Germany, which would allow him to claim ownership of the ancient legacy.

There was no easy way to do this except to repeatedly state it as fact and give the idea time to become embedded in the national psyche. It would require considerable falsification of history and obfuscation of contradictions, but the rewards in terms its propaganda value were immense. There was, of course, a significant barrier to overcome if the people were to be convinced that the ancients were the ideal role model. All that was left of Classical Greece and Rome were ruins. Why would anyone want to associate themselves with a civilisations that had fallen into decay? The solution was to find a reason for their demise and one that could form the basis of why a modern version of their empires could avoid the same fate. Academics came up with the ideal explanation: the Greeks, especially the Spartans, once a supremely powerful race had been weakened catastrophically through racial mixing, which had diluted the blood line. Having made their point, there was nothing to be gained by overplaying it and so, having got that out of the way, it was the symbolism of the ancient world that came to the fore and obscured the somewhat questionable pseudo-historical connection.

One of the most powerful ways of creating a link between the ancient cultures and the present was through the built environment. Hitler wanted buildings that would 'tower over the millennia of the future like cathedrals [providing a] measure of the truly monumental cultural spirit of their time'. Using huge blocks of granite, their gargantuan scale would become an evocation of timeless values and supplant religious dogmas by guaranteeing continued existence of the individual within 'the visible immortality of the nation'.[4] The extravagant use of the expensive materials of stone and marble would signify the end of commercialism, utilitarianism, individualism and 'Jewish' economic interests and, at the same time, would demonstrate the immense force and creativity that only the Third Reich could release under Hitler's leadership.

It had been an obsession of Hitler since his time in Landsberg Prison to transform the country and proclaim the values of a nation reborn through architecture. As his political career developed, he tried to consolidate his grip on the NSDAP by promoting the victims of the abortive Beer Hall Putsch as martyrs and etching their memory in stone. He moved the party headquarters to Munich where, in 1930, they bought a large Neoclassical house at 45 Brienner Straße, situated between Karolinenplatz and Königsplatz. Renaming it the Brown

House, they began extensive renovations funded by the industrial tycoon Fritz Thyssen. Hitler's biographer, Konrad Heiden, says that tackling the redesigning of this former Italian Legation building allowed Hitler 'to abandon himself to his passion for building and design…for the first time in his life'.[5]

To oversee the project, Hitler chose an architect of the reactionary movement, Paul Ludwig Troost, who proved to be sufficiently malleable to accomodate Hitler's constant interference and modification of plans and models, which he insisted should be based upon classical styles. Troost had actually been a classical architect and interior designer of modest ability, but his style had pleased Hitler when they met in 1929 and Hitler gave him a small commission.[6] It was obviously completed to Hitler's satisfaction and Troost was given responsibility for work on the Brown House. The Brown House already had significant Neoclassical elements in its design, including strong vertical and horizontal lines on the facade, but plans now included a balcony from which Hitler could 'look down upon a crowd of followers in fervent celebration'.[7]

Attention now turned towards the Königsplatz, where Hitler intended to creat a monumant to the Nazis killed in the Beer Hall Putsch as part of his ambition to consolidate a cult of personality. The large open space was surrounded on three sides by Neoclassical buildings that had been designed for Crown Prince Ludwig of Bavaria by Leo von Klenze and were based on the Acropolis. The square, which already had the shape of a classical meeting space, was fronted by two Greek-style buildings, the *Glyptothek* with its an Ionic porch, and the *Neue Staatsgalerie,* with a Corinthian one. It also already had a large Doric gate called the *Propyläen*. Although deliberately in a Greek style, the Königsplatz was designed more as a Roman forum, whose purpose was to serve as a public space for major events displaying the grandeur of the state, rather than a Greek *agora,* which was more of a commercial marketplace for everyday use.

When the Nazis added their own buildings they were more Roman in style, showing less curvature and ornamentation than Greek, which added a note of incongruity given the style of the existing buildings. Clearly, while Classicism was the overall style, the Nazis were not rigorous in its application, but the richly evocative *Gesamtkunstwerk* (total arwork) endowed every part of the square with meaning and uncompromising ambition. Three buildings were added. The imposing *Führerbau* (Führer building) was built as a symbol of Hitler's leadership, while the other two, the *Ehrentempel* (Honour Temples), erected in memory of the sixteen Nazis who died in the failed 1923 coup, were the true focal points. The *Ehrentempel* were square buildings with open spaces in the *atria* (centre). Twenty-four fluted columns surrounded a sunken space housing sixteen *sarcophagi*. The name implies some attempt to give the buildings religious significance, although the Nazi movement itself had no religious tenets, but the Honour Temples, with their architectural references to ancient history, gave the site huge cultural and political relevance. It was here that the first book-burning events took place in 1933. Goebbels said of the Königsplatz that 'Here the Führer wrote his will in stone'.[8]

These buildings were in the stark and imposing 'stripped classical' style, where only the bare structure is visible. This became a feature of much of Hitler's architectural planning. Nazi buildings were designed to convey to the viewer a sense of endurance stretching from a distant past long into the future. Troost was selected to design the new *Haus der Deutschen Kunst*, which he did in the same Roman classical style, but he died in 1934 before the building was completed.

In 1931, the Weimar government had made a successful bid to host the 1936 Olympic Games, despite the dire state of government finances. By the following year it was looking increasingly likely that the government could not raise the necessary money, so a new body, the Organisation Committee for the XI Olympic Games, was set up on 27 January 1933. It had little hope of making progress, however, especially when, days later, the Nazis took over the government as it was well known that they had no interest in the games, which they saw as an artificial bourgeois-internationalist concept. It did not help their cause that Theodor Lewald, the man who had done most to win the bid and was the driving force behind the project, was Jewish. When international pressure mounted on the International Olympic Committee (IOC) to withdraw the invitation to host the games, it was quite another matter. It was acceptable for the Nazis to back out of the deal, but to be rejected would be an insult. The original budget had been 1.5 million Reichsmarks and the organisers asked for an extra 6 million to start work on a new stadium, but this was flatly rejected. Then a personal plea to Hitler offering him the Presidency of the German Olympic Committee received an enthusiastic response. He agreed to a state guarantee for a loan of 28 million Reichsmarks which, in the end, was only about a third of the eventual cost. There was no indication as to who might come up with the actual cash, but at least this got the ball rolling.

Planning went ahead but with strict limits on the budget since there was still no actual money on offer, just a loan guarantee. By the end of the summer, it was clear that the Berlin city administration would have to take on the bulk of the financial burden if the whole thing was not to be completely abandoned. After all, the Organisation Committee argued, it was Berlin that would most benefit from the huge influx of foreign visitors, but the city authorities were reluctant to agree to signing a blank cheque. Much of the land earmarked for Olympic development was owned by Prussia and let on a long-term lease to a third party. They would be asked to pay for and build the new stadium on land they did not and could not own. Who would lend the city the money to do that? The national government had put up some money to start preparing the site, but the project was foundering. A number of different individuals and agencies were angling to derive profit from construction, but nobody wanted to take responsibility for it.

Then on 5 October, Hitler visited the site along with the Reich Interior Minister Hans Pfundtner, who had been given overall responsibility for organising the games as part of the public works and employment creation programmes. They found only 'scrubby grass on sandy earth'.[9] Hitler took the immediate decision to abandon any idea of renovating the 1916 stadium and threw his weight behind a new plan for the entire Reich Sports Field. It would include the construction of a 100,000-seat stadium, 'the largest structure of its kind to date', and a massive open-air theatre next to it. The problem of finance disappeared overnight. The money would come from the 1.5 billion Reichsmarks fund that was set up to finance infrastructure projects across the country and was authorised by Hitler personally. On 10 October, he told the Reichstag that

> Germany must [therefore] try to win over world opinion through [a display of its] great cultural achievements. If we are to invite the world's nations to such an event, then they must be shown the cultural achievements of the new Germany.[10]

Once the idea of hosting the games took hold, widespread enthusiasm for the project grew rapidly and many agencies saw benefit for themselves in promoting them. The propaganda appeal was obvious and it was not long before the *Völkischer Beobachter* was proudly proclaiming that, contrary to all available evidence, the Olympic Games themselves were a German creation. Winckelmann was the authority they had turned to calling him 'the veritable discoverer of Hellenism, who was the first to highlight the racial foundations of art and culture'.[11] In 1852, it had been two other Germans the archaeologists Ernst Curtius and Wilhelm Dörpfeld who had begun excavations on the site of ancient Olympia, the original home of the games on the Peloponnesian peninsula in

Greece, which also added to the narrative of German-Greek cultural links. Hitler ordered those excavations at Olympia be revitalised under Hans Schlief, a member of Himmler's Black Order, which had been established to explore the origins of the race and preserve its heritage. He asked for regular briefings on the findings.

Hitler also saw the games as an opportunity to draw in foreign currency which the country was desperately short of. It was an ideal form of currency exchange. The games would be paid for in Reichsmarks and the revenue from them would be in the form of foreign currency. Neither was it lost on Hitler that construction of a new stadium would absorb a significant number of the unemployed. The whole thing could be funded through the national Work Creation Programme and a small tax on wages levied to provide additional revenue for work creation. Hitler was already working on plans for the rebuilding of public spaces in Berlin with 'monuments of pride', and a new stadium fitted in comfortably with that idea. By taking this decision, he would take all the credit for the whole project. It would become a personal triumph and a huge propaganda victory for him but, of course, would cost him neither time, money nor effort. In the end, the city of Berlin paid for the streets, bridges and parking lot surrounding the Olympic site, though not before trying to push this bill, too, onto the German state. Pfundtner would have none of it and even denied the city a share of the income from ticket sales to help cover its loan repayments.

Hitler then told Pfundtner of his ambition to raise up a structure on the site that would 'reflect the dignity of the Olympic idea and the honour of the German people'. It was still early days, but it was already becoming commonplace for those around Hitler to begin speaking of the 'will of the Führer' that was replacing government. It was convenient for Goebbels to promote this idea of Hitler as almost superhuman, but in reality, behind the scenes there lay a disorderly and at times confusing administrative process involving different individuals and agencies, all of whom wanted to profit from construction without taking responsibility. These agencies would often work against each other to pursue their own interests, some even risking Hitler's wrath by working against his expressed wishes. Hitler was never interested in the details of how any scheme would be implemented. All he was concerned with were the 'big ideas' he would lay out and let others bring to life. All his big ideas would require a complex government apparatus to implement them, and the Olympic project would be no different in that respect. He would, however, retain complete control over the design of the *Olympiastadion*.

Hitler's first decision was to appoint Werner March to be the architect. March's father, Otto, had designed the Berlin Stadium for the 1916 Olympic Games that had been abandoned because of the First World War. This stadium was no longer suitable to hold the games twenty years later, but the nearby unfinished German Sport Forum training facility could be incorporated into any new design. When March brought Hitler the first rough plans, however, Hitler was less than pleased. March had completely failed to understand what was expected of him. He had come up with a steel and glass main structure similar to the Vienna Stadium. Speer was with Hitler as the Führer flew into a rage and called Pfundtner, telling him to cancel the games. Speer stayed with Hitler until he had calmed down and managed to start up a conversation about Hitler's own vision for the Olympic site. With the plans laid out before them, the two men started covering up the steel frames with stone and getting rid of all the glass. What had started out as a design based on Greek lines had turned more into a Roman Neoclassical amphitheatre. By the end of the evening Hitler had rescinded his earlier decision to cancel the games. The new design saw the *Olympiastadion* jutting up from a flat surface and emulating the oval shape of the Roman Colosseum.

The completed stadium would go on to feature prominently in Riefenstahl's film of the games. In the introductory sequence, images of ancient ruins and statues fade into the Athenian Parthenon, which is replaced by the new *Olympiastadion*. The obvious message is that the *Olympiastadion* would stand as a symbol of Reich grandeur thousands of years into the future in the same way that the Parthenon did for the Greeks.

There is an interesting concept inherent in the view where both Hitler and Speer seem fascinated by the idea that a building should have 'ruin value'. The concept of lasting power came up often as they walked together, stimulated by the existence of edifices of Rome, Greece and Karnak that still existed and spoke of their power many hundreds of years after the civilisations that built them had disappeared. This meant that even when a building had fallen into ruins, it should still imitate the classical legacy and have aesthetic appeal. Often, when discussing projects in later years, Hitler would spend hours considering how a building would eventually decay and how its original construction might determine how that collapse would occur. When presenting plans for new buildings, architects would often be asked to produce drawings showing what they might look like in a ruined state. Although Speer claimed it was he who had first conceived this idea, it was not a new one. When designs had been called for the Bank of England building in the early nineteenth century, the architect Sir John Soane had submitted an oil sketch of how the building might look after a thousand years.

After 1935, Hitler began to modify his architectural aesthetic to include more decoration, as was apparent in his ideas for a new *Naziparteitagsgelände* (Nazi Party Rally Ground) at Nuremberg. No place was as symbolically important to the Nazis as this city, where rallies had been held since 1927, despite it never having been a particular stronghold of Nazi fervour. While the municipal government was no more than lukewarm to the idea of the Nazis descending on them, there was a well-organised local party machine and the police in the city were particularly well-disposed to give all assistance. The Nazis loved the city for its symbolic connection to German history, art and culture.

The party rallies had grown in size and importance during the 1930s, with huge theatrical celebrations of Nazi power incorporating pageantry, historical allusions and national pride. Hitler's architectural concepts for cities of the future all contained huge symbolic open areas around which monumental buildings would rise. National greatness would express itself through the spectacular scale and grandeur of these spaces. At the same time as creating the modern *Naziparteitagsgelände*, the whole Nuremberg city centre was earmarked for a restoration programme to preserve its historic character. In this way the Nazi concept of linking the past and future could manifest itself through spectacular architecture. It was undoubtedly true that one of the reasons Hitler was so popular was that he created a mood of excitement through pageant that had been totally lacking during the austere Weimar years, and this helped the German people to recapture a sense of national pride and feel part of the political process.

In 1933, the improvised and haphazard organisation of the 1927 and 1929 rallies in the city had given way to a much more sophisticated and elaborate, not to say efficient, staging of the event which Hitler planned to make an annual occurrence and would become important in the wider international community, drawing audiences from around the world. Riefenstahl's film of the 1934 rally, *Triumph des Willens* (Triumph of the Will), did much to cement the importance of the annual rallies, so much so that it was felt they needed their own bespoke arena to do them justice. The area chosen had been a park during the Weimar years, a largely open space except for two buildings which were incorporated into the plans and had been utilised for the two previous rallies in the city.

The pleasure and recreation ground already had the Dutzendteich Lake, with lakeside café and the Luitpold Grove landscaped park, designed for the 1906 Bavarian Jubilee Exhibition. There was an emotional component in the form of the *Ehrenhalle,* a memorial to the city's First World War dead, which particularly appealed to the Nazis. Of less importance was a small zoo and a public swimming pool. Initial plans drawn up by Schultze-Naumburg were thrown back at him by a singularly unimpressed Hitler, who thought they looked like a provincial marketplace. Speer was quick to step in with his own ideas based on what he knew would be much more acceptable to his Führer and would enhance the leader's standing as a cult figure. Speer well knew how to evoke an emotional response from Hitler, even if it was 'at the expense of practicality and proportion'.[12] His love of architecture matched that of Hitler and he seemed to understand completely what Hitler wanted. He became a trusted adviser who did not pester his leader with annoying questions once the overall concept of a project had been agreed.

Speer designed most of the buildings in the *Naziparteitagsgelände.* His preference was for Greek rather than Roman styles, but the buildings would tend more towards the Roman indicating the strong influence that Hitler had on the designs at all stages. What Hitler found particularly appealing about Speer was his penchant for 'over-the-top' designs, which Hitler was ever willing to finance. A special corporation, the *Zweckverband Reichsparteitag Nürnberg* (Special Purpose Association for the Nuremberg Party Rally), was created to oversee the whole redevelopment project. It included representatives from the city of Nuremberg, the state of Bavaria, the Reich and the Nazi Party. Right from the start, Hitler ensured it had priority status when it came to finance and material resources. The whole project comprised six components.

The *Luitpoldarena* (Luitpold Grove), and war memorial area was completely levelled and opened up into a space that could accommodate 150,000 standing figures between two massive stone grandstands. It was envisaged that during a rally, Hitler would walk solemnly between the massed ranks of SA and SS stormtroopers and pay his respects at the war memorial. Next to this open area was the Luitpold Hall, a remodelling of one of the existing buildings on the site.

The Zeppelin Field was a stadium built where the sports field had been. All along one side of the field would be a massive stone grandstand-like structure, designed by Speer. The nearly square complex looked toward this grandstand with its central podium from where Hitler could review the whole parade. Behind this and high above was a giant swastika set in an oak leaf wreath. Another similar, much bigger, area, the *Märzfeld* (March Field), was planned as a parade ground for the Wehrmacht. It was begun in 1938 but never completed.

Having been lukewarm about the idea of hosting the Olympic Games, Hitler now planned an arena, fashioned on the Panathenaic Stadium of Athens, which would become a permanent home for the games and where they could be held every four years and renamed the Germanic World Festival. This was the horseshoe-shaped *Deutsches Stadion* (German Stadium), to be built entirely of stone and which would hold nearly 500,000 spectators. It would be decorated with massive spread-winged eagles and 25-metre-high equestrian statues. A cornerstone was laid in 1937 but very little work was ever done on the project.

The semi-circular *Neue Kongresshalle* (New Congress Hall) was designed by Ludwig and Franz Ruff in 1934 as an immense 50,000-seat auditorium where party meetings would be held. It was sited along the north shore of the Dutzendteich Lake. Most of the outer shell of the building was completed but the interior remained unfinished.

The rallies themselves were extraordinary spectacles, drawing heavily on tradition and public celebrations that had been taking place in the country for more than 100 years. Yet while the architecture hearkened back to the past, the celebrations were greatly enhanced by very modern theatrical devices used effectively to heighten the drama and mystical experience for the crowds, who became an essential part of the *Gesamtkunstwerk*. The proceedings relied heavily on the

> Stirring and anticipatory effects of martial music, trumpeted fanfares and thundering drums; on the visually exhilarating effects of massed blocks of uniformed marching men and women, phalanxes of flags and standards, and the surreal effects cast by thousands of flickering torches; and on the ecstatic effects of spellbindingly bombastic oratory and mass proclamations of undying loyalty.[13]

The designs of the rally venues were primarily influenced by their propaganda value. A mock-up scale model of the whole project was in place by 1935 and Hitler spent hours poring over it with Speer. Hitler seemed to have had a keen perception of grandeur and spatial layout, which Speer had been quick to understand and apply. The two most significant facets of Hitler's aesthetic vision for architecture that Speer shared were firstly that monuments should be constructed out of natural, traditional, hard-wearing materials like granite and marble, and secondly, that they should be built to last as enduring evidence of the nation's achievements. In terms of spatial awareness within the designs, plans ensured that inside the arenas, all eyes of the many tens of thousands in there would be focused on the place where the Führer stood, and all spectacle was designed to create a sense of overwhelming power and endurance. The architecture itself, in the manner of medieval cathedrals, was meant to instruct and educate all who witnessed it. The message was simple and it was delivered with panache. The heroic achievements of the Nazis were set in stone and the Reich would last 'a thousand years'. Designed to overwhelm the senses with awe and inspiration on a grand scale, the gigantist monuments would epitomise the state as it towered over and protected the people, whose individuality was diminished and subsumed into the mass.

To some extent Nuremberg had been chosen for the annual Nazi rallies because of its historic symbolism, and within its medieval walls, the old city itself became part of the overall experience for the many thousands of visitors. The urban landscape as a stage for public performance and mass spectacle was a concept that had become part of the process of creating a new German identity. Far from serving as mere passive scenery, it was destined to play a more dynamic role in the cultural life of the community. The old city was a little dowdy, however, and not quite in keeping with the sense of national pride and greatness the rallies were designed to create. At the same time that the *Naziparteitagsgelände* was taking shape, a decision was taken to upgrade the city centre, whose historic squares, buildings and fortifications had been allowed to lose much of their character and appeal. These would now be restored and integrated into an orderly and disciplined urban landscape.

There were many historical structures in dire need of restoration, while others were sound but had lost their character through cheap modification of their facades. In some places the whole medieval character had been diluted by the construction of modernist buildings alongside historic ones, some of which had connections to the time of the Holy Roman Empire. All in all, the city was suffering from what might be called cultural degeneration. The Nazi mayor of the city, Willy Liebel, was keen for the city to reflect the basic tenets of Nazi ideology and, with the support of the middle- and upper-class inhabitants, made a start on the historic centre, which hosted parades and other festivities during the times of the rallies. Liebel was a long-time member of the Nazi party and a man well attuned to the mood, so as his first step, the *Hauptkarkt* was renamed Adolf-Hitler-Platz. He then turned his focus on buildings such as the neogothic Telegraph Building, built in 1870, which was 'an unbearable foreign body'.[14] Rather than pull it down, the building was given a dramatic facelift and an 'old German look', as were so many others around the central square. Where owners resisted change, pressure was brought to bear. All in all, some 400 buildings were modified to some degree. One building of 'foreign [Moorish] architectural style' that officials were not prepared to see modified was the city's synagogue, which was demolished under questionable legal pretext.

Meanwhile, the Bavarian president Ludwig Siebert and the *Zweckverband Reichsparteitag Nürnberg* stumped up the cash for the restoration of Nuremberg's imperial castle, which was seen as a potent symbol of Germany's medieval greatness. Outwardly the castle looked authentic, but the interior had undergone modifications and was now seen as requiring a 'thorough cleansing' to restore it to its simple, modest 'pure and unadulterated state, monumental character and powerful dignity'. The city's fortifications were stripped of vegetation and footpaths were laid out around the walls and moat. The castle was now connected to the modern *Naziparteitagsgelände* via Adolf-Hitler-Platz, which sent out a powerful symbolic message showing the Führer to be the link between the past and the future. Leni Riefenstahl was to make good use of the cityscape in *Triumph des Willens*.

Hitler was very 'hands-on' with all of his major building projects, but would have to rely on his architects to convert his rough sketches into working plans. Sometimes these were hasty scribbles and other times it was obvious that Hitler had spent some time making them. Whichever they were, Speer said of them that they were always to scale and proportion and 'accurate in perspective'.[15] So that they all were left in doubt as to what the overall aesthetic would be, Hitler gave a speech at the 1935 Party Rally referring to cultural issues in which he stipulated that:

Germany's architectural achievements must reflect its cultural values.

- Buildings must have greatness of conception, clarity of plan and harmony of proportions (Neoclassical but one that is more in keeping with simpler forms).
- 'Stupid imitators of the past' were 'charlatans [and] imbeciles' (a reference to Schultze-Naumberg).
- Public buildings should be 'monumental but not bombastic' and be grander than private buildings. Romanticism was out.
- Lesser public buildings could follow local architectural traditions, but even so a petrol station must not look as if it sold hay for horses.
- Public buildings would be designed for maximum effect and rival great structures of the past.

- A building's design must be 'unambiguously' consistent with its purpose. Form must follow function.
- Modernism was not totally shunned and modern materials such as steel and glass should be used where appropriate.[16]

A year later, he told construction workers that

> buildings exist to strengthen our authority [and] are to serve the interests of this authority.[17]

In 1937, with his power inside Germany consolidated, he passed a law allowing him to seize any property and replace it with a new building of his own choosing. This heralded the start of his Berlin project. When finished, the size and power of the Reich would completely overwhelm statesmen from 'little countries [who have] a pathetic sense of their own greatness'.[18]

Now Hitler set about conceiving vast construction programmes for five major cities: Berlin, Hamburg, Nuremberg, Munich and Linz that would transform them into monuments of Reich power. At least thirty smaller cities were designated for some level of redevelopment in line with these major projects. Speaking later of this time in Hitler's life, von Schirach said of him that 'he was absolutely obsessed with building'.[19]

Chapter 10

GERMANIA

> 'They follow the Führer's own ideas. Now they make sense and have shape.'[1]

Berthold Konrad Hermann Albert Speer was born in 1905 into a family of architects, so it was no surprise when he too chose to study architecture, first at the University of Karlsruhe then at Munich Technische Hochschule and finally at Berlin Technische Hochschule, under Heinrich Tessenow, where he became Tessenow's teaching assistant after graduation. He tried to get private commissions, but it was during the depression years and such things were rare. His prospects improved somewhat after April 1930, however, when he joined the National Socialist Automobile Korps. Nazi district leader in West Berlin, Karl Hanke, commissioned him to convert a rented villa in Berlin-Grunewald into a party office. It was work and a chance to impress, but unfortunately the commission did not command a fee.

In January of the following year, he joined the Nazi Party proper (membership number 474,481). This brought him into contact with Joseph Goebbels, who commissioned him to convert the new Gauhaus at Voßstraße 10 into the Party's Berlin headquarters. This went well enough for Goebbels to take him on to revamp a former government press office building, the Leopold Palais on Wilhelmplatz, to be the headquarters of his new *Propagandaministerium*.

It was in Karl Hanke's office that Speer noticed plans for the speaker's platform at the Nazi Party rally due to take place on 1 May at Tempelhof Field, and he suggested modifications using searchlights to produce a striking effect. When Hitler saw the new plans he was most impressed, but he was not told about Speer's contribution. Soon afterwards Speer redesigned Goebbels' private apartment and again Hitler approved and again Goebbels took all the credit for himself.

Hitler was less impressed with plans for the Nuremberg rally later that year and asked Goebbels to get hold of the architect who had designed the Tempelhof Field rally. Goebbels duly called on Speer to submit plans, which he delivered personally to Hitler. They were quickly approved. Subsequently Speer was taken on as assistant to Paul Ludwig Troost, who was in charge of redesigning the Reich Chancellor's apartment in Berlin. During the course of this work, Speer met Hitler on a number of occasions and was surprised to be invited to Hitler's private apartment for lunch with senior party officials. Apparently, Hitler spent the whole mealtime discussing architecture with Speer, who found him both knowledgeable and enthusiastic about the subject.

Almost immediately after the lunch Speer found himself part of Hitler's inner circle and was called in frequently to discuss architectural ideas. Göring was present on many occasions and he also was sufficiently impressed by Speer to invite him to redesign his own official residence. Rudolf Hess gave Speer his own department which was more or less an honorary position, but it came with a personal staff. Goebbels was put out since it was he who had actually found Speer in the first place so he, too, gave Speer a department, this one in the *Propagandaministerium*. They all wanted to be on the side of this new shooting star in the Nazi firmament.

Speer worked closely with Leni Riefenstahl on *Triumph des Willens*. An avid skier himself, he had long been a big fan of hers from watching Fanck's alpine films in which she had appeared. Speer and Riefenstahl had become friends almost as soon as they met, and both found themselves being accepted into Hitler's inner circle at about the same time. Their bond was strengthened by a mutual dislike and distrust of Goebbels, who constantly tried to claim more credit than he was due for pretty much everything that Speer did, especially the organisation of the rally and filming of *Triumph des Willens.* Both Goebbels and Hess resented Speer and Riefenstahl's rapid rise in popularity with Hitler, but while they could not touch Speer, they started a whispering campaign against Riefenstahl, claiming that she had Jewish blood. To counter this Speer continued to give Riefenstahl all the support she needed to make the sort of films that Hitler appreciated. In this way it was Hitler's patronage that protected her.

Speer had obviously made a big impression on Hitler because he rented a holiday home close to Hitler's *Berghof* (residence) near Berchtesgaden and after Troost's death in 1934, he became Hitler's principal architect. His work for the 1933 party rally encouraged Hitler to invite him to work on the Nuremberg Zeppelin Field site for future rallies; the first major project that Hitler was able to commission with state funds. The building designs Speer came up with envisaged structures that would be the biggest of their kind in the world. The *Zeppelintribüne* (the main stands), were influenced by the Pergamon Altar on the Acropolis, but would be much larger. The Congress Hall, a venue for the annual Nazi Party Congress, took its design inspiration from the Colosseum in Rome.

Both Speer and Hitler were fascinated by spatial environments that not only captured an observer's attention but made them feel intimidated by the sheer size of the building. Speer later wrote that he had intended to overwhelm people with the power of the Reich. The German Stadium at the Nuremberg complex was designed to be bigger than the Circus Maximus in Rome. A skyscraper intended for Hamburg would be taller than the Empire State Building in New York, and a new railway station planned for Berlin was intended to be larger than New York's Grand Central. The level of Hitler's preoccupation with architecture is evidenced by Goebbels recording in his diaries that Hitler spoke to him at length on eleven separate occasions during the first two months of 1937, about the various building projects he planned.

All of Hitler's plan for monumental buildings had but one purpose; to impress. No consideration was given for people who had to live in or around them. Houses, apartments, shops, bars, libraries and the like were of no interest to him whatsoever. Such plans were completely sterile. When Speer's father, an architect, saw the plans Hitler and Speer hatched up for the redevelopment of Berlin, he said, 'You have all gone mad!'[2] This was Hitler's single biggest idea that had grown from an obsession since as early as his time in Landsberg Prison to a real project he set in motion in 1936.

Hitler had already discussed a redesign of Berlin's city centre with the city's mayor, Dr Julius Lippert, but when he saw the plans the Berlin City Council had approved, he was infuriated to discover that his own ideas he had floated to Lippert had been scaled down. He abandoned any idea of going any further with Lippert, whom he dismissed as 'an incompetent, an idiot, a flop, a nonentity', and called for Speer who was appointed *Generalbauinspektor* (Inspector General) with virtually unlimited state funds for the implementation of his plans for Berlin. The municipal authorities could accept his decision, or Hitler would choose Mecklenburg as his capital. Speer's office was not only connected to Hitler's *Reichskanzlei* (Reich Chancellery) by a private garden, thus giving him permanent access to Hitler, but his new department was accorded status as an independent research institute, making him directly responsible to the Führer with no intermediaries to worry about.

Hitler invited Speer to share his vision for a new Berlin, which would be renamed Germania, and would be a city celebrating Nazi power and ideology. Speer was not the only one, however. There were a dozen architects Hitler had taken on to develop sketches he had been making since as early as 1924 and turn them into proper architectural drawings. All the basic ideas for the most important buildings in the new Germania were Hitler's. He drew rough sketches to follow, chose the sites, authorised the budget, finalised the plans and approved the work at each stage before it could move on to the next. Where these projects were concerned, Speer was little more than what Frederic Spotts called the 'contractor'.[3]

There were lesser projects where Speer had more leeway, such as the Zeppelin Field and the *Reichskanzlei,* and architects designing projects that were too small to engage Hitler's attention were also left pretty much to their own devices. Hermann Giesler designed the Ordensburg Training School at Sonthofen without too much interference. Ernst Sagebiel was left to get on with Tempelhof and Wilhelm Kreis the new Berlin museums. Despite Hitler's aversion to Modernism, it should be noted that several ex-*Bauhaus* architects including Hanns Dustmann, Ernst Neufert and Herbert Rimpl were also given commissions.

Hitler's plans for Germania assumed that Berlin's population would double to 8 million. Right in the centre of the new city would be two streets: one running east–west for 50 kilometres and the other, the Prachtstraße, running north–south for 38 kilometres. They would intersect near the Brandenburg Gate and be cut across by four ring roads, the outermost one linking to the autobahn network. Visiting statesmen would arrive at a mammoth Lehrter railway station and be driven down the 7-kilometre-long Via Triumphalis, an avenue wider than the Champs Elysee, under a triumphal arch six times bigger in overall volume than the Arc de Triomphe and be welcomed at the *Volkshalle* (People's Hall) or *Große Halle* (Great Hall), which would be the world's largest building.

At the other end of the Via Triumphalis would be the physical and symbolic threshold of the Reich. A monumental Arch of Triumph 117 metres high, more than twice the height of the Arc de Triomphe in Paris, six times higher than the nearby Brandenburg Gate and 170 metres wide. On the arch would be carved the names of all the German soldiers who died in the First World War. It would be the clearest allusion yet to Hitler's obsession with classical antiquity. The idea for the arch is thought to have come from a design first made by Friedrich Gilly in 1794, but also owes something to the Arch of Titus in Rome's Forum. The design lacked taste and seemed to be concerned primarily with the impact of its dimensions. It would be the one thing that Speer found Hitler most obsessive about. It was this obsession with triumphant monuments, said Speer, that showed Hitler's passion for imperial glory that could only be acquired through war, and all this at a time when he was asking the world to accept that he had only peaceful ambitions. It is more telling in that Hitler had been creating these imperial designs since the mid-1920s.

The concept of a triumphal victory procession to the temple of Jupiter Optimus Maximus was begun even before the recorded history of Rome and it would pass through the *porta triumphalis* (gates), whose use was reserved solely for this occasion. These became profoundly political occasions, and it was to celebrate the victories of Vespasian and Titus that a monumental arch was built in 80 CE. While the Roman arch has been described as a 'remarkably harmonious structure of elegant proportions' the design for Hitler's speaks of power and dominance over aesthetics.[4]

Speer claims to have urged Hitler to modify the structure's proportions and simplify its design but Hitler refused to compromise. Speer had a reputation for encouraging Hitler to ever more extremes, but in the case of the arch, he was probably concerned about the difficulty in providing a solid foundation for a structure of such massive weight. He tried to protect his professional reputation by distancing himself from what he called Hitler's architectural fantasies.

The dimensions of the arch were such that it was necessary to carry out tests to determine whether or not the ground would support its weight without subsidence. A structure called the *Schwerbelastungskörper* (heavy-loading body) was called for and built in Schöneburg later in 1941. First a base of a large cylindrical concrete structure 11 metres in diameter was sunk 18 metres into the ground and on top of this, another 21 metres in diameter and 14 metres high was built, the whole weighing some 12,600 tons. It would later be found that it had sunk by some 19 centimetres.

Monumentalism in architecture is symptomatic of a culture that resists evolution. It tries to enshrine within a structure a set of ideological values that remain changeless through time. When Hitler envisaged his grand avenue lined with massive, solid buildings, he was showing contempt for new concepts in urbanisation and was laying down a challenge to the future. His vision allowed for no modification and no matter how much the people wanted to change, they would forever be surrounded, stifled and inhibited by a stone and concrete environment propagandising the Nazi ideal. It would be an 'architectural expression of boundless ambition that bore no relation whatsoever to Berlin's immediate needs or future requirements'.[5]

The Via Triumphalis was a purely monumental construct with no pretension to form any part of the circulatory thoroughfares. Traffic and residential concerns were of no interest to Hitler. Just under half of the boulevard would be lined with government buildings. There would also be two cinemas, an opera house, three theatres, a concert hall, and a twenty-one-storey hotel and restaurants. The north and south axes of the central boulevard would see two new 'mile-wide' train stations at Anhalter and Lehrter, bigger then Grand Central in New York, needless to say, the whole concept seem to suggest that people would arrive at the north station, for example, pass along the boulevard, through the Arch of Triumph, admire the *Volkshalle* and leave by the south station. It would be a form of pilgrimage to experience the Reich's statues as leader of the world. It was not a place for the residents of Berlin.

In 1933, the Berlin authorities already had many problems to contend with. There had been a rapid rise in its population. There were housing and job shortages, class divisions, and administrative chaos as a leftover from the war and the years of austerity. Where new buildings went up they were necessarily of cheap construction, which allowed for little elaboration thus producing a uniform but austere effect. Their modernist design clashed with the ideals of National Socialism. Hitler knew that if he was going to change the character of Berlin, he was going to encounter a great deal of opposition both from the population and the city authorities, but he also knew that all he had to do was send in the SS to 'come rolling up here in their armoured vehicles the full width of the street' to restore order.[6]

The *pièce de résistance*, however, was to be the gigantic *Volkshalle*. This proved to be the other building, apart from the Arch of Triumph, that Hitler was most concerned with. Again, there was Roman influence. Hitler had sketched out his first ideas for the *Volkshalle* in the 1920s and they were obviously influenced by the design of the Pantheon in Rome. Hitler rarely travelled outside Germany, but he did make a trip to Italy in May 1938, during which he spent a whole day walking round the ancient ruins, museums and galleries in Rome and was able, at last, to see the Pantheon for himself. He was not disappointed, calling it 'one of the most perfect [buildings] ever built'.[7] When he returned home, he made new sketches of the *Volkshalle*. Whatever Hitler came up with, however, in terms of size, Speer was ever ready to suggest a little more height, a little more length, a bit more grandeur. When Speer called for the dome of the *Volkshalle* to be no less than 300 metres high and

250 metres in diameter, it was Hitler who objected on the grounds that such a structure was bound to collapse.

The *Volkshalle* was designed to hold 180,000 people in three tiers and, naturally pandering to Hitler's megalomania, it would be the biggest building in the world. To set it off it would be surrounded on three sides by water from the River Spree and on the fourth side would be a granite-paved square, Adolf-Hitler-Platz, big enough to hold a million people. The entrance was to be flanked by two massive Breker's sculptures, one of Atlas holding the heavens and the other of Tellus holding the earth. On top of the building would be a globe with a German eagle perched on top, and the whole edifice would, according to Speer, be 'a place to worship the Führer'.[8]

The interior chamber was round and marble-walled with a diameter of 250 metres and height of 220 metres. A golden arched recess opposite the entrance would house a marble pillar supporting a gilded eagle clutching a swastika in its talons, and it would be in front of this where Hitler would stand to make his speeches. Attached to the *Volkshalle* via a series of covered galleries would be Hitler's new palace, which by contrast would be 'a fiasco of opulent ornamentation'.[9]

Speer and his handpicked team of young architects would not have to worry about minor issues like planning permission. All they needed to do was to come up with plans that Hitler approved of. 'Berlin must change its face in order to adapt to its new great mission' was the task set them.[10] This was no overnight fad of Hitler. He had been working on these ideas on and off since his time in prison. The rough sketches he made while incarcerated he kept with him all his life, refining them, reworking them, planning each detail of his *Welthaupstadt* (world capital). Its Latin name, Germania, harked back to the glory of Rome but also bore witness to the ancient people of northern Europe that Tacitus had named but which the legions had failed to conquer.

Apart from buildings assigned to Speer, there were other major projects. Wilhelm Kreis was commissioned to create a new centre for the army High Command from which they would conduct future wars and also a *Ruhmeshalle* (Hall of Fame, although known informally as the 'Soldiers' Hall') to honour the dead heroes of all such wars, which says much about Hitler's territorial ambitions. The *Ruhmeshalle* would be 230 metres long and 73 metres high. Kreis was also to design a weapons and armour museum as one of four new museums to be built along the Via Triumphalis.

On a postcard of the Kaiser Friedrich Museum Hitler sent to a friend during 1917 while on leave from the front, he mentioned having 'studied' the building. Now in 1938, he planned to replace it with four new ones. As well as the weapons museum there would also be one dedicated to nineteenth-century German art, one for Germanic culture and one for Egyptian and Middle Eastern art. An idea for a fifth museum of ethnology, or race, was mooted for consideration at a later date.

Hitler gave his sketches to Speer and made him *Generalbauinspektor für die Rauchhaupstadt Berlin* (General Building Inspector for Berlin (GBI)) branch of the Reich and the plans for the redevelopment of Berlin were made public on 28 January 1938. The GBI was given special powers as the supreme planning authority for the city answerable only to Hitler. It was a mammoth opportunity for the Nazis to promote their ideological connection to classical civilisations and use architecture to both reinforce a theory of racial history and create a monument celebrating the essence of German culture as they saw it. Within six months Speer and his team had come up with a gigantic model showing in the tiniest detail exactly how the new centre of Berlin would look after redevelopment. Hitler would often now pop along through the connecting garden and sit gazing at this model in rapt admiration. He would bend down to see what the *Volkshalle* looked like when viewed though the arch of the Arch of Triumph, taking guests across to Speer's studio and proudly show it off.

When the Nazis took control of the government in January 1933, they were still a very long way from having the sort of power they craved. Getting to a position of total dominance over the country would take a few years of plotting and manoeuvre yet. For them Berlin had always been the goal. To control the administration of the capital and seat of government would be to control the country. One of the problems for them was that Berlin was also the centre of what they saw as degeneracy, economic liberalism and a hotbed of communist labour movements. Furthermore, a quarter of Berlin's residents were Jews. The redevelopment of Berlin would both stamp Hitler's authority on the country and clear out many of those subversive elements within the city, showing to the world a new, cleaner image of Germany.

Central to the project for Berlin was the immense scale of destruction of the city centre that would have been required to realise such grandiose ambitions. At a time when Berlin was already suffering from a critical shortage of housing due to the inexorable rise of the industrial working population, Speer estimated that some 54,000 dwellings would have to go as well as churches, industrial sites, embassies, offices and shopping centres. This would require the GBI to work closely with every major political, social and economic institution in the city, although it had the powers to set funding and demand property acquisition in dictatorial fashion if need be. Straight away, Speer recognised the opportunity to link the redevelopment of Berlin with Nazi anti-Semitic ideology to dislodge the Berlin Jewish population by manipulating those parts of the plans that referenced housing policy. He was the architect not only of the buildings but of the ethnic cleansing of the city centre. Urban planning had become a tool of Nazi propaganda in a very big way.

As the plans were reaching completion it was obvious that there would need to be a revision of the laws governing property ownership and a strategy for rehousing the displaced population. As a first measure the GBI asked the Berlin city authorities to purchase properties designated by them which included all property around the Potsdamer Platz in the heart of the capital. To clear the way for this the GBI, through the Nuremberg Laws enacted in 1935, took steps to deprive Jews of tenancy rights and would later extend this to property ownership rights, thus depriving them of any claim to social and economic justice. The first laws were passed on 25 July 1938, which gave landlords the right to evict Jewish professionals, such a doctors, from commercial premises.

Speer called a meeting on 14 September 1938 between the GBI and Berlin city officials to discuss the clearing of specific sites so that construction could begin. It was clear that there was an urgent need for rehousing of displaced people. It was Speer who suggested that, as a first measure, all Jews should be moved out through compulsory evictions despite there being no alternative accommodation available for them. His proposals went far beyond anything that had been attempted before in relation to policies against the Jews. There was liaison with the somewhat ironically named Ministry of Justice, which was also in the process of drafting legislation to restrict Jewish rights. Speer sought Hitler's approval to deprive Jews of all property rights, which he never doubted would be forthcoming, and then enacted the necessary legislation. This showed just how far beyond its architectural brief the GBI was allowed to go, knowing that its policies would be enforced by the Gestapo. It now remained only to specify a date when evictions would start, but there was still the issue of where the homeless Jewish population would go.

Two weeks later there was a special meeting of the *Stadtplanungsamt* (City Planning Office) attended by representatives of the German Labour Front, the police, local Nazi leaders and the GBI. The main item of discussion was the acquisition of property and the relaxation of tenancy rights for the whole population of Berlin. The meeting agreed to

> Register immediately all Jewish-occupied, Aryan-owned dwellings of 4 rooms or more in the areas of Charlottenburg, Tiergarten, Wilmersdorf, Shöneberg and Steglitz.

This would be the first phase of the separation of the Berlin Jews from the rest of the population of the city under the guise of architectural policies, but that was not enough for Speer. Knowing he could count on Hitler's full support, he enacted an independent policy as shown by a letter of 6 October in which he writes to the Ministry of Economics restating his need for more dwellings and urging an accelerated evacuation of Jews into what was beginning to take on all the characteristics of a ghetto. After the Kristallnacht pogroms on 9–10 November 1938, this process became so much easier.

As State Plenipotentiary for the Implementation of the Four-Year Plan, Göring, along with SS chiefs Heydrich and Goebbels, now stepped in and added his weight to the argument. They met to discuss the Aryanisation of the economy and how to deal with Jewish businesses and property rights. In particular, they considered the pros and cons of creating a Jewish ghetto in Berlin and eventually decided against it on the grounds that it would become a hiding place for criminals and a breeding ground for epidemics. In a letter to Reich ministers following this meeting, Göring banned Jews from all sleeping carriages on trains and from certain hotels favoured by party officials. He proposed that instead of depriving Jews of property or tenancy rights, they should simply be separated from non-Jews. Nazi policy at this time was still to encourage Jews to emigrate.

It was only on 30 April 1939 that Hitler finally approved a law allowing the eviction of Jewish tenants, provided alternative accommodation was available. It was not as wide-ranging as Speer would have liked, but it gave him enough leeway to start evicting Jews. Afterwards the slide to war meant that anti-Jewish policies could be firmed up, in practice if not in law.

It was hardly the case that Speer had merely followed orders in his attempted resolution of Berlin's 'Jewish problem' and neither could it be said that he was just taking advantage of situations that others had engineered. He had a direct hand in formulation of policy. Knowing that Hitler would never actually put his name to anti-Jewish directives (in an effort to avoid international criticism), Speer was confident that he would back him to the hilt unofficially and he was left to create a policy through the GBI. Speer's accepted defence at the Nuremberg War Trials that it had been

> no affair of [his] when open season on Jews' was proclaimed, absolutely does not stand up to scrutiny. His claim that 'I myself did not take part.

Is plainly a lie. It is not simply that Speeer's architecture was of use to anti-Semitic propaganda, but rather that Speer and his staff formulated an anti-Semitic policy meant to realise key aspects of the architectural plans.[11]

Others apart from Jews were affected by the GBI's plans, although, of course, with lesser consequences. The city authorities had been forced to cut back drastically on plans to expand green space within the city after the economic crash of 1929–1930, when welfare programmes and unemployment ravaged the city's finances. Its Comprehensive Green Space Plan had been adopted in 1929 to ensure that any future growth of the city would take into consideration the provision of a diversity of green space through parks, gardens, lakes and forest on the outer edges. It clearly took into consideration the importance such amenities in the preservation of the health and wellbeing of the population. While economic constraints had slowed progress on these plans, it was the new Nazi regime that scuppered them despite the introduction of the Nazi Reich Nature Protection Law passed in 1935. While this protected forests, for instance, it abandoned any ambition to preserve parks and playgrounds.

Speer's GBI had apparently taken the Green Plan into their deliberations, but it would not be allowed to restrict his redevelopment plans. He asked his friend and colleague, Willi Schelkes, to draft a new plan that would redefine its objectives strictly in line with the requirements of the architectural plans for Germania. Berlin's municipal authorities had little choice but to approve Schelkes' plans in May 1938, but it was evident the GBI had little interest in it. This was manifestly clear when thousands of Berlin allotments were taken over and tenants were evicted. Although they were promised alternative sites elsewhere, little was ever done in that regard. This would have a profound influence on the severe food shortages that the capital would endure during the coming war.

The *Grunewald*, as the name implies, was a region of undeveloped forested area west of Berlin that was easily accessible to the city's population. The Prussian aristocracy had used it as a private hunting preserve but in the late nineteenth century they sold off a large part of the east forest for the development of an exclusive city residential suburb. To prevent further erosion of the area, the *Zweckverband Groß-Berlin* (Special Purpose Association Greater Berlin) was formed after Charlottenburg, Schöneberg, Wilmersdorf, Lichtenberg, Neukölln and Spandau as well as the Niederbarnim and Teltow had been incorporated into Greater Berlin. Through the *Zweckverband* the city formally purchased the whole of the remaining *Grunewald* and was tasked with preserving it in its natural state. The area became hugely popular with Berlin's population, but financial constraints meant that some parts of the preservation plans had not been implemented, and then along came Schelkes.

The Grunewald was a key part of Schelkes' plans. With his own department, the *Grunewald-Büro,* he set about turning it into a *Volkpark* with the addition of sports fields, playgrounds, swimming beaches and camping areas, as well as restaurants and beer gardens. The problem was that the GBI's plans for the east-west axis route passed right through the northern part. There were also plans for a huge new national forestry office, a national hunting museum, a hospital and a new university all within the forested area.[12]

Plans for the new city centre of Germania had stipulated all buildings be made primarily of stone. Any steel supports had to be completely invisible to the viewer. There was going to be a massive requirement for stone which would have to be quarried. This meant a huge demand for manual labourers, far more than Germany could provide from its own work force. Demolition of old buildings and construction of the new would also demand huge labour resources. The Nazis met these demands through forced labour, initially by using inmates from their concentration camps that had been filled, partly as a response to the need for labour, by the mass arrests of homeless people, the unemployed, and the mentally ill. For instance, Flossenbürg in northern Bavaria was sited next to a quarry where white-flecked granite came from to face many of the new buildings. After the occupation of France in June 1940, at the suggestion of Speer, the *Natzweiler-Struthof* concentration camp was created in Alsace in order to quarry the red granite found there. Later, prisoners of war would be used as slave labour on a massive scale. Plans were agreed between Speer and Himmler to organise the production and delivery of building materials by concentration camp prisoners. The company responsible for this was *Deutsche Erd und Steinwerke GmbH* (DEST) run by the SS but financed by the various departments now under Speer's control. He would often specify the location of new camps close to the sources of building materials.

Of the buildings planned, few were begun and even less completed. The *Reichskanzlei* was completed in 1941 but was damaged during the Allied bombing attacks on Berlin and was almost completely destroyed by the Soviets when they entered Berlin in April 1945. No trace of the *Reichskanzlei* remains today. Göring's new Air Ministry headquarters, the

Reichsluftfahrtministerium, on Wilhelmstraße had been designed by Ernst Sagebiel, and when completed in 1936 was the largest office building in the world. It was incorporated in the plans for Germania and survived the war, becoming, for a while, the Soviet military headquarters. It now houses the German Finance Ministry. Another of Sagebiel's projects was the redesign of Tempelhof Airport just south of the city centre. The plan was to create a combined Luftwaffe and civilian airport and for a time it included the biggest airport buildings in the world.

As part of the overall concept of a Greater Reich that would dominate the European landscape with its *Kultur*, Hitler conceived of a plan to re-create the city of Linz as its centre. Not for him the Vienna that had so easily crushed his artistic ambitions. Linz might one day even supplant it as the capital of Austria, binding that country and Germany together in a new, more permanent relationship. It was even mooted as the future capital of the whole Reich; the 'Führer City Linz'.[13] Right at the end of the Second World War, as Hitler sat in his bunker awaiting the inevitable, he spent hours sitting and gazing at a scale model of the city he had dreamed of building. A city that was meant to be the most beautiful city on the Danube and embody the whole idea of the new Third Reich.

The city had been the centre of German nationalist agitation since the turn of the century and showed the greatest enthusiasm for the Anschluss in 1938. It was the indigenous Germans, rather than German nationals, who controlled the *Reichsgau Oberdonau* (Upper Danube administrative region) thereafter under the 'tenaciously brutal' *Gauleiter* (Nazi political official) August Eigruber.[14] Local police chief Josef Plakolm held a high position in the Gestapo, as did the future commandant of the Treblinka concentration camp, Franz Stangl.

Between the Anschluss and the start of the war, Hitler spent a considerable amount of time working on his plans for Linz. His private library included scores of completed architectural drawings for the Linz project. Amongst them were plans for a *Führermuseum,* comprising a great library, a theatre, and a separate collection of weapons of war. The project was given to official architect Roderich Fick, who made his working drawings entirely from Hitler's personal sketches. The museum, with a colonnaded façade about 150 metres long, would resemble the *Haus für Deutsche Kunst* in Munich and be built on the site of the Linz railway station, which would be relocated. The whole city would eventually be transformed in line with plans also in his library under the title of *Die wirtschaftliche Zukunft der Stadt Linz* (The Future Economic Status of the City of Linz). Hitler chose Fick because his *Heimatschutz* (homeland protection) approach was to protect the traditional Germanic landscape, which neatly coincided with the Nazi concept of blood and soil.

Fick had worked for Martin Bormann, designing his villa in the Obersalzberg, and later was involved in projects to create the site for Hitler's Eagle's Nest on top of the Kehlstein, which Bormann gifted to Hitler for his fiftieth birthday. Fick, however, was not enthused by Hitler's megalomania. Speer, perhaps driven by jealousy at another architect getting centre-stage, was quick to bring this to Hitler's attention. Hitler was easily swayed by Speer and soon replaced Fick with Hermann Giesler, a man much more in the Nazi mould. While Giesler was given overall control, Fick was still kept on to design the *Führermuseum*. This did not please Speer either since Giesler was even more of a threat to his position as Hitler's favourite architect.

Initially Hitler ordered that the Linz project be kept secret, primarily because of plans for a new art museum that would be filled with great works that could only be acquired through military conquest. Already, Dr Hans Posse, director of the *Sonderauftrag Linz* (Special Commission Linz), that had been set up to oversee the collection, had presented Hitler with a list of 182 pictures he had confiscated from the Viennese branch of the Rothschild family. Posse was by no means an ardent Nazi, but his expertise was such that Hitler was willing to overlook this minor detail. Ernst Kaltenbrunner, the Austrian chief of the Gestapo, had made his headquarters in the Rothschild house in *Theresianumgasse* after which the whole art collection had been handed over by Louis de Rothschild in return for his brother's release from Dachau concentration camp. Other Jewish collections were confiscated and placed in the *Hofburg* (the former imperial palace of the Hapsburgs), awaiting an inventory and an examination of legal pretexts under which they could become property of the German government. Members of the *Sonderauftrag* then went to the *Kunsthistorisches Museum,* which was reputed to have one of the finest art collections in the world, but the museum authorities had been quick to act. They had boxed up many of those paintings most coveted by the Nazis, including Breughels and Cranachs, and put them in a secret depository. When the Germans arrived, they confessed themselves disappointed at the exhibits which were much below what they had been led to expect. They left empty-handed. The *Sonderauftrag* (special orders), however, made a selection for Hitler's approval but had to contend with Göring's, whose acquisitive drive had drawn him to the feeding frenzy, and who took some for himself. A furious Hitler made him hand them back and further ordered that all works of art must remain in the country unless purchased through official channels.

Chapter 11

PROPAGANDA THROUGH FILM

> 'Film is one of the most modern and far-reaching means of influencing the masses.'[1]
>
> Joseph Goebbels

There are three important reasons why films are such a good vehicle for propaganda:

- They can be transparent in as much as they can disguise the message as entertainment. The viewer watches in passive mode, wrapped up in the narrative, which itself is the message, and rarely has time or inclination to peer through the veil of deception.
- The narrative, by creating a dynamic, albeit passive, experience can easily overcome critical appraisal of its logical progression, meaning that truthful and reasonable premises can be used as a foundation upon which, through mendacious manipulation of false argument, a totally unjustified conclusion might be arrived at.
- Rather than promulgate a falsehood in print, it is much more persuasive if an actor masquerading as an important figure from history or a contemporary politician is seen and heard making a false assertion. The message is absorbed much more easily and carries with it the power of verisimilitude. Allied with indoctrination within the education system and suppression of critical appraisal, film is therefore a prime agent of propaganda.

Up until 1933, the Germany film industry was renowned for its bold experimentation which thrived on the support of brilliant technical and artistic filmmakers such as Walter Ruttmann, Viking Eggeling and Oskar Fischinger. These pioneers of avant-garde cinema had produced classics of revolutionary art form like Ruttmann's social commentary *Berlin*. Feature films grabbed the world's attention through expressionist fantasies such as *The Cabinet of Dr Caligari* and historical pageants. Many technological innovations such as moving cameras, close-ups, special effects and complex editing saw their first application. The whole industry was so successful that many of its leading lights, including Billy Wilder and Marlene Dietrich, were lured away to Hollywood. This all changed in 1933.

It was clear that Hitler had been aware of the power of film when he wrote in *Mein Kampf*,

> One must also remember that of itself the multitude is mentally inert, that it remains attached to its old habits and that it is not naturally prone to read something which does not conform with its own pre-established beliefs…The picture, in all its forms, including the film, has better prospects [for propaganda] people will understand a pictorial presentation of something which it would take them a long and laborious effort of reading to understand.[2]

Neither was Goebbels slow to see the potential of film as a means of mass communication as well as a vital source of foreign currency but, unfortunately for his ambitions, many film personnel fell foul of early Nazi discrimination. As early as 1933, communists, socialists, homosexuals and Jews who worked in the film industry had been arrested and thrown into Dachau and Oranienburg concentration camps. More than 1,500 others fled the country, leaving the industry without many of its leading lights. Desperate to halt the exodus, when Goebbels was faced with losing so many Jewish directors such as the Jewish Fritz Lang, he famously said, 'I'll decide who's Jewish'.[3] He offered Lang the position of Head of the German Film Studio, UFA. Lang demurred then fled the country on 31 July 1933.

Clearly for Goebbels, propaganda was as much to do with what the people did not see or hear as much as what they were spoon-fed. Censorship was a vital component of his strategy. Initially, the Nazis used existing regulations to control artistic expression, especially in the film industry, but they soon wanted more powers and brought in the *Reichsfilmgesetz* (Reich Film Law) on 16 February 1934, designed to take thematic control of the German film industry. Amongst other things it required new film scripts and cast lists to be handed to the Goebbels-controlled *Reichsfilmdramaturg* (National Film Dramaturgists) before any work could begin, and people employed in the film industry were obliged to attend classes at the Nazi Film School. In the context of film, Goebbels was particularly conscious of the need to put entertainment as the main requirement and then, having acquired an emotional response from the audience, deliver a message through engagement with character or storyline.

The vast majority of films produced by the Nazis were not overtly political but were certainly produced within a broad ideological context and subject to strict censorship. In this sense, it is hard to see how any of these films might be considered to be 'pure' entertainment devoid of any propaganda. Of course, it was not only the Nazis who produced propaganda films, especially once the war had started. The use of actual film footage added weight to any argument even if it was selective and manipulative in its use. This particular device had become widely used by all sides during the First World War to maintain morale and support for the war effort throughout the populations.

Before the Nazis could implement their film propaganda programme, they would have to acquire control of the German film industry. Their method was to simply buy up film companies and bring them under the control of the state. The following is a list of films produced by the Nazis that are usually categorised as propaganda. The title is followed by the name of the director and its release date.

Eine Symphonie des Kampfwillens (A Symphony of the Will to Fight), Julius Lippert, 1927
This was the first film documentary of a Nuremberg Rally. It is a short record of the conference, where meetings were held in parks. It shows the various Nazi contingents arriving at Nuremberg by train, trucks, bus and on foot. The most significant moment in the film is when Hitler vows that areas of Germany that had been lost at Versailles will be reunited with the Reich and all foreigners will be expelled. The film ends with a parade of the *Sturmabteilung* (SA) past Hitler.

Der Nürnberger Parteitag der NSDAP (The Nuremberg Convention of the NSDAP), Baldur von Schirach, 1929
A film about the fourth Nazi Party convention held in August 1929.

S.A. Mann Brand (Storm Trooper Brand), Franz Seitz, 1933
Made just after Hitler became Chancellor of Germany. Despite its high production values, it has an essentially unsophisticated plot which revolves around a truck driver, Fritz Brand, who joins the SA to defend the country against communist subversion. The simple, clear

message was that the country must support Hitler in the forthcoming federal elections.

Hitlerjunge Quex (Hitler Youth Quex or Our Flags Lead Us Forward), Hans Steinhoff, 1933

Seldom have film, myth and history been so integrated as they were in *Hitlerjunge Quex*, one of the most important films produced during the early years of the Third Reich.[4] It was advertised as 'A film about the sacrificial spirit of German youth' and premiered at the Uta Phoebus Palace in Munich, where long lines of Hitler Youth formed a ceremonial guard, and was attended by Hitler, Göring, Hess, Ernst Röhm, von Papen and von Blomberg. In a foretaste of their use at Nuremberg, searchlights lit up the sky and Nazi flags festooned the inside of the cinema. A floral swastika sat at the foot of the stage and the Reich Symphony Orchestra played Bruckner's Fourth Symphony. Just before the film started, the director of the Bavarian State Theatre, Hans Schlenk, read out the prologue of Kurt Klawwiter's *Ours the Victory – Ours the Power*.

The film was loosely based on the best-selling 1932 novel *Der Hitlerjunge Quex* by Karl Aloys Schenzinger, which in turn was based on the life of Herbert Norkus, nicknamed Quex (quicksilver), who as a 15-year-old member of the Hitler Youth was murdered by communists while distributing leaflets advertising a forthcoming Nazi rally in Beusselkeitz. Goebbels had attended Norkus' funeral where he called for revenge and, almost overnight, the grave became a Nazi shrine. The date of his death, 24 January 1932, was remembered in an annual event as a memorial to all fallen Hitler Youths. Throughout the country memorial plaques were erected proclaiming that Norkus had given his life 'for Germany's freedom'.[5]

Norkus becomes Heini Völker in the film, which was made incorporating a blend of fact and myth to give the feel of a passion play, where the victim's innocence becomes intertwined with the promise of national regeneration through the person of the Führer. In Völker, the director had embodied all the qualities of idealistic youth, courage, vision and unselfishness. His impoverished background, physically abusive unemployed father and his murder are effectively combined to condemn both the heartless capitalism of the Weimar years and ever-present communist threat. As he lay dying at the end of the film, Völker has enough strength to sing a few words of *Unsere Fahne flattert uns voran* (Our flag flutters ahead of us) after which a heavenly scene of resurrection opens up, where his soul is united with those of his fallen comrades. Oddly, it does not seem to have been apparent to the audiences that this film is indebted to Weimar-era film. In particular, it contains allusions to *Kuhle Wampe* (Who Owns the World) made in 1932 and *Die Dreigroschenoper* (The Threepenny Opera) of 1931, both of which were examples of Expressionist cinema.[6]

The *Kinematograph* film magazine described what followed the end of the premiere:

> The shouts and Heils were heard throughout the neighbourhood...as the Führer left the theatre, the Hitler Youth band played the *Badenweiler Marsch*.[7]

Goebbels praised the film for contributing significantly to the development of film but also to the aesthetic configuration of National Socialist ideology. He portrayed the film as murderous 'Bolshevik sub-humanity' running rampant in the streets of Berlin. Hitler Youth leader Baldur von Schirach, who was involved in producing the film, added his appreciation of Norkus, the 'symbol of the self-sacrificial spirit of all the young who hear Hitler's name'. The Hitler Youth were bound together by their link to 'this dead boy', he said.[8] The film about Norkus' heroic life and death played an important role in persuading millions of young Germans to sign up to the Nazi cause.

Der Sieg des Glaubens (Victory of the Faith), Leni Riefenstahl, 1933

This was Leni Riefenstahl's first propaganda film for the Nazis and covers the fifth Nazi Party rally at Nuremberg from 30 August to 3 September 1933. Described as 'short, powerful [yet] modest', it revealed 'great gifts in the realm of editing for maximum mass effects'.[9] The film documents the rally in strict chronological order, starting with the arrival of foreign diplomats and other guests at the Nuremberg train station followed by Hitler's arrival by aircraft. The welcoming ceremony is followed by the rally on the immense stretches of Speer's parade ground, as a Zeppelin airship passes overhead. After a Hitler Youth Rally, there is a march through the streets of the old city by massed SA and SS units passing before Hitler, who takes the salute. Marching troops feature again in the final sequences in the main parade ground, with tributes to the fallen laid by Hitler and Ernst Röhm. One of the most interesting features of the film is the apparently close relationship depicted between Hitler and Röhm just months before Hitler had him murdered in the Night of the Long Knives on 1 July 1934. He later demanded that all known copies of the film be located and destroyed to erase Röhm from history, but at least one survived.

Flüchtlinge (Refugees), Gustav Ucicky, 1933
This drama portrays Volga German refugees persecuted by the Bolsheviks on the Sino-Russian border in Manchuria in 1928. The film had been produced before the Nazis took power and had not been under Goebbels' control, but it nevertheless won a state prize and was praised by Goebbels for its embodiment of the National Socialist spirit. In it some refugees are rescued by a heroic leader, obviously a symbolic representation of Hitler, while others, deemed worthless, are left to perish. Those rescued are expected to submit themselves to complete obedience as a gesture of thanks for their deliverance. The communists who had abducted them are shown as brutal murderers.

Hans Westmar. Einer von vielen. Ein Deutsches Schicksal aus dem Jahre 1929 (Hans Westmar. One of Many. A German Fate from the Year 1929), Franz Wenzler, 1933
This film was a celebration of the Nazi's rise to power and a partly fictionalised biography of the Nazi hero, Horst Wessel. The plot has communists parading through the Berlin of the late 1920s as the hero, Hans Westmar arrives. He is horrified by the black jazz and Jewish nightclub singers as, in his mind, he sees his fallen comrades from the war. When he joins the Nazi Party and helps them to electoral victory, Westmar is killed. Communists and Jews are portrayed as equally guilty of his murder.

The film was initially banned by Goebbels after the Nazi Film Review Office said it 'neither does justice to Horst Wessel's personality nor to the National Socialist movement as the leader of the state', but it was allowed to go on release after some alterations to show stormtroopers in a less violent light. It was one of the first films to suggest that to die for Hitler's Germany was a glorious end.

Nur nicht weich werden, Susanne! (Don't Lose Heart, Susanne!), Arzén von Cserépy, 1935
The film is set at the end of the Weimar Republic at the height of the world economic crisis. In it, Susanne is an unemployed extra on a film set run by Jewish producers, who are portrayed as greedy and lustful gamblers. When the National Socialists seize power, Susanne exposes the producers as murderers and they are arrested. The film had powerful support in the person of Goebbels, but it was poorly received and the producer never made another film for the Nazis. It did, however, launch the career of actress Hilde Krüger who, with the patronage of Goebbels, went on to make twenty more films for the Nazis.

Der alte und der junge König (The Old and the Young King), Hans Steinhoff, 1935
The film portrays the well-known dramatic conflict in the eighteenth century between the Prussian King Friedrich Wilhelm I and his son, who would become Friedrich II (Frederick the Great). The way the story is told emphasises the duty of the people to offer blind obedience to their leader. Although in the film the leader was the king, the clear contemporary analogy was to Hitler. The story also touches on the situation of Germany being 'encircled' by enemies.

Triumph des Willens (Triumph of the Will), Leni Riefenstahl, 1935
'Most historians would agree', wrote the academic Vicki O'Donnell Stupp in 1978, that 'Leni Riefenstahl's chronicle of the Nuremberg Rally of 1934 is one of the greatest propaganda films of all time,' but in the fifty years since then, the balance of opinion has swung back and forth in ways that, at times, denied the truth of her assertion.[10] The film was also described by the American writer Susan Sontag as the 'quintessential example of the art of political film propaganda' made by 'a filmmaker of genius'.[11] There are many who disagree, however, and critique the film both for its artistic and propaganda values. The media scholar, Brian Winston, sees it as the opposite of propaganda and can equally be thought of as a warning against the very ideas it is accused of propagating. Riefenstahl herself always claimed that the film was apolitical and merely a documentary record of events.

It is undoubtedly one of the most important films made by the Nazis and was released on 28 March 1935. Commissioned by Hitler as a record of the event held between 4 and 10 September 1934, officially referred to as the Reich Party Rally of Unity and Strength, it was directed, produced, edited and co-written by Leni Riefenstahl. She was given unprecedented support and funding, which allowed her to use as many as eighteen film cameramen, sixteen newsreel cameramen, thirty cameras and twenty-two chauffeur-driven cars, not to mention an airship and aircraft. Her filming techniques employed moving cameras, aerial photography and the use of long-focus lenses to create a distorted perspective. Music for the film was specially composed by Herbert Windte and used in a revolutionary new way to dramatise events. It would be Hitler, also, who chose the title for the film, which was designed to show not only his own personal triumph over adversity but also the way in which the German people can be the authors of their own destiny.

Simple recording of events, however, does not absolve a filmmaker from a charge of propaganda. The way in which a shot is constructed might distort the impression given and the reality of the image on screen. This is particularly true of *Triumph des Willens* since some preparations for the rally were made specifically according to the way the film was planned. The film producer, David Gunston, later went so far as to claim that the whole Party Congress was staged specifically according to Riefenstahl's direction. This was supported by Iris Barry, who said that it was 'actually staged for the camera like some colossal Hollywood production'.[12] Riefenstahl herself would admit that 'the preparations...were made in concert with the preparations for the camerawork.'[13] At the very least it was a 'staged' documentary.[14] The film follows a script similar to that used in *Der Sieg des Glaubens* and much of the musical score from that film is recycled here. Pits were dug in front of the speakers' platform so that Riefenstahl could get the camera angles she wanted, and lines were laid so that the cameras could capture traveling shots of the crowd. If Riefenstahl was unhappy with some scenes, she was allowed to recall major party leaders and high-ranking public officials to re-enact their speeches in a studio.

When sixty-one hours of filming was reduced to two hours during the editing process, what was called a documentary took on the qualities of an epic feature film, with Hitler playing the leading role. The film portrayed him as a person of unchallenged legitimacy. Riefenstahl had clearly learned a lesson from *Der Sieg des Glaubens*, when Röhm had been given far too much prominence. Who knew which of the current crop of Nazi leaders might soon suffer Röhm's fate?

The film opens with Hitler's aircraft descending through cloud 'like a god arriving at a festival to his honour' onto a vista of Nuremberg's medieval spires laid out beneath.[15] The opening titles begin

> On September 5, 1934, twenty years after the outbreak of the World War, sixteen years after the start of German suffering, nineteen months after the beginning of Germany's rebirth, Adolf Hitler flew to Nuremberg to review the columns of his faithful followers.[16]

The cruciform shadow of Hitler's aircraft passes over the tiny figures marching below as it descends as if out of the sun, bringing light with it. After landing, Hitler steps from his aircraft to be greeted by thunderous applause and a cheering crowd, before being driven to his hotel through streets lined with more enthusiastic supporters waving Nazi flags.

As dawn breaks over Nuremberg on the following day, the spires are seen again in a dim morning light, mysterious and evocative of a distant past. The picture then dissolves into a scene of Hitler Youth at camp as a symbol of the future of Germany. While these scenes play out, the audience hears the music 'Awake, the dawn draws near' from Act III of Wagner's *Die Meistersinger von Nürnberg* and the screen again dissolves, this time to see Hitler emerging from his hotel. Later in the day, we see a smiling Hitler being greeted by people bedecked with floral garlands wearing traditional peasant costumes from various parts of Germany. When he politely refuses a gift of flowers, Hitler subtly hints that while he may be one of the people, he is also unique, aloof and existing on a higher plane. After opening speeches at an outdoor rally for the Labour Service by various leading Nazis such as Goebbels, Hitler addresses the crowds, and the day ends with a torchlit parade and firework display. Dramatic SA and SS silhouettes against bonfires signify mystery and strength.

A powerful, possibly the most powerful, message to come out of the film is the idea that Hitler is the link between a past that is idyllic but scarred by internal conflict and military defeat and a glorious future. The idea of consigning violence to the past is reinforced by the sight of Viktor Lutze walking closely beside Hitler. Lutze is the man who took command of the SA after the murder of its previous leader, Ernst Röhm, who was demonised in a speech as the man who had been holding Germany back from its path to greatness because of his crude personal ambition, disloyalty and vicious personality. With the stormtroopers now fully on the side of the Nazi Party, there would be no more disruptive behaviour from them. Again, it was the person of Hitler who had bridged the chasm between internal strife and harmony. When a scene shows Hitler, Himmler and Lutze walking side-by-side towards the cenotaph at the Luitpold arena in front of 100,000 soldiers, an image of the Reich eagle perched on top of a swastika is superimposed over them to signify the unity of leader, soldiers and state. In early shots, people are shown in close-up as individuals, but as the story evolves, they become seen more and more only in log-shots, denying their separateness and accentuating their duty as a component part of a whole. Their destiny is inextricably bound up with that of the state, personified by Hitler, to which they must show complete obedience and their will must be subsumed into the will of the nation.

On the following day, Hitler addresses a crowd of Hitler Youth, telling them they must prepare themselves for sacrifice. This is followed by a procession of cavalry and armour. The climax of the rally follows on the fourth day and it is here that the most memorable images are shown. Over 150,000 SA and SS troops stand to attention as Hitler lays a wreath at a First World War memorial. Later Hitler delivers his final speech, calling on all loyal Germans to join the National Socialist Party.

Hess then leads the assembled throng in a 'Sieg Heil' salute to Hitler as the image fades to the sound of the Horst Wessel Song.

This god-like aura is reinforced by close-up shots of Hitler speaking from a position above and apart from the mass of people, who are shown not as a collection of individuals but as a single unit. Each shot of Hitler in the film is calculated to impress on the audience that Hitler is the embodiment of a Germany awakening from its nightmare. He stands out from the crowd in iconic silhouette, with a transcendental aura. Everyone is diminished in size except for Hitler. Backlit by the sun, he is the divine leader promising salvation and rebirth in a myth more powerful than any the German people have ever known. Even other leading Nazis are kept at arm's length from the camera. A powerful musical accompaniment reinforces the Führer's dominance of the nation. The film remains famous for probably what are the most enduring images of the Nazi regime and its leader. In his opening address, Hess turns to Hitler and says, 'You are Germany' and he ends the film by saying, 'Hitler is Germany. Germany is Hitler.'

After massive pre-release publicity, the film had its premiere on 28 March 1935 at the Ufa Palast am Zoo in Berlin. It was an instant success. It then went on general distribution to seventy regional cinemas and was shown to capacity audiences wherever it went. Goebbels praised it and, under his influence, the film was awarded the *Deutscher Filmpreis* (German Film Prize), which he presented to Riefenstahl, personally praising the film for its artistic merit.[17] The *London Observer* reported that it had captured 'the intoxicating spirit which is moving Germany'.[18] Riefenstahl would later be awarded a gold medal at the 1935 Venice Biennial and the Grand Prix at the 1937 World Exhibition in Paris. She would later cite this as evidence for the film's aesthetic qualities when defending herself against charges that it was pure propaganda.

There has been much debate over the extent to which the film enhanced Hitler's position either internally or internationally at a time when his grip on the nation was far from complete. Unemployment figures were still very high, food shortages still existed and the fillip the regime had received after the recovery of the Saarland was just a memory. Historian Ian Kershaw describes a 'gloomy economic situation' and 'wide-ranging dissatisfaction' with the Nazi Party.[19] Any real improvement in Hitler's ratings with the people would have to wait for the German re-occupation of the Rhineland.

Some ask why such a boring film should ever have been given such accolades. Given Speer's choreography of the rally and the spectacle of the event itself, they maintain that any competent newsreel photographer might have been expected to capture the flavour of the event, even without all the special privileges afforded Riefenstahl, but others feel that this view underestimates the special qualities Riefenstahl brought to the film such as its rhythmic editing and the religious imagery of the opening sequence as Hitler's aircraft breaks out of the cloud. Close-ups of adoring spectators, they claim, draws them into the narrative in a way that newsreel does not.

The question remains as to whether *Triumph des Willens* is an artistic film with propagandist overtones, or pure propaganda presented aesthetically. In his biography of Riefenstahl, Steven Bach says, 'She sought credit for art and craft while rejecting to the end of her life all moral responsibility for content or consequences'.[20] Riefenstahl, of course, always insisted that she had no responsibility for the political content, but it is doubtful that distilling a dozen lengthy and mostly boring speeches into a few dramatic soundbites was entirely without political judgement. Creating the narrative drive of the film and capturing the overall atmosphere of the event was entirely Riefenstahl's work. Contemporary sources such as the pamphlet put out by the Nazis to celebrate the making of the film speak of the intention to create 'a dramatic impression in showing Germany on its triumphant march forwards', which seems to imply that there was a clear propagandist ambition right from the start.[21] Indeed, Riefenstahl herself spoke of her decisions when choosing camera angles and marrying image to soundtrack in a way that suggests she was perfectly aware she was reinforcing a political message and promoting the person of Hitler as a superior being.

Whatever the intention it is self-evident that the film conveys a clear set of, almost religious, values that are constructed around a core of, mostly invented, historical ideas and cultural symbols. The rally itself, of course, was a supremely political event and it might be argued that any film recording it cannot but be political also. When it was widely shown to the German people, the intention was to deliver a message of a unified nation moving forward with military power and political vision under the leadership of a single man, Hitler.

Triumph des Willens is often compared to Fritz Lang's 1927 science-fiction epic *Metropolis*. Lang's film depicts a fascist state in which the oppressed majority are forced into hard labour while the rich minority dwells in peace and comfort. From this mass of proletariat one hero rises to challenge the regime and it is this theme that is reprised in *Triumph des Willens* in the person of Hitler, who will guide the people to their salvation. It is one of the important similarities between the two films that it is an heroic individual who stands above the masses and offers hope. Ironically, however, Riefenstahl portrays Hitler as not rising from the masses but descending on them from above and representing every ideal of totalitarianism the original *Metropolis* hero stood against.

Both Hitler and Goebbels were great film enthusiasts and huge fans of *Metropolis.* They both fully understood the power of cinema as a tool of propaganda and films became an integral part of the Nazi campaign to gain control of public opinion in Germany. Hitler had reputedly wept when he watched Lang's *Die Nibelungen* and told Goebbels 'Here is a man who will give us great Nazi films', but Lang, whose mother was Jewish, wanted none of it and fled to America.[22]

In Lang's film, Maria is a robotic blond larger than life individual who dominates every scene, standing out from the masses in heroic isolation and leading the oppressed and mistreated people, who are seen only as a collective, in a revolution of hope. Through her the fascist state is overthrown but it is the people who are the real heroes, and the viewer is drawn in to identify as one of the liberated many. In *Triumph des Willens,* Riefenstahl seems to create a similar sensation by bringing Hitler to the forefront of the film in a similar manner using low camera angles to accentuate his dominance and heroic stature, but there is no sense here that the hero is one of the people in the way that Maria purports to be, despite the fact that she is a robot. Riefenstahl shows the German people oppressed not by an elite within but by the international community outside Germany and painfully climbing back to relevance through the leadership of their leader and saviour, Adolph Hitler.

Friesennot (Frisians in Peril), Peter Hagan, 1935
A film about a village of Volga Germans being harassed and persecuted by Soviet authorities. When Mette, a half-Russian, half-Frisian woman, becomes the girlfriend of the Russian, the Frisians murder her and kill all the Red Army soldiers stationed nearby and flee the village. The film exudes hypocrisy by portraying the oppression of Christian Germans by godless Bolsheviks at the same time the Nazis themselves were throwing German religious leaders into concentration camps.

Der höhere Befehl (The Higher Command), Gerhard Lamprecht, 1935
Goebbels called this film 'engrossing'. It recalled the historic Anglo-Prussian partnership in liberating Europe from Napoleon. It was released around the time of the Anglo-German Naval Agreement (June 1935), when the German government was still optimistic about forming an alliance with the British.

Tag der Freiheit: Unsere Wehrmacht (Day of Freedom: Our Armed Forces), Leni Riefenstahl, 1935
This was the third documentary made by Leni Riefenstahl and recounts the seventh Nazi Party Rally at Nuremberg. It closely follows the pattern of *Triumph des Willens* but with a slightly more audacious style.

The film shows a mock battle staged by German troops in which new German tanks are seen for the first time. The film ends with a shot of German fighter biplanes flying overhead in a swastika formation.

Traumulus (The Dreamer), Carl Froehlich, 1936
This historical drama tells of a student, Kurt von Zedlitz, who is disgraced over an affair with an actress and commits suicide. His tutor, Professor Niemeyer, tells the other students that von Zedlitz was no hero and that they must harden themselves and conquer their weaknesses.

Ewiger Wald (Enchanted Forest), Hanns Springer, 1936
This feature-length film was commissioned by Alfred Rosenberg's Militant League for German Culture. It draws a connection between German woods and the German people, showing the perfect symbiosis of an eternal forest and an eternal people.

Verräter (The Traitor), Karl Ritter, 9 September 1936
When foreign agents, assisted by traitors, infiltrate the German arms industry, they are defeated by the Wehrmacht and the Gestapo.

Weisse Sklaven (White Slaves), Karl Anton, 1937
An anti-Soviet propaganda film set during the Russian Revolution and designed as an anti-Communist response to Sergei Eisenstein's famous 1925 Soviet film, *Battleship Potemkin*. It was withdrawn for political reasons following the Ribbentrop-Molotov Pact, but after the German invasion of the Soviet Union in June 1941, it was once more shown in German cinemas.

Der Herrscher (The Ruler), Veit Harlan, 1937
A drama proclaiming the duty of industry to serve the community.

Festliches Nürnberg (Festive Nuremberg), Hans Weidermann, 1937
It was Weidermann who was called on to chronicle the 1936 and 1937 Nazi rallies at Nuremberg. The film is relatively short at twenty-one minutes, but it adopts the same themes of adoration of Hitler and scenes of marching SS men and Wehrmacht soldiers that Riefenstahl

had used for her films. Its most memorable scene is the where Speer lights up 134 Luftwaffe searchlights directed straight up into the sky to create his 'cathedral of light', which he said was his 'most beautiful architectural concept'.[23] The film concludes with sequences of folk dances and gymnastic displays, followed by a torchlit parade and a brief speech from Hitler.

Urlaub auf Ehrenwort (Leave on Word of Honour), Karl Ritter, 1938
Set late in 1918, during the final stages of the First World War, as a troop of German infantry pass through Berlin on their way from the Eastern Front to the Western Front. They are tempted by family connections to desert, but they resist after encountering communist revolutionaries and continue to the front to do their duty.

Wort und Tat (Words and Deeds), Fritz Hippler, 1938
This ten-minute film was commissioned by Goebbels to show how life had improved for the German people under the Nazis.

Olympia, Leni Riefenstahl, 1938
The film documents the 1936 Olympics held in Berlin. The games themselves were an unwanted inheritance, having been arranged by the Weimar government in 1931, before the Nazis came to power. The Olympic movement, with its ideology of internationalism and pacifism, at first thought the Nazis would cancel the games but, in the end, they delivered up a show on what William Shirer called a 'lavish scale never before experienced', designed to show the new Germany as a decent, friendly, peace-loving nation.[24] Leni Riefenstahl was again called upon to direct and given lavish funding by Goebbels through a shell company.

Strictly speaking *Olympia* should have been pure sports coverage, but it was different from the normal newsreels in so many ways. Details of the various events and the results were of less importance to Riefenstahl than the competitors, whose aesthetic lines, grace, poise and strength she was determined to capture. This opened her up to criticism for the portrayal of athletes as 'mere models [for] cultural display'.[25] As in *Triumph des Willens*, she again employed striking composition, unusual camera angles with imaginative framing, smash cuts jumping from scene to another, tracking shots and dramatic backdrops. Typically, the heads of athletes would be shot from below against a cloud-dotted sky. Cameras were sited in many unconventional places, including amongst the crowds in the grandstands. Automatic cameras were attached to balloons and in boats, but the greatest innovation seen in *Olympia* was the use of an underwater camera that followed divers through the air and, as soon as they hit the water, the cameraman dived down with them, all the while changing focus and aperture.

Nazi pageantry is again to the fore, which some have criticised for making it an 'intensely political film'.[26] The first Olympic flame of modern times had been ignited at the Olympisch Stadion in Amsterdam for the 1928 games and had been repeated in Los Angeles in 1932, but the torch relay in which runners carried the sacred flame from the archaeological site at Olympia in Greece to the Berlin *Olympiastadion* was introduced for the first time in 1936. Its significance was to create in the mind of the viewer a direct link between Ancient Greece and modern Germany through the symbolism of fire. The Olympic flame covered over 3,000 kilometres in twelve days by a total of 3,400 couriers, before arriving in Berlin on 1 August for the opening ceremony. It had passed through Bulgaria, Austria and Czechoslovakia before crossing the German border at the appropriately named village of Hellendorf.

At the Berlin torch-lighting ceremony, 3,000 girls each held a stainless steel and chrome magnesium torch and the Olympic flame itself was lit using a parabolic mirror that concentrated the rays of the sun. It was 'a modern, technological, mass-media event masquerading as an authentic re-enactment of ancient Greek ritual'.[27] The staging of this moment was under the complete control of Riefenstahl. The first film opens with a fifteen-minute sequence devoted to Greek antiquity using dramatic effects such as chiaroscuro and shallow depth of field. The transformation of a classical Greek statue into the body of a modern athlete is particularly effective in cementing the link between ancient and modern. It is suggested by Spotts that it might well have been Hitler's own decision to use Myron's *Discus Thrower* for this scene, in keeping with his concept of creating a new man, 'slender and supple, swift as a greyhound, tough as leather and hard as Krupp steel'.[28]

One of Riefenstahl's most vociferous critics, Susan Sontag, accused her of employing fascist aesthetics which she describes in her 1974 essay 'Fascinating Fascism' as:

> a preoccupation with situations of control, submissive behaviour, extravagant effort, and the endurance of pain... The relations of domination and enslavement take the form of a characteristic pageantry: the massing of groups of people; the turning of people into things; and the grouping of people/things around an all- powerful, hypnotic leader-figure or force... Fascist art glorifies sur- render, it exalts mindlessness, it glamorizes death.[29]

Riefenstahl defended herself against such attacks by saying that not only was she free of any sort of political control during the making of the film, but she was also subjected to various forms of harassment and obstruction by Goebbels, never more so in disputes over the black American athlete Jesse Owens. Goebbels had demanded that Riefenstahl play down his achievements, but she claims to have shown a clear rejection of Nazi racial policies in her film. The figure of Owens is captured beautifully by Riefenstahl in the track and field section of the film, and it is Owens, 'the personification of all that contradicts Hitler and his theories of a master race', who dominates the film overall.[30]

The film was released in two parts. *Olympia 1: Teil Fest der Völker* (Festival of Nations) lasting 126 minutes and *Olympia 2: Teil Fest der Schönheit* (Festival of Beauty) lasting 100 minutes. Neither part sticks to the chronology of the games, but both are montages of short segments put together with a Wagnerian soundtrack to give narrative energy and momentum. It went on to win the grand prize at the 1938 Venice International Film Festival, beating Walt Disney's *Snow White and the Seven Dwarves* into second place.

Pour le Mérite, Karl Ritter, 1938

The film follows the story of officers of the Luftstreitkräfte in the First World War, who later became the core of officers in the Luftwaffe. An important message of the film is the 'stab in the back' theory that the German people had been betrayed by their politicians. Set in the 1920s, it castigates the 'weak and unpatriotic' Weimar government for betraying the country and its armed forces and calls for strong men to overthrow it. It ends with a call for the Nazis to rebuild Germany's military might, especially its air force. In its final sequence the film includes a cameo by First World War fighter ace, now head of the Luftwaffe, Hermann Göring.

Aufruhr in Damaskus (Uproar in Damascus), Gustav Ucicky, 1939

A thriller set during the First World War in which German forces battle Arabs led by Lawrence of Arabia.

Robert und Bertram (Robert und Bertram), Hans H. Zerlett, 1939

An anti-Semitic musical comedy about two wandering vagrants set in 1839.

Der Westwall (The West Wall), Fritz Hippler, 1939
Released three weeks before the German invasion of Poland, the film features the Siegfried Line defences around the German borders with France, Belgium, Luxembourg and the Netherlands.

Kadetten (Cadets), Karl Ritter, 1939
A historical war film set in the Seven Years' War in which a group of Prussian cadets hold off superior Russian forces.

The following films were part of a series produced by the National Socialist Racial and Political Office to demonise people in Germany diagnosed with mental illness.

Das Erbe (The Inheritance) Carl C. Hartmann, 1935
This short (twelve-minute) film was an attempt to justify the compulsory sterilisation of anyone who, in the opinion of an *Erbgesundheitsgericht* (Genetic Health Court), suffered from a list of alleged genetic disorders. It was shown as a trailer to the main event in contemporary German cinemas. The simple brutal message was that only the strong and healthy are victorious. The film includes shocking sequences of asylum patients and shows the high cost of caring for them. It marks the moment when Social Darwinism becomes official Nazi racial policy that allows for euthanasia.

Erbkrank (The Hereditary Defective), Herbert Gerdes, 1936

Alles Leben ist Kampf (All Life is Struggle), Herbert Gerdes, 1937
Two films about disabled people which promoted forced sterilisation and demonised people diagnosed with mental illnesses.

Opfer der Vergangenheit: Die Sünde wider Blut und Rasse (Victims of the Past: The Sin against Blood and Race), Gernot Bock-Stieber and Kurt Botner, 1937
This film showed images of inmates of German asylums to bolster public support for the planned T-4 euthanasia programme for the mentally ill.

Chapter 12

PROPAGANDA THROUGH MUSIC AND THEATRE

'A Babylon of sin.'

Joseph Goebbels on the Weimar music scene

Already during the late 1920s there had been a noticeable change in the public attitude to modernist music, which may well have been a natural retrenchment into traditional cultural values brought on by the chaos and uncertainty of the economic depression. This continued into the 1930s, when the annual contemporary music festivals at Baden-Baden were abandoned and the experimental Kroll Opera in Berlin was abolished. As the Nazis gained more power, the music of Ernst Krenek and Kurt Weill was heard less and less, and modernist composers had a choice if they wanted to continue writing music; they could bend with the wind and reach a compromise with Nazi aesthetics or leave the country. For those who remained, the question was 'what exactly was acceptable'? Bitter rivalries between the three main codifiers of acceptability, Goebbels, Göring and Rosenberg, were not helped by Hitler's capricious attitudes towards the medium.

For the Nazis music had unique significance and power. The German nation took great pride in its long history of producing great classical composers, which led musicologist Pamela Potter to think of music as 'the most German of all the arts'. However, all this was threatened by modernist and cosmopolitan trends which the Nazis saw as the degeneration of German music in line with the Weimar abandonment of national pride. It was convenient for them to claim it was no coincidence that the introduction of swing, jazz, avant-garde experimentation, African-American and Jewish music had coincided with the collapse of German society during the depression years. The music magazine *Die Musik* called avant-garde music 'a foul, anti-Volk bacillus that denigrated the cultural body through cynicism and calculation'.[1] This was more than what might be thought of as a natural reaction from a conservative bourgeoisie to youthful exuberance. Music was political and a natural target for Goebbels' propaganda machine. The *Völkisch* tradition in music was redolent with themes of heroism, love of nation, a society rooted in blood and soil, but this new music was called sensational and superficial, appealing only to the moment and condemned as exploitative with nothing but the profit motive to sustain it.

The perversion of German values was its ultimate aim, and this required a strong defence of the Aryan people against the intellectual and economic tyranny forced on them by Jewry. 'What was required,' said Ziegler, 'was a wholesale eradication of the Jewish influence in all aspects of German musical life, so that capable and gifted true-blooded German musicians could once again work together for the common good.'[2] Now, of course, they would be tyrannised by the aesthetics of a man who was essentially anti-intellectual. It was enough that Arnold Schoenberg was an ethnic Jew, but asking Hitler to appreciate the complex forms and patterns of a Schoenberg composition was beyond him. Ziegler put it into words for him when he said, 'Atonality in music signifies degeneracy and artistic bolshevism' and Rosenberg was ever willing to add his voice, saying, 'The whole atonal movement in music is contradictory to the rhythm of blood and soul of the German nation'.[3] It was to Wagner that Hitler turned to give dramatic expression to what he saw as the purity and greatness of German race, culture and art.

Hitler had first encountered Wagner's *Lohengrin* in Linz in 1901, when it left him 'Wagner's prisoner for life'.[4] Thereafter, during his time in Linz, he had attended Wagner's operas at every opportunity. Moving to Vienna, one of the first things he did was go to the opera to see Wagner's *Tristan and Isolde,* followed immediately afterwards by the *Flying Dutchman.* Often, in later life, Hitler would emerge from the Bayreuth Festival where had had got his fill of Wagner and, filled with inspiration, immediately retired to his Berghof retreat to write. However, the total extent of Hitler's enthusiasm for Wagner has recently come into question by Frederic Spotts, who questions some of the factual entries in August Kubizek's book *Young Hitler,* and the descriptions of Hitler being 'intoxicated and bewitched', which Spotts says have obviously been exaggerated for effect.[5] Wilhelm Furtwängler said of Hitler, after meeting him in 1933 to discuss music, that he was absolutely devoted to opera, especially the works of

Wagner and Puccini, whereas symphonies and chamber music left him cold. If he agreed to go to a Verdi opera it would be most likely as a sop to Mussolini. Where Wagner was concerned, money was no object. In December 1938, by which time Hitler had control of all state expenditure, he authorised a payment of 150,000 Reichsmarks to Clemens Kraus to put on *Tannhäuiser* and *Arabella* at the Munich State Theatre. It must be said, however, that the music-loving population of Germany did not share Hitler's love of Wagner as much as he would have hoped. With its escapist theme, the inclusion of Richard Strauss' lyrical comedy, *Arabella,* was significantly the more popular of the two.

How Hitler used music as propaganda can be illustrated by his decision to invite the Hungarian Regent Admiral Horthy to a performance of *Lohengrin* at the Berlin State Opera in 1938. The storyline had Germany defending itself against an attack by Hungary. It is thought by some to have been a diplomatic gaffe, but perhaps Hitler was having a wry joke by suggesting the boot was now on the other foot.

Goebbels was quick to recognise the power of music to seduce and influence crowds. 'Music affects the heart and emotions more than the intellect', he said. From the earliest days of Nazi rule, they had energetically sought to 'purify' German music, and this inevitably involved anti-Semitic action. Members of the *Kampfbund für deutsche Kultur* felt empowered to disrupt musical performances by Jewish artists. In March 1933, Goebbels gained control of all German radio stations and fired art and music critics who did not support the Nazi agenda. Then, six months later, the *Reichsmusikkammer* (Reich Chamber of Music, (RMK)) was formed, requiring all working musicians to become members. It was essentially completely under Goebbels' control and, naturally, undesirable elements were denied entry. Then in late 1935, Goebbels put out a list of 108 composers, most of whom were Jewish, whose works were blacklisted. To emphasise his point, Goebbels held a ceremony outside the Leipzig Gewandhaus where he instructed local official Rudolph Haake to pull down Mendelsohn's statue, which had stood there since 1892.

The mass exodus of musicians and theatricals in 1933 had left the German stage and concert halls bereft of quality productions, and critics were getting frustrated. To counter the bad impression the public was getting, in November 1936 Goebbels ordered that all criticism of the arts was forbidden. From this point only 'commentaries' were permitted. This was little more than a list of contributors to any given production. Two years later, after becoming frustrated by innuendo and satire, Goebbels banned all reference to politics and politicians in theatres, music halls and cabarets.

Hitler took an intense personal interest in the arts generally, but his vague, turgid memos left much confusion amongst those who carried out his policies. Control of musical theatre in 1933 was shared over a number of agencies, but Goebbels soon brought them all to heel. He immediately saw an opportunity to impose his will on the impecunious Berlin Philharmonic Orchestra, which was seeking state support and patronage. Of course, Goebbels was more than willing to step in with funding, but on the understanding that the orchestra, whose appeal was mainly within the German elites, would perform only those pieces specifically designated as wholesome and in conformity with Nazi ideals, such as those by Beethoven, Wagner and Bruckner.

By 1937, the RMK had tens of thousands of members, but commitment to Nazi ideology tended to count more than musical talent, ensuring that mediocrity thrived. Marches and light music to distract and entertain the population was the order of the day and numerous compositions were created for Nazi Party events and rallies to celebrated Hitler, Germany, and the glorious future of Nazism. In terms of whether there was ever a particular Nazi music aesthetic, it is likely that the most important factor in the popularity of a musician was more to do with their personal and political connections.

Music was clearly used as an important means of instilling 'German values' and was broadcast into homes, schools and military barracks through the medium of radio. Music also featured prominently at party rallies and other public events. Under Baldur von Schirach, the *Hitlerjungend* (Hitler Youth) had over 900 musical groups, including choirs and orchestras. All were encouraged to sing patriotic songs, many of which were German folk tunes with new words added reinforcing Nazi ideals. According to music professor Fritz Stein, folk music was the key to unifying a fragmented people.[6] The *Hitlerjungend* would feature prominently in Riefenstahl's *Triumph des Willens* and would go on to play a crucial role in state propaganda and public morale, especially during the war years. Even infants were not forgotten. A National Socialist music educator, Fritz Jöde, emphasised the important role played by music in kindergarten, where he believed overt state control over children should begin. Prisons and concentration camps were also not allowed to escape the propaganda drive, while the SS even had its own music corps.

A law had been passed on 5 May 1934 under which Goebbels appointed Rainer Schlösser to take regulatory control of theatre, opera, and operetta in all areas except Prussia, where Göring retained authority as Minister President. Such divisions of authority soon showed up the way in which policy was driven by personal preference rather that central dictat. When Goebbels tried to ban a staging of Shakespeare's *Richard II* at the Vienna Reich Theatre Week, Göring protested and forced Goebbels to back down, yet then when Göring tried to ban Werner Egk's opera *Peer Gynt*, Hitler overruled him. Hitler may have made clear his opposition to Modernism in the visual arts, but musically he was not so easy to read. While Göring might well have assumed he was massaging Hitler's prejudices by damning what was clearly an example of provocative modernist music, Hitler approved and adopted Egk as a personal favourite.

The lack of total control of live theatre tended to leave Goebbels less interested in the stage than the screen. Theatres, like cinemas, were in poor financial shape in 1933, but Goebbels was sufficiently interested to increase funding which brought life back to many venues, but only after many Jewish owners such as Max Reinhardt had been hounded out. Four main theatres were chosen for special attention, Göring's *Preussisches Staatstheater* being the most prominent, but elsewhere, other party leaders had ambitions to control the arts. Rosenberg's KfdK and Robert Ley's *Gemeinschaft Kraft durch Freude* (Community Strength through Joy (KdF)) funded their own theatres.

Those plays deemed suitable to be performed were, in the main, without much artistic value, but it was necessary to entertain the people. Many serious playwrights, directors and actors were shunned in favour of others favoured by party hacks. The quality of performances plummeted, with plays now suffused with Nazi clichés and turgid plots often involving a strong leader who saves his community from disaster. Any producer who wanted to succeed under the Nazis very soon learned to 'work towards the Führer' when choosing plots or infusing standards with a 'new spirit'.[7] Many groups, including communists, non-Aryans, Poles, Czechs and war profiteers were demonised. Women's rights were ridiculed. At long last, even Goebbels was able to get his play *Der Wanderer* performed in Leipzig.

At first, theatres were encouraged to portray revolutionary characters, but after the Röhm purges left Hitler in sole charge, revolutionary concepts were abjured. Goebbels promoted popular playwrights like Ludwig Thoma but was acutely aware a sizeable portion of the audiences wanted to see works by classic German playwrights such as Schiller and Goethe, not forgetting William Shakespeare, who was almost thought of as an 'honorary' German. It was equally important to have a classic repertoire for the benefit of visiting dignitaries.

To see how the Nazis imposed their will and transformed cultural life, it is instructive to look in detail at how they took over Max Reinhardt's *Deutches Theater* in Berlin. As a director, Reinhardt was involved with eleven theatres in 1930, staging classics of Ibsen, Strindberg, Tolstoy and Brecht. He also directed at the Viennese *Theater in der Josefstadt* as well as working in both England and the US. He was perhaps Europe's most famous theatre director, having a worldwide reputation for revolutionising the traditional theatre by drawing emotional responses from his audiences through the enhancement of design, music and expressive acting. Together with Richard Strauss and Hugo von Hofmannsthal, he founded the Salzburg Festival in 1920.

Reinhardt's style of theatre was entirely at odds with the Nazi aesthetic, however, and he soon became a target for their criticism. His theatres were becoming economically stretched during the depression and he chose to cut back his investment, handing over control of both the *Deutches Theater* and the adjoining *Kammerspiele* to Karl Heinz Martin and Rudolf Beer in 1932.

The Nazi press ramped up its invective against the *Deutches Theater* and its production of *Gott, Kaiser und Bauer* starring Fritz Kortner, who, like Beer, was Jewish. On its first few nights, performances had been interrupted by a rowdy element in the audience protesting at the unedifying depiction of medieval Germany. On the fifth day, the play was banned by the Berlin police and the theatre was temporarily closed down. After Beer resigned, a few weeks later Reinhardt handed a new contract for the running of the two theatres to Dr Carl Ludwig Achaz-Duisberg and Heinrich Neft. After the Reichstag fire on 27 February 1933, Reinhardt had seen enough. Days later, after attending the first night of *Das Grosse Weltheater,* which he had co-directed, he left the country.

Goebbels condemned the production in his newspaper *Der Angriff* but found Achaz-Duisberg willing to bend with the wind and help transform the theatre into a vehicle for Nazi propaganda. The growing influence of Rosenberg's *Kampfbund für deutsche Kultur* saw Wulf Bley appointed to act as special adviser to Achaz-Duisberg and Neft. Heinz Martin was persuaded to stay and produce *Ewiges Volk,* written by the Nazi Kurt Kluge, indicating that the theatre had turned a political corner. This time the *Völkischer Beobachter* was effusive in its praise of Achaz-Duisberg and Neft for 'an attempt to perform a cultural service in accord with the interests of a national Germany'.[8] This was in spite of what others called the shrill, bombastic rhetoric that alienated the audience from the characters. Whatever the tame Nazi press called it, *Ewiges Volk* was closed down after only five performances. It was clear that Reinhardt's predominantly Jewish audiences had refused to turn up, and the theatre suffered severe financial losses as a result.

Meanwhile, the ground upon which German theatre stood was being shaken by several tremors. Otto Laubinger, the former head of the *Kampfbund für deutsche Kultur* Theatre Division, was taken on by Goebbels at his Propaganda Ministry. After a battle with Goebbels, Göring retained control of the Prussian State Theatre and the Berlin opera, and the ever-active Rosenberg took over two national theatre organisations: the *Volksbühnenverband* and the *Bühnenvolksbund*, with 350,000 members. He combined them to form the *Reichsverband Deutsche Bühne*, which was now the only officially recognised theatre-subscription organisation.

To celebrate his victory in retaining control, Göring commissioned a heavily pro-Nazi production of Hanns Johst's *Schlageter* for the Prussian State Theatre in honour of Hitler's forty-fourth birthday on 20 April 1933. At the close of the play on the first night, Goebbels and Frick were present, along with a number of leading Nazis who led the audience in the singing of the national anthem. Reinhardt's predominantly Jewish audiences had been replaced overnight by Goebbels' Nazis. Neft was sickened by the Nazification of the theatre and resigned.

The next production put on by Achaz-Duisberg was Schiller's *William Tell*. Goebbels was sure that had Schiller been alive, he would undoubtedly have been a Nazi. Just to be on the safe side, however, Achaz-Duisberg modified the script to simplify characterisation and emphasise the heroic character of Tell, who was cast in Nazi fashion as a good-hearted courageous folk hero. The last act was rounded off with flag waving and singing. In fact, the play ended up as something of an *Ewiges Volk* pastiche in which an oppressed German-speaking people with deep agrarian roots is saved by a charismatic leader. 'Surely', said one critic, 'Schiller did not intend it to be all that simple'.[9] To ensure the production was a success, he instructed political organisations to attend and thus ensure six weeks of capacity audiences. All around the theatre Nazi flags were flown and inside the audiences responded with great enthusiasm. The Nazi press was ecstatic. *Der Tag* said it 'captured the spirit of our times'. The *Rheinisch-Westfälische Zeitung* excelled in its sycophancy by saying,

> The action springs across the eternal dividing line out into the auditorium, and its pulse beats suddenly among us...The fateful words of the dramatist have melted everything in glowing flames to communal experience. The theatre becomes cultlike in the antique sense, becomes once again the showpiece of the nation.[10]

Goebbels called *William Tell* 'absolutely suited to the times...as if it had been written yesterday.' Encouraged by its success, Goebbels now laid out the mission theatre directors were to carry out. 'The German art of the decade,' he said, 'will be heroic...romantic...without sentimentality [and] relevant to the concept of *Volksgemeinschaft*'. It would not be so much a question of what material to use but how it was interpreted and how it related to the audience. It was at this point that Goebbels tried to take full control of the arts by appointing Rainer Schlösser as head of the new office of *Reichsdramaturg* to be the official censor of the theatre, which would now become 'an institution of the national education'. At the same time, he aimed a barb at Rosenberg's conservative *Kampfbund* approach by saying that he rejected 'all moral prudishness in the area of the arts' and repudiated 'every pedantic objection to the German dramatist's choice of subject matter decisively'.[11]

On 22 May 1938, Goebbels held a *Reichsmusiktage* (Reich Music Festival) in Düsseldorf in which German folk songs, which appealed to the German soul, were lauded as the epitome of 'simplicity and elementary greatness in art' and would defeat 'all intellectual constructivism [and remove] the last vestiges of cultural Bolshevism... in the area of music and the visual arts.'[12] It proved to be a dull and boring experience for visitors.

Inspired by the success of the *Ausstellung Entartete Kunst*, an *Entartete Musik* (degenerate music) exhibition was set up alongside Goebbels' festival by Ziegler to make sure the German public knew exactly what 'degenerate' music was. Again, the 'degenerate' aspect of culture proved to be the more popular. Ziegler's plans almost backfired when it became clear that many of the pieces of music he featured were actually immensely popular with the public, such as Felix Mendelssohn's *A Midsummer Night's Dream*, which was still being performed as late as 1935, as was Stravinsky's *Firebird*. What started out as a blatant attempt to please Hitler by acolytes who knew little about music or what was popular with the public had now become muddled. Was it acceptable to listen to Mozart opera when his librettist had been a Jew? Were Handel's Old Testament themes and Schumann and Schubert's settings of the Jewish Heinrich Heine's poetry to music to be allowed? Who could tell?

When Ernst Krenek's opera *Jonny spielt auf* had premiered in 1927 it had been an instant hit through most of Germany and Austria, but when it opened in Munich in 1928, it was roundly condemned by the local Nazi Party. In the show, Jonny, a black American jazz violinist, has an affair with a white girl and steals a priceless European violin, and it is he who was featured prominently on the advertising posters.

The success of the opera was not at all surprising given the way in which American music and black performers such as Josephine Baker had become hugely popular, especially in Berlin. Neither was it a surprise that the Nazis, in their Bavarian stronghold, reacted so strongly to non-Aryan culture, especially that which seemed to have such a hold on the popular imagination.

Sections of the Munich audience booed the black performers and started a riot by releasing stink bombs and tear gas in the auditorium, but they were thrown out. The local press was less than enthusiastic, but after this initial disturbance the show continued and ran for some years. Krenek, however, became a marked man for the Nazis. This modernist composer who had achieved international fame was targeted after 1933 when the state brought pressure to bear to have his works banned from the stage. *Jonny spielt auf* was, however, resurrected in a macabre way at the *Ententarte Musik* exhibition in 1938, when the poster advertising the exhibition lampooned the original poster by featuring a blackface saxophonist with a Star of David on his lapel. Anyone attending the exhibit would see this work as a reference to Krenek's opera, leaving them in no doubt what the official opinion of him was. Krenek emigrated to the US that same year.

Postscript

ARCHITECTURAL DEBATE IN POST-WAR MUNICH

> 'Few issues have possessed the centrality or sparked as much controversy in the post-war history of the Federal republic of Germany as the struggle to come to terms with the nation's Nazi past.'[1]

In the ruins that was Germany in 1945, the population was faced with coming to terms with its past and finding some foundation on which to build a future. Architecture was fundamental to that process, but it had also been a central component of Nazi propaganda and the echoes of the 1930s could be detected throughout the early post-war years as the cities were gradually rebuilt from ruins. Many city centres carried the legacy of large-scale Nazi reconstruction projects, as well as considerable bomb damage. There was an urgent need for development and new construction, but the question was what style should be adopted. Just like in the 1930s, the modernists favoured a complete break with the past. The past in this case being anything that could be labelled as 'Nazi'. Traditionalists, however, saw Nazi architecture as modernist and urged a return to traditional styles. Architecture was still highly symbolic and, perhaps more than ever before, found itself at the forefront of political discourse. German cities had different traditions. While Berlin and Frankfurt saw themselves as modern, others such as Freiburg and Nuremberg favoured traditional architecture. Perhaps none were as conservative as Munich, however, and it is this city which encapsulates the whole debate. Up until 1945, Munich had been designated as the capital of German art and one of the five *Führerstadt* (Führer city) and arguably had to deal with the greater burden of Nazism.

Naturally there were a number of competing philosophies which fell roughly into the two camps of modern and traditional, although there were many nuanced opinions within those broad concepts, each wanting to imbue their architectural style with political and historic symbolism as a reaction to Nazism. To the modernists, anything resembling the Neoclassicist styles of the *Haus der Deutschen Kunst* implied fascism. Natural stone, symmetry and heavy enclosed monumentalism were abandoned in favour of light, transparent structures of glass, steel and concrete that encompassed the ideals of democracy and openness. Architectural innovation was essential to break with the past. For them, opponents of Modernism were reactionary adherents of a traditionalist, conservative mentality that produced the Third Reich. The modernist architect Hans Eckstein said that it was necessary to fundamentally revise ideas 'that people [had] allowed themselves to be misled by' and embrace new forms so that the 'sources of Nazi disaster' could be permanently left behind.

For their part, traditionalists were represented by the chief Munich architect Karl Meitinger, who rejected Modernism for being 'infected with the spirit of Nazism'.[2] Technology, materialism, utilitarianism, and belief in progress were all forces that had led to disaster. For this group, the only solution was an architecture rooted in tradition to restore the *Geist* (spirit) which Munich's mayor Karl Scharnagl said had been 'eroded by modern forces [which] had led to catastrophe'.

It was the traditionalists, defying taboos of Nazism, who held sway in the immediate post-war years, as evinced by the large number of Neoclassical buildings going up at the time. The first was the *Neues Residenztheater*, completed in 1951, closely followed by the *Neuer Herkulessaal*, the *Starnberger Bahnhof* and the *Bayerische Hypotheken-undf-Wechselbank*, and many other buildings designed by architects such as Roderick Fick and Paul Schmitthenner, who had worked closely with the Nazis. Modernist plans to clear the ruins of the fifteenth-century city hall site in favour of a thoroughfare were widely condemned by grassroots opposition as 'on the same lines as the Nazi propensity to tear everything down' and were eventually thrown out. Where modernist designs were tolerated, they were denied full expression by being heavily modified before being allowed to go ahead. The Herzog-Max-Burg building was only allowed on condition that it was harmoniously integrated with the tower of a sixteenth-century building that had been extensively damaged by wartime bombing.

By the end of the 1950s, however, the traditionalists were losing their control and increasingly modern architectural design was favoured when Munich underwent a rapid phase of urban modernisation. The *Deutsche Kaiser Hotel* went up in 1959, followed by the *Hertie* department store in 1964, signalling that the city was now ready to embrace the new with open arms. Debate between traditionalists and modernists became a thing of the past and architecture took on a much less political significance. The city looked to the future, not the past.

Appendix 1

NAZI ARCHITECTURE THAT CAN STILL BE SEEN IN GERMANY

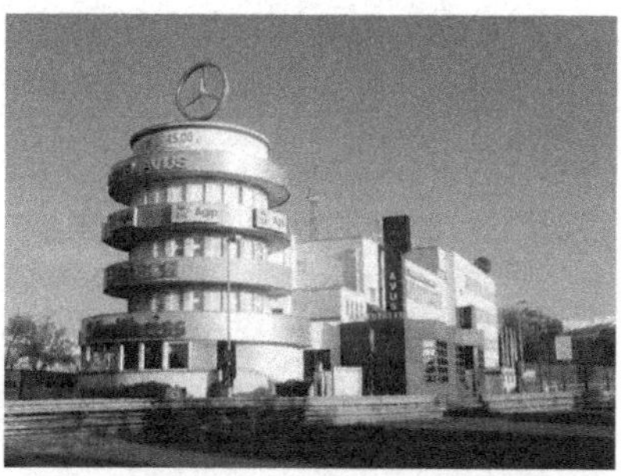

AVUS Grandstand and Motel

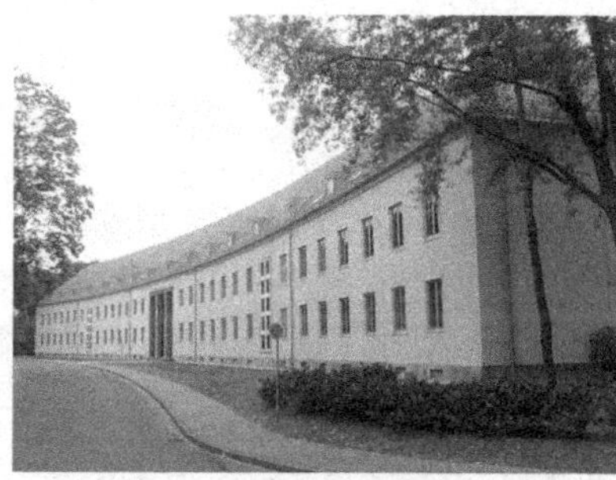

Julius Leber Barracks

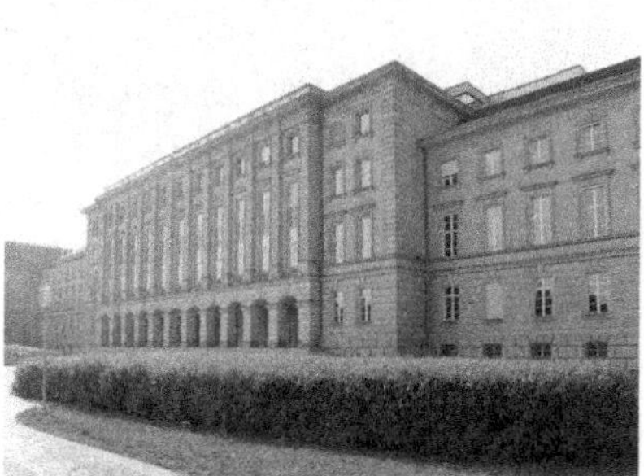

Ernst-Reuter-Haus

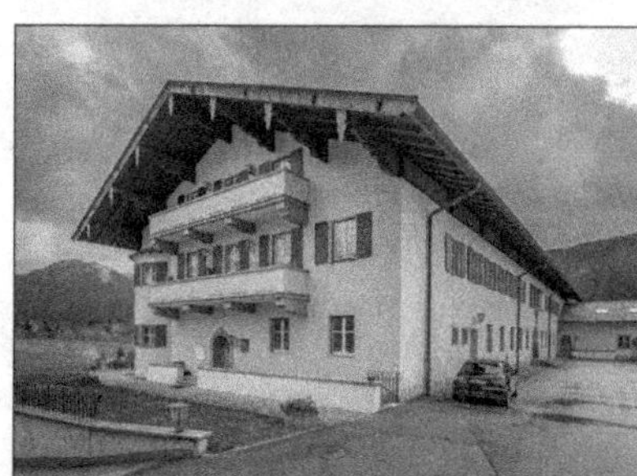

Fehrbelliner Platz Senate Department for Urban Development and the Environment

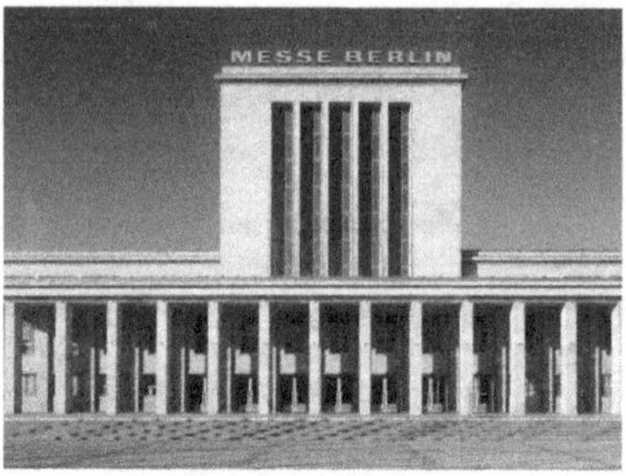

Funkturm: Haupthalle and Messegelände

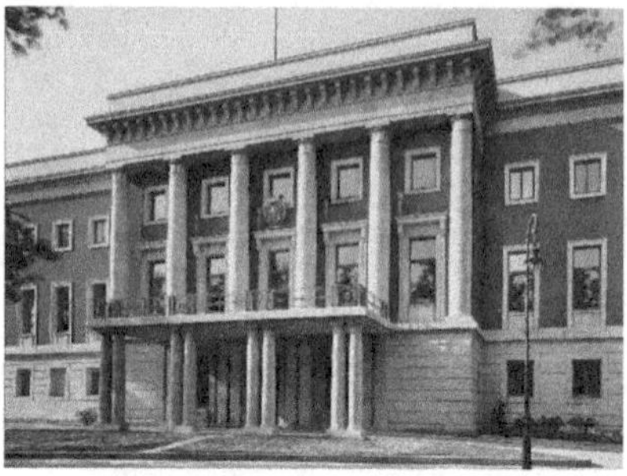

Italian Embassy in Berlin

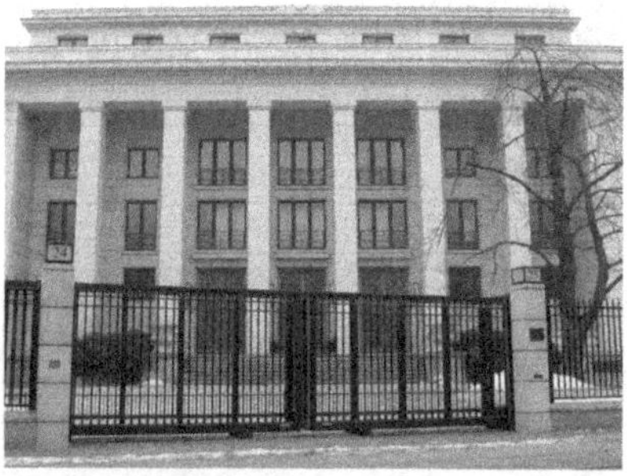

Japanese Embassy in Berlin

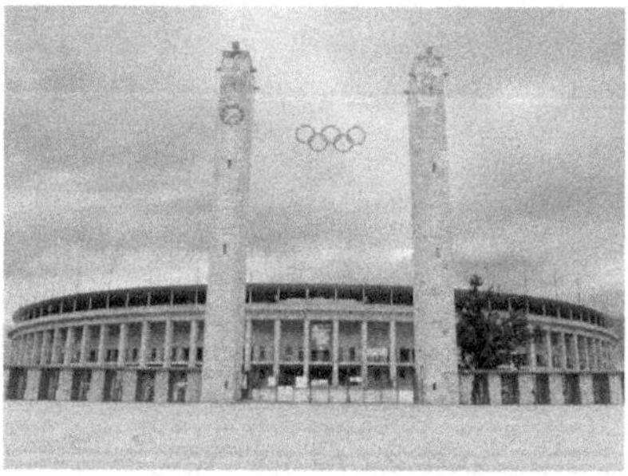

Olympiastadion

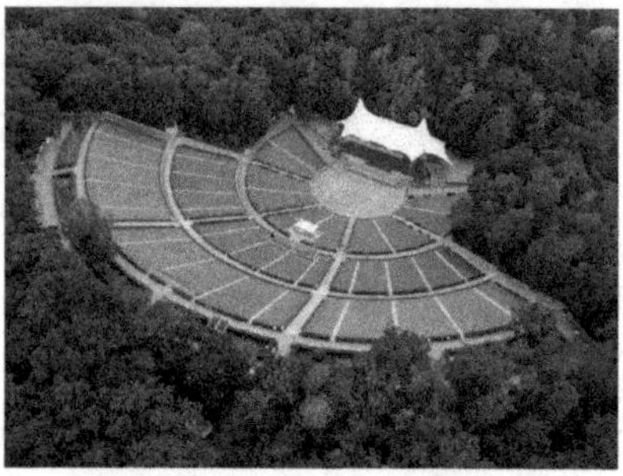

Dietrich-Eckart-Bühne

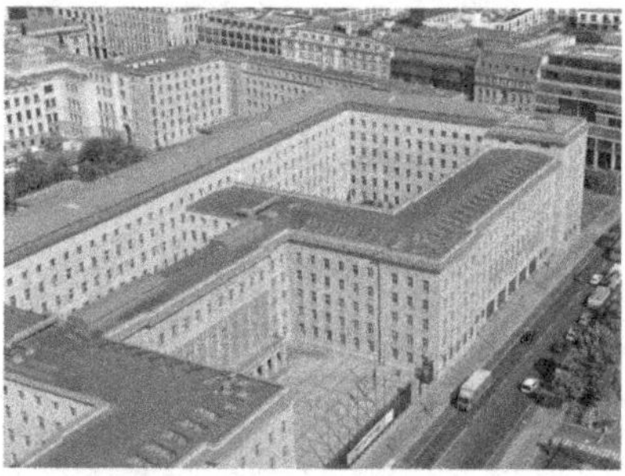

Senate Department for Urban Development and the Environment

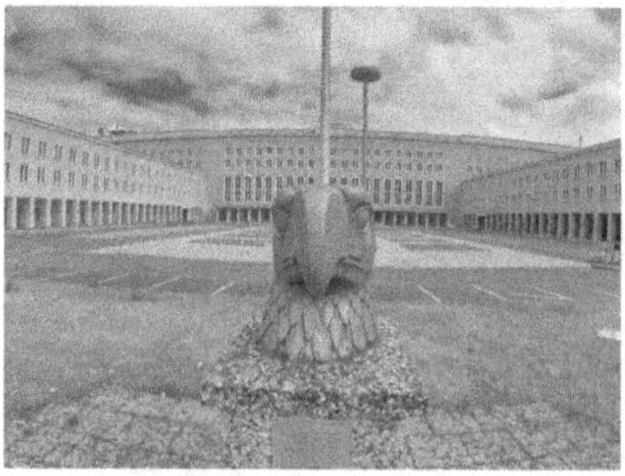

Flughafen Tempelhof

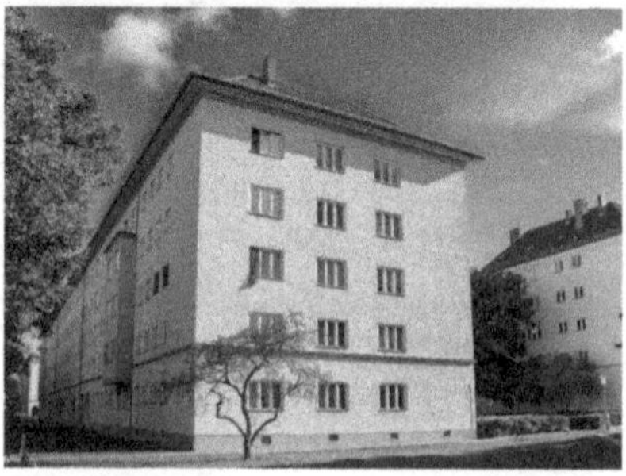

Housing estate on Grazer Damm

Appendix 2

ARTISTS IN THE 1937 *AUSSTELLUNG ENTARTETE KUNST* (DEGENERATE ART EXHIBITION)

Jankel Adler, Ernst Barlach, Rudolf Bauer, Philipp Bauknecht, Otto Baum, Willi Baumeister, Herbert Bayer, Max Beckmann, Rudolf Belling, Paul Bindel, Theo Brün, Max Burchartz, Fritz Burger-Mühlfeld, Paul Camenisch, Heinrich Campendonk, Karl Caspar, Maria Caspar-Filser, Pol Cassel, Marc Chagall, Lovis Corint, Heinrich Maria Davringhausen, Walter Dexel, Johannes Diesner, Otto Dix, Pranas Domšaitis, Hans Drexel, Johannes Driesch, Heinrich Eberhard, Max Ernst, Hans Feibusch, Lyonel Feininger, Conrad Felixmüller, Otto Freundlich, Xavier Fuhr, Ludwig Gies, Werner Gilles, Otto Gleichmann, Rudolph Grossmann, Georg Grosz, Hans Grundig, Rudolf Haizmann, Raoul Hausmann, Guido Hebert, Erich Heckel, Wilhelm Heckrott, Jacoba van Heemskerck, Hans Siebert von Heister, Oswald Herzog, Werner Heuser, Heinrich Hoerle, Karl Hofer, Eugen Hoffmann, Johannes Itten, Alexej Jawlensky, Eric Johanson, Hans Jürgen Kallmann, Wassily Kandinsky, Hanns Kat, Ernst Kirchner, Paul Klee, Cesar Klein, Paul Kleinschmidt, Oskar Kokoschka, Otto Lange, Wilhelm Lehmbruck, El Lissitzky, Oskar Lüthy, Franz Marc, Gerhard Marcks, Ewald Mataré, Ludwig Meidner, Jean Metzinger, Constantin von Mitschke-Collande, Laszlo Moholy-Nagy, Margarethe (Marg) Moll, Oskar Moll, Johannes Molzahn, Piet Mondrian, Georg Muche, Otto Mueller, Erich Nagel, Heinrich Nauen, Ernst Wilhelm Nay, Karel Niestrath, Emil Nolde, Otto Pankok, Max Pechstein, Max Peiffer-Watenphul, Hans Purrmann, Max Rauh, Hans Richter, Emy Röder, Christian Rohlfs, Edwin Scharff,

Oskar Schlemmer, Rudolf Schlichter, Karl Schmidt-Rottluff, Werner Scholz, Lothar Schreyer, Otto Schubert, Kurt Schwitters, Lasar Segall, Friedrich Skade, Friedrich (Fritz) Stuckenberg, Paul Thalheimer, Johannes Tietz, Arnold Topp, Karl Völker, Christoph Voll, Friedrich Vordemberge-Gildewart, William Wauer, Gert Heinrich Wollheim

Artistic movements condemned as degenerate

- Bauhaus, Cubism, Dada, Expressionism, Fauvism, Impressionism, New Objectivity, Surrealism

Appendix 3

A GUIDE TO THE *AUSSTELLUNG ENTARTETE KUNST* EXHIBITION

Translation of the catalogue accompanying the exhibition.

Purposes of the Exhibition

At the outset of a new era for the German people [*Volk*], *it wants* to offer a first-hand overview of the dreadful concluding chapter of those decades of cultural deterioration preceding the great change.

By appealing to the sound judgment of the people, *it wants* to put a stop to the palaver and claptrap of all those literary cliques and hangers-on, many of whom would still try to deny that we ever experienced artistic degeneracy.

It wants to make clear that this degeneracy in art was more than just passing foolishness, idiocy, and rash experimentation that might have run its course and died out even without the National Socialist revolution.

It wants to show that this was not a "necessary ferment", but rather a deliberate and calculated attack on the very essence and ongoing existence of art itself.

It wants to point out the common roots of *political* anarchy and *cultural* anarchy and to unmask degenerate art as *art-Bolshevism* in every sense of the term.

It wants to make clear the philosophical, political, racial, and moral goals and intentions of those who were the driving forces behind the subversion.

It also wants to show the extent to which these symptoms of degeneracy spread from those driving forces who were acting deliberately to infect more or less unwitting acolytes, who, despite *previous* – and in some cases also *subsequent* – evidence of formal artistic talent, were so lacking in *conscience, character,* or *common sense* as to participate in the general Jewish and Bolshevik hype.

By doing so, *it also wants* to show the true danger of a development that, steered by a few Jewish and openly Bolshevik leaders, could succeed in putting such individuals into the service of Bolshevik anarchy in *cultural politics,* when those very same individuals might very well have eschewed any affiliation with Bolshevism in *party politics.*

It wants to prove above all that *not one* of the men who were involved in any way in the degeneracy of art can now dismiss this activity as "harmless youthful folly".

Out of all this comes, finally, what the "Degenerate Art" exhibition does *not* want to do.

It does not want to assert that *all* the names attached to the sorry artworks shown here also appeared on the membership lists of the *Communist* party. Since *no* such assertion is made, *no refutation* is necessary.

It does not want to deny that one or another of the artists represented here has at some point – either before or since – "been capable of something different". Yet this exhibition must not gloss over the fact that in the years of the major Bolshevik-Jewish attack on German art such men stood on the side of subversion.

It does not want to prevent those featured artists who are of German blood – and who have not followed their former Jewish friends abroad – from now *honestly striving* and *fighting* for the foundations of a new and healthy creativity. It *wants* and *must* prevent a situation, however, in which such men are foisted on the new state and its future-oriented people as "the natural standard-bearers of Third Reich art" by the circles and cliques of that dark past.

Exhibits

Group 1

This room gives a general overview of *representational barbarism* from the point of view of craftsmanship. This group illustrates the progressive *degradation of the sense for form and colour,* the *deliberate contempt for all the technical foundations* of the visual arts, the *garish blurring of colour* combined with the deliberate *distortion* of drawing, the absolute *stupidity of subject choice* – all of them things that gradually assumed the character of an impertinent provocation to any normal viewer interested in the arts.

Group 2

This room brings together pictorial works that deal with *religious content*. In the Jewish press, these horrors were once described as "revelations of German religiosity". To a person of normal sense, however, these "revelations" rather seem like *witchcraft*, which he, regardless of the religious denomination to which he belongs, perceives as an impertinent of subject *mockery of all religious ideas*. Especially noteworthy is the fact that painted and carved mockeries of *Jewish Old Testament legends* are not to be found. By contrast, the figures of *Christian* legends grin at us with ever new and diabolic grimaces.

Group 3

The graphic works shown in this section are conclusive evidence for the *political roots of degenerate art*. Using the expressive devices of *artistic anarchy*, these works preach *political anarchy as a demand*. Every single picture in this group calls for *class warfare* in the Bolshevist sense. By means of a coarsely tendentious proletarian art, the creative human being is supposed to be confirmed in his conviction that he will remain a slave languishing in spiritual chains until the very last property owner, the very last non-proletarian has been removed by the hoped-for *Bolshevist revolution*. Workers, workers' wives, and workers' children with the grey and green *faces of misery* stare out at the viewer. The drawings depict all imaginable kinds of "capitalists" and "exploiters" who mockingly disregard the misery of working people. From butcher to banker, all of these "slaveholders" are depicted. Noticeably overlooked by the painters of class warfare were certain Jewish art dealers, who certainly were not starving at the time and who enriched themselves significantly by this proletarian art.

Group 4

This section, too, is of a marked *political tendentiousness*. Here, "art" is put into the service of Marxist propaganda for conscientious objection. The intention is clear: the viewer is meant to recognise the soldier as a murderer or as the pointlessly butchered victim of a "capitalist world order" in the sense of Bolshevist class warfare. Most of all, the intention is to eradicate the populace's deeply rooted respect for all soldierly virtues, namely courage, bravery, and the willingness to fight. Thus, in addition to distorted images of crippled veterans designed to evoke disgust and views into mass graves painted with great sophistication, the drawings in this section depict German soldiers as fools, common erotic lechers, and drunkards. The fact that, with their base efforts, not only Jews but also "artists" of German blood thus retroactively *once again reinforce,* without being asked, enemy *propaganda about wartime atrocities,* propaganda that had already been exposed as a web of lies at the time – this fact will forever remain *a blot on German cultural history.*

Group 5

This section of the exhibition provides insight into the *moral* side of degenerate art. For the "artists" represented here, the entire world apparently is one big *brothel,* and to them humanity is made up of *harlots* and *pimps.* Among this painted and drawn pornography are drawings and paintings that cannot even be shown in the context of the exhibition "Degenerate Art" when one considers that women will visit this show as well. It is completely incomprehensible to any individual of today's Germany that just a few years ago, even in the times of Centre Party rule under Heinrich Brüning, such abysmal vulgarity, such squalidness and clearly exposed criminality was allowed to appeal to the basest instinct of sub-human beings unhindered. Yet one thing must not be overlooked: the ultimate objective of this side of degenerate art, too, is political. This can be seen from the fact that almost all these vulgarities also display clear Marxist-class warfare tendencies. Time and again, we see drawings on which lechers from the "propertied class" and their harlots are contrasted with the starving figures of "proletarians" tiredly dragging themselves along in the background. In other drawings, the harlot is idealised and contrasted with the woman of bourgeois society, who, according to the creators of this "art", is much more morally corrupt than the prostitute. In short: *the moral agenda of Bolshevism screams at the viewer from all walls in this section.*

Group 6

Here, a larger number of works serve to illustrate how degenerate art often served that part of Marxist and Bolshevist ideology whose goal is this: *the systematic elimination of the last remnants of all race consciousness.* While the harlot was portrayed as a moral ideal in the pictures in the previous section, we now encounter the *Negro* and the *South Sea Islander* as the apparent *racial ideal* of "modern art". It is hard to believe that the creators of these images call Germany or Europe home, or at least did so at the time. Yet it must be stressed that this n[*****] art also is so barbaric in terms of craftsmanship that many a Negro would justifiably refuse to see people of his own kind in these figures or even be accused of being the creator of such pictorial works.

Group 7

This section of the exhibition makes clear that apart from the Negro as a racial ideal, the "modern" art of the time also had one very special *intellectual ideal,* namely the *idiot,* the *cretin* and the *paralytic*. Where these "artists" portrayed themselves or each other, the results are extremely cretinous faces and figures. Judging by the rest of the works, this may not always be a fundamental decision against actual likeness. It is certain, however, that each stupid, idiot-like face has *particularly* inspired the creativity of the "modernists" represented here. Otherwise, it cannot be explained why this section of the exhibition is so rich in sculpture, graphic works, and painting. It shows human figures who, in fact, have more in common with gorillas than with humans. There are portraits compared to which the first historically verified attempts at depicting humans found in Stone Age caves are mature masterpieces. *Yet until a few years ago, as the purchase prices show, the highest prices were demanded and paid even for such atrocious pieces.*

Group 8

For the sake of variety, *only Jews* are represented in this small room. In order to avoid any misunderstandings, it should be mentioned that this is only a small selection of the numerous sorry efforts by Jews that the exhibition shows overall. The great "merit" that the Jewish spokespersons, dealers, and supporters of degenerate art have doubtless earned, sufficiently justifies this "*special honouring*". It is here that we can find, among other things, "the new human being", as the Jew *Freundlich* has conjured him. Other sculpted and painted desert dreams can be found standing and hanging here as well, in the face of which words must fail us.

Group 9

This section can only be titled "*Complete Lunacy*". It takes up the largest part of the exhibition and includes a cross section of the spawn of all the "*isms*" that Flechtheim, Wollheim, and the "Cohn-sorts" have hatched, promoted, and flogged over the years. In the pictures and drawings of this chamber of horrors it is impossible to tell in most cases what those sick minds were thinking when they picked up the brush or pencil. While one eventually "painted" using only the contents of garbage cans, another made do with three black lines and a piece of wood on a large white background. A third had the bright idea to paint "some circles" onto two square meters of canvas. A fourth consecutively used a good three kilograms of paint for three self-portraits because he could not decide whether his head ought to be green or sulphur yellow, round or rectangular, and whether his eyes are red or sky blue or whatever. In this group of madness, visitors to the exhibition only shake their heads and laugh. Certainly not without reason. Yet when one considers that all of these "artworks" were taken not from the dusty corners of deserted studios but from the art collections and museums of major German cities, where some of them still hung in the initial years after the National Socialist takeover and were presented to the astonished public, one can laugh no longer: *all one can do is grapple with one's anger at the fact that a people as decent as the Germans have been so gravely abused in such a manner to begin with.*

SOURCES

Abendroth, Walter, *Kunstmusik und Volstümlichkeit in Die Musik* (März, 1934)

Adam, Peter, *Art of the Third Reich* (Harry N. Abrams, 1991)

Arendt, Hannah, *The Origins of Totalitarianism* (World Publishing, 1958)

Bach, Steven, *Leni, The Life and Works of Leni Riefenstahl* (Little Brown, 2007)

Baird, Jay W., 'From Berlin to Neubabelsberg: Nazi Film Propaganda and Hitler Youth Quex' (*Journal of Contemporary History*, Vol. 18, No. 3, 1983)

Barr, Alfred H., 'Art in the Third Reich' (*Magazine of Art*, October, 1945)

Barron, Stephanie, *Degenerate Art:' The Fate of the Avant-Garde in Nazi Germany* (Harry N. Abrams, 1991)

Barron, Stephanie, *Modern Art and Politics in Prewar Germany* (Harry N. Abrams, 1991)

Barron, Stephanie, *The Gallery Fischer Auction* (Harry N. Abrams, 1991)

Batty, Ginny, *The Political Picture: How the Nazis Created a Distinctly Fascist Art* (ginnyandthemoon.wordpress.com, 2015)

Belikova, Maria, *Weimar Art: Between Tradition and Avant-Garde* (State Institute of Art Studies (SIAS)

Boehlert, Mumford Aaron, *Hitler's Germania: Propaganda Writ in Stone* (Bard College, 2017)

Brecker, Arno, *Im Strahlungsfeld Der Ereignisse* (Preussisch Oldendorf: Schütz, 1972)

Bucherer, Fritz, *Humanistische Bildung im nationalsozialistischen Staate* (Teubner, 1933)

Bukey, Evan B., 'Hitler's Hometown under Nazi Rule: Linz, Austria, 1938–45' (*Central European History*, Vol. 16, No. 2, 1983)

Cathcart, Adam, 'Music and Politics in Hitler's Germany' (*Madison Historical Review*, Vol. 3, Article 1, 2006)

Chapoutot, Johann, *Greeks, Romans, Germans: How the Nazis Usurped Europe's Classical Past* (University of California Press, Kindle Edition)

Chiew-Lee, Khut, *Primacy of Ideology? The Confiscation and Exchange of 'degenerate art' in the Third Reich* (University of Adelaide, 2001)

Clinefelter, Joan, *Artists for the Reich* (Berg, 2005)

Diebold, W.J., 'The Politics of Derestoration: The Aegina Pediments and the German Confrontation with the Past' (*Art Journal*, 1995)

Dix, Otto, *Neues Deutschland*, December 1964

Downing, Taylor, *Olympia* (British Film Institute, 1992)

Droste, Magdalena, *The Bauhaus 1919–1933* (Taschen, 2006)

El-Mecky, Nausikaa, *Hitler's destruction of Modern Art* (smarthistory.org/art-in-nazi-germany)

English, Charlie, *The Gallery of Miracles and Madness* (William Collins, 2021)

Evans, Richard J., *The Coming of the Third Reich* (Penguin, 2004)

Fischer-Defoy, Christine, 'Artists and Art Institutions in Germany 1933–1945' (*Oxford Art Journal*, Vol. 9, Issue 2, 1986)

Gay, Peter, *Weimar Culture: The Outsider as Insider* (Secker and Warburg, 1968)

Gittler, L.F., 'Nazi Propaganda at Work' (*Current History*, December, 1937)

Grosshans, Henry, *Hitler and the Artists* (Holmes and Meyer, 1983)

Grosz, Georg, *A Small Yes and a Big No: The Autobiography of Georg Grosz* (University of California Press, 1998)

Guenther, Peter, *Three Days in Munich* (Harry N. Abrams, 1991)

Gunston, David, 'Leni Riefenstahl' (*Film Quarterly*, Vol. 14, No. 1, 1960)

Hagan, Joshua, 'Parades, Public Space, and Propaganda: The Nazi Culture Parades in Munich' (*Geografiska Annaler*. Series B, Human Geography, Vol. 90, No. 4, 2008)

Hagen, Joshua and Ostergren, Robert, 'Spectacle, architecture and place at the Nuremberg Party Rallies: projecting a Nazi vision of past, present and future' (*Cultural Geographies*, Vol. 13, No. 2, 2006)

Hamann, Brigitte, *Hitler's Vienna; a Portrait of the Tyrant as a Young Man* (Tauris Parke, 2010)

Heiber, Helmut (ed.), *Das Tagebuch von Joseph Goebbels 1925–26* (Deutsche Verlags, 1961)

Heiden, Konrad, *The Führer* (Castle Books, 2002)

Heilborn, Adolf, *Die Zeichner des Volks: Käthe Kollwitz – Heinrich Zille* (Saxoniabuch, 2021)

Hertzfelde, Wieland, *Heartfield's Photomontages and Contemporary History* (1972)

Hickley, Catherine, *The Munich Art Hoard* (Thames and Hudson, 2015)

Hinz, Berthold, *Art in the Third Reich* (Oxford University Press, 1979)

Hitler, Adolf, *Mein Kampf*, (Franz Eher Nachfolger GmbH, 1925)

Hünke, Andreas, *On the Trail of Missing Masterpieces* (Harry N. Abrams, 1991)

Huxley, Aldous, 'Notes on Propaganda' (*Harpers' Magazine*, December, 1936)

Irvine, David T., *Albert Speer* (Kindle Edition)

Jakisch, Barry A., 'The Nature of Berlin: Green Space and Visions of a New German Capital, 1900-45' (*Central European History*, Vol. 47, No. 2, 2014)

Jaskot, Paul B., 'Anti-Semitic Policy in Albert Speer's Plans for the Rebuilding of Berlin' (*The Art Bulletin*, Vol. 78, No. 4, 1996)

Jason, Gary, *Film and Propaganda: The Lessons of the Nazi Film Industry* (California State University, 2013)

Jekeli, Hermann, *Rasse ist Verpflichtung* (Nazi Party Publication)

Jones, Derek, *Censorship; A World Encyclopedia* (Kindle Edition, 2001) Routledge, 2001

Kasher, Steven, *The Art of Hitler* (Vol. 59, winter 1992)

Kater, Michael H., *Culture in Nazi Germany* (Yale University Press, Kindle Edition) 2019

Kearns, Martha, *Käthe Kollwitz* (The Feminist Press at CUNY, 1976)

Kennedy, Shane Michael, *Expressionist Art and Drama Before, During, and After the Weimar Republic* (Portland State University, 2015)

Kershaw, Ian, *Hitler 1889–1936: Hubris* (Penguin, 1999)

Kollwitze, Käthe, *Diary and Letters of Kaethe Kollwitz* (Northwestern University Press, 1989)

Krippendorf, Kurt, *Grundsätzliche Erwägungen zur Neugestaltung des Geschichtsunterrichts, Vergangenheit und Gegenwart: Zeitschrift für den Geschichtsunterricht und staatsbürgerliche Erziehung in allen Schulgattungen* (Heft, 1933)

Kuiper, Kathleen, *The Britannica Guide to Theories and Ideas That Changed the Modern World* (Britannica Educational, 2010)

Kyam, Wayne, 'The Nazification of Max Reinhardt's Deutsches Theater' (*Theatre Journal*, Vol. 40, No. 3, 1998)

Lacqueur, Walter, 'Weimar; A Cultutal History' (*Kirkus Review*, December, 1974)

Lane, Barbara Miller, *Interpreting Nazi Architecture: The Case of Albert Speer* (Bryn Mawr College, 1997)

Lane, Mary M., *Time Magazine* (18 September, 2019)

Levi, Erik, *Music in the Third Reich* (St. Martin's Press, 1994)

Levi, Erik, *Atonality, 12-Tone Music and the Third Reich* (Tempo, 1991)

Lüttichau, Mario von, *Entartete Kunst, Munich 1937 A Reconstruction* (Harry N. Abrams, 1991)

Mackenzie, Michael, 'From Athens to Berlin: The 1936 Olympics and Leni Riefenstahl's Olympia' (*Critical Inquiry*, Vol. 29, No. 2, 2003)

McGilligan, Patrick, *Fritz Lang: The Nature of the Beast, a Biography* (St. Martin's Press, 1997)

Michalski, Sergiusz, *New Objectivity* (Taschen America, 1994)

Modersohn-Becker, Paula, *magazine.artland.com*

Moritz, William, *Film Censorship during the Nazi Era* (Harry N. Abrams, 1991)

Moss, Timothy, *Hitler's Noxious Plan to 'Restructure' Berlin* (thereader.mitpress.mit.edu/hitlers-noxious-plan-to-restructure-berlin, 2021)

Mosse, George L., *Beauty without Sensuality The Exhibition Entartet Kunst* (Harry N. Abrams, 1991)

Mosse, George L., *Nazi Culture: Intellectual, Cultural and Social Life in the Third Reich* (University of Wisconsin Press, 1966)

Nelson, Roger B., 'Hitler's Propaganda Machine' (*Current History (1916–1940)*, Vol. 38, No. 3, 1933)

Neuschwander, Del ora J., 'Music in the Third Reich' (*Musical Offerings*: Vol. 3: No. 2, Article 3, 2012)

Nicholas, Lynn H., *The Rape of Europa* (Knopf Doubleday Publishing Group, Kindle Edition,1994)

Nordau, Max, *Entartung* (Duncker, 1893)

O'Byrne, Darren M. and Young, Christopher, *The Will of the Führer? Financing Construction for the 1936 Olympics* (University of Cambridge, 2022)

Petropoulos, Jonathan, *Faustian Bargain: The Art World in Nazi Germany* (Oxford University Press, 2000)

Petropoulos, Jonathan, *From Seduction to Denial' Art, Culture, and Media under the Third Reich* (University of Chicago Press, 2002)

Reeves, Nicholas, *Power of Film Propaganda; Myth or Reality* (Continuum, 2004)

Riefenstahl, Leni, *Hinter den Kulissen des Reichsparteitag* (International Historic Films, Inc., 1935)

Ritchie, J.M., 'The Nazi Book-Burning' (*The Modern Language Review*, July, 1988)

Roh, Franz, *German Art in the 20th Century* (New York Graphic Society, 1958)

Rosenberg, Alfred, *Race and Race History and Older Essays, ed Robert Pois* (Harper and Row, 1970)

Rosenfeld, Gavriel D., 'Architecture and the Memory of Nazism in Postwar Munich' (*German Politics & Society*, Vol. 16, No. 4, 1998)

Schachermeyr, Fritz, *Die Aufgaben der Alten Geschichte im Rahmen der nordischen Weltgeschichte* (Vergangenheit und Gegenwart, 1933)

Schmidt, Diether, *Otto Dix* (Painter and Work, 1977)

Schroeder, Christa, *He was my Chief: The Memoirs of Adolf Hitler's Secretary* (Kindle Edition, 2009)

Sennett, Alan, 'Film Propaganda: Triumph of the Will as a Case Study' (*Framework: The Journal of Cinema and Media*, Vol. 55, No. 1, 2014)

Simkin, John, *Dramatize-educational.com/Adolf_Ziegler.htm*

Simkin, John, *spartacus-educational.com*, (September 1997)

Smith, Maggie L., *Germania: The Nazi Party and the Third Reich through the lens of Classical Architecture* (University of Mississippi, 2021)

Sontag, Susan, *Fascinating Fascism, Under the Sign of Saturn* (Penguin, 2013)

Speer, Albert, *Spandau, the Secret Diaries* (Macmillan 1976)

Speer, Albert, *Inside the Third Reich* (Simon and Schuster, 1970)

Spotts, Frederic, *Hitler and the Power of Aesthetics* (Abrams Press, 2021)

Stupp, Vicki O'Donnell, 'Myth, Meaning, and Message in "The Triumph of the Will"' (*Film Criticism*, Vol. 2, No. 2/3, 1978)

Taper, Bernard, 'Hitler's Photographer An intimate friend of the Führer' (*The New Yorker*, 27 October, 1950)

Thies, Jochen, 'Hitler's European Building Programme' (*Journal of Contemporary History*, Vol. 13, No. 3, 1978)

Thomas, Friedrich, *Hitler's Berlin: Abused City* (Yale University Press, 2006)

Werckmeister, O.K., 'Hitler the Artist' (*Critical Inquiry*, Vol. 23, No. 2, 1997)

Werner, Alfred, 'Hitler's Kampf against Modern Art' (*Antioch Review*, Spring, 1966)

Werner, Alfred, 'Ernst Barlach' (*The Kenyon Review*, Vol. 24, No. 4, 1962)

Werner, Alfred, *An Artist against the Third Reich: Ernst Barlach, 1933–1938* (Cambridge University Press, 2002)

Werner, Bruno E., *Deutsche Allgemeine Zeitung, 20 July 1937*

Willet, John, *Art and Politics in the Weimar Period* (Thames and Hudson, 1978)

Yourman, Julius, 'Propaganda Techniques Within Nazi Germany' (*The Journal of Educational Sociology*, November, 1939)

Zeman, Zbyněk, *Heckling Hitler: Caricatures of the Third Reich* (I.B. Tauris, 1987)

Alldeutsches Tagblatt, 18 April 1908

Berliner Illustrirte Zeitung, 27 October 1937

Close Up, Territet, December 1929

Daily Mail, 3 February 1960

Frankfurter Zeitung, 8 October 1937

Goebbels' Diary, 14 March 1937

Goebbels' Diary, 8 March 1937

Joseph Goebbels in Der Autor, January 1934

Letter from Lewald to Pfundtner, 5 October 1933, Barch B R 1501/5608.

Weimar Republic Sourcebook, (Berkeley: University of California Press, 1994)

Rheinisch- Westfdlische Zeitung, 11 June 1933, *Wilhelm Tell in der Westfalenhalle*,

Designmanifestos.org / walter-gropius-manifesto-of-the-staatliches-bauhaus

Dramatize.org/wiki/Neue_Künstlervereinigung_München

NOTES

Chapter 1: Nazi Propaganda Techniques

1 Reeves, Nicholas, *Power of Film Propaganda: Myth or Reality,* (Continuum, 2004), p. 5.
2 Huxley, Aldous, 'Notes on Propaganda' (*Harpers' Magazine,* December, 1936), p. 39.
3 Sennett, Alan, 'Film Propaganda: Triumph of the Will as a Case Study' (Framework: *The Journal of Cinema and Media,* Vol. 55, No. 1, 2014), p. 54.
4 Evans, Richard J., *The Coming of the Third Reich* (Penguin, 2004), p. 204.
5 Heiber, Helmut (ed.), *Das Tagebuch von Joseph Goebbels 1925–26* (Deutsche Verlags, 1961).
6 Thomas, Friedrich, *Hitler's Berlin: Abused City* (Yale University Press, 2006).
7 Gittler, L.F., 'Nazi Propaganda at Work' (*Current History,* December, 1937), p. 37.
8 Chapoutot, Johann, *Greeks, Romans, Germans: How the Nazis Usurped Europe's Classical Past* (University of California Press, Kindle Edition), p. 8.
9 Ibid, p. 10.
10 Yourman, Julius, *Propaganda Techniques Within Nazi Germany* (The Journal of Educational Sociology, November, 1939), p. 155.
11 Ibid, p. 158.
12 Krippendorf, Kurt, *'Grundsätzliche Erwägungen zur Neugestaltung des Geschichtsunterrichts', Vergangenheit und Gegenwart: Zeitschrift für den Geschichtsunterricht und staatsbürgerliche Erziehung in allen Schulgattungen* (Heft, 1933), p. 483.
13 Bucherer, Fritz, *Humanistische Bildung im nationalsozialistischen Staate* (Teubner, 1933), p. 7.
14 Chapoutot, p. 114.
15 Schachermeyr, Fritz, *Die Aufgaben der Alten Geschichte im Rahmen der nordischen Weltgeschichte* (Vergangenheit und Gegenwart, 1933), p. 599.
16 Chapoutot, p. 102.
17 Hitler, Adolf, *Mein Kampf,* (Franz Eher Nachfolger GmbH, 1925), p. 14.
18 Chapoutot, p. 140.
19 Nelson, Roger B., 'Hitler's Propaganda Machine' (*Current History (1916–1940),* Vol. 38, No. 3, 1933), p. 287.
20 Ibid, p. 288.
21 Ibid, p. 290.
22 Ibid.
23 Gittler, p. 35.
24 Ibid, p. 37.

Chapter 2: Hitler and Art

1 Kasher, Steven, 'The Art of Hitler' (Vol 59. Winter 1992), p. 275.
2 Hamann, Brigitte, *Hitler's Vienna;: a Portrait of the Tyrant as a Young Man* (Tauris Parke, 2010), p. 21.
3 Spotts, Frederic, *Hitler and the Power of Aesthetics* (Abrams Press, 2021), p. 124.
4 Hamann, p. 35.
5 *Alldeutsches Tagblatt*, 18 April 1908.
6 Hamann, p. 85.
7 Spotts, p. 138.
8 Ibid, p. 129.
9 Werckmeister, O.K., 'Hitler the Artist' (*Critical Inquiry*, Vol. 23, No. 2, 1997), p. 277.
10 Hamann, p. 173.
11 Spotts, p. 130.
12 Werckmeister, p. 279.
13 Ibid, p. 80.
14 Ibid, p. 284.
15 Ibid, p. 285.
16 Grosshans, Henry, *Hitler and the Artists* (Holmes and Meyer, 1983), p. 74.
17 Ibid, p. 80.
18 Ibid, p. 86.
19 Roh, Franz, *German Art in the 20th Century* (New York Graphic Society, 1958), p. 152.

Chapter 3: Art in Weimar Germany

1 Lacqueur, Walter, 'Weimar; A Cultutal History' (*Kirkus Review*, December, 1974).
2 Belikova, Maria, *Weimar Art: Between Tradition and Avant-Garde* (State Institute of Art Studies (SIAS)), p. 222.
3 Rosenberg, Alfred, 'Race and Race History' and Older Essays, ed Robert Pois, (Harper and Row, 1970), p. 154.
4 Modersohn-Becker, Paula, magazine.artland.com.
5 dramatize.org/wiki/Neue_Künstlervereinigung_München.
6 Kennedy, Shane Michael, *Expressionist Art and Drama Before, During, and After the Weimar Republic* (Portland State University, 2015), p. 6.
7 Kuiper, Kathleen, *The Britannica Guide to Theories and Ideas That Changed the Modern World* (Britannica Educational, 2010), p. 150.
8 Willet, John, *Art and politics in the Weimar Period* (Thames and Hudson, 1978), p. 114.
9 Gay, Peter, *Weimar Culture: The Outsider as Insider* (Secker and Warburg, 1968).
10 Weimar Republic Sourcebook, (Berkeley: University of California Press, 1994), p. 721.
11 Kleinfelter, Joan, *Artists for the Reich* (Berg, 2005), p. 65.
12 Jones, Derek, *Censorship; A World Encyclopedia* (Kindle Edition, 2001).
13 Grosshans, p. 9.
14 Willet, John, *Art and Politics in the Weimar Period* (Thames and Hudson, 1978), p. 187.
15 Designmanifestos.org/walter-gropius-manifesto-of-the-staatliches-bauhaus.
16 Droste, Magdalena, *The Bauhaus 1919–1933* (Taschen, 2006), p. 60.
17 Kater, Michael H., *Culture in Nazi Germany* (Yale University Press, Kindle Edition), p. 2.
18 English, Charlie, *The Gallery of Miracles and Madness* (William Collins, 2021), p. 90.
19 Kater, p. 5.
20 Gittler, p. 36.

Chapter 4: Art under the Nazis

1 El-Mecky, Nausikaa, 'Hitler's destruction of Modern Art', smarthistory.org/art-in-nazi-germany.
2 Mosse, George L., *Beauty without Sensuality The Exhibition Entartet Kunst* (Harry N. Abrams, 1991), p. 26.
3 Nordau, Max, *Entartung* (Duncker, 1893), p. 498.
4 Hamann, p. 84.
5 Kater, p. 9.
6 Ibid, p. 12.
7 English, p. 16.
8 Ibid, p. 41.
9 Ibid, p. 51.
10 Batty, Ginny, 'The Political Picture: How the Nazis Created a Distinctly Fascist Art' (ginnyandthemoon.wordpress.com, 2015).
11 Kater, p. 62.
12 Chiew-Lee, Khut, *Primacy of Ideology? The Confiscation and Exchange of 'degenerate art' in the Third Reich* (University of Adelaide, 2001), p. 24.
13 Nicholas, Lynn H., *The Rape of Europa* (Knopf Doubleday Publishing Group, Kindle Edition), p. 6.
14 Barr, Alfred H., 'Art in the Third Reich' (*Magazine of Art*, October, 1945), p. 213.
15 Fischer-Defoy, Christine, 'Artists and Art Institutions in Germany 1933–1945' (*Oxford Art Journal*, Volume 9, Issue 2, 1986), p. 19.
16 English, p. 106.
17 Spotts, p. 155.
18 Kater, p. 35.
19 English, p. 110.
20 Nicholas, p. 11.
21 Barron, Stephanie, *Modern Art and Politics in Prewar Germany* (Harry N. Abrams, 1991), p. 17.
22 Spotts, p. 156.
23 Chapoutot, p. 90.
24 Hagan, Joshua, 'Parades, Public Space, and Propaganda: The Nazi Culture Parades in Munich' (*Geografiska Annaler*. Series B, Human Geography, Vol. 90, No. 4, 2008), p. 355.
25 English, p. 110.
26 Adam, Peter, *Art of the Third Reich* (Harry N. Abrams, 1991), p. 56.
27 Werner, Alfred, 'Hitler's Kampf against Modern Art' (*Antioch Review*, Spring, 1966), p. 60.
28 Kater, p. 38.
29 Werner, Alfred, Hitler's Kampf against Modern Art, p. 60.
30 Ritchie, J.M., 'The Nazi Book-Burning' (*The Modern Language Review*, July, 1988), p. 628.
31 Spotts, p. 156.
32 Ibid, p. 158.
33 Willets, p. 221.

Chapter 5: The Good the Bad and the Ugly

1 Guenther, Peter, *Three Days in Munich* (Harry N. Abrams, 1991), p. 34.
2 Werner, Bruno E., *Deutsche Allgemeine Zeitung*, 20 July 1937.
3 *Berliner Illustrirte Zeitung*, 27 October 1937.
4 *Frankfurter Zeitung*, 8 October 1937.

5 Simkin, John, spartacus-educational.com, (September 1997).
6 English, p. 139.
7 Werner, Alfred, 'Hitler's Kampf against Modern Art', p. 62.
8 Mosse, George L., *Nazi Culture: Intellectual, Cultural and Social Life in the Third Reich* (University of Wisconsin Press, 1966), p. 14.
9 Werner, Alfred, 'Hitler's Kampf against Modern Art', p. 63.
10 English, p. 146.
11 Barron, Stephanie, *Modern Art and Politics in Prewar Germany*, p. 17.
12 Hagan, p. 355.
13 Barron, Stephanie, *Modern Art and Politics in Prewar Germany*, p. 18.
14 Werner, Alfred, 'Hitler's Kampf against Modern Art', p. 65.
15 Guenther, p. 35.
16 English, p. 135.
17 Barron, Stephanie, *Modern Art and Politics in Prewar Germany*, p. 19.
18 Mosse, George L., Beauty without Sensuality, p. 27.
19 Lüttichau, Mario von, *Entartete Kunst, Munich 1937 A Reconstruction* (Harry N. Abrams, 1991), p. 26.
20 Kater, p. 43.
21 Werner, Alfred, 'Hitler's Kampf against Modern Art', p. 65.
22 Guenther, p. 38.
23 Hünke, Andreas, *On the Trail of Missing Masterpieces* (Harry N. Abrams, 1991), p. 122.
24 Hickley, Catherine, *The Munich Art Hoard* (Thames and Hudson, 2015), p. 51.
25 Barron, Stephanie, *The Gallery Fischer Auction* (Harry N. Abrams, 1991), p. 139.
26 Ibid, p. 144.

Chapter 6: Artist Outcast of the Third Reich

1 Spotts, p. 88.
2 Ibid, p. 341.
3 Werner, Alfred, 'Ernst Barlach' (*The Kenyon Review*, Vol. 24, No. 4, 1962), p. 632.
4 Ibid, p. 627.
5 Kater, p. 32.
6 Werner, Alfred, 'Ernst Barlach', p. 631.
7 Ibid, p. 630.
8 Ibid, p. 639.
9 Spotts, p. 153.
10 Dix, Otto, *Neues Deutschland*, December 1964.
11 Schmidt, Diether, *Otto Dix* (Painter and Work, 1977), p. 252.
12 Michalski, Sergiusz, *New Objectivity* (Taschen America, 1994), p. 62.
13 Kater, p. 19.
14 Grosz, Georg, *A Small Yes and a Big No: The Autobiography of Georg Grosz* (University of California Press 1998), p. 79.
15 ibid, p. 119.
16 Zeman, Zbyněk, *Heckling Hitler: Caricatures of the Third Reich* (I.B. Tauris, 1987), p. 22.
17 Lane. Mary M, *Time Magazine* (18 September, 2019).
18 Hertzfelde, Wieland, *Heartfield's Photomontages and Contemporary History* (1972), p. 22.
19 Zeman, p. 37.
20 Kollwitze Käthe, *Diary and Letters of Kaethe Kollwitz* (Northwestern University Press. 1989), p. 38.
21 Ibid, p. 40.

22 Heilborn, Adolf, *Die Zeichner des Volks: Käthe Kollwitz - Heinrich Zille* (saxoniabuch, 2021), p. 33.
23 Kearns, Martha, *Käthe Kollwitz* (The Feminist Press at CUNY, 1976), p. 81.
24 Kollwitze, p. 44.
25 Ibid, p. 96.
26 Ibid, p. 9.
27 Ibid, p. 180.

Chapter 7: Artistic Champions of the Third Reich

1 Petropoulos, Jonathan, *Faustian Bargain: The Art World in Nazi Germany* (Oxford University Press, 2000), p. 221.
2 Ibid, p. 223.
3 Ibid, p. 222.
4 Ibid, p. 223.
5 Kasher, p. 55.
6 Petropoulos, p. 212.
7 Adam, p. 199.
8 Spotts, p. 185.
9 Ibid.
10 Chapoutot, p. 156.
11 Nelson, p. 292.
12 Simkin, John, spartacus-educational.com September 1997.
13 Taper, Bernard, 'Hitler's Photographer: An intimate friend of the Führer' (*The New Yorker*, 27 October, 1950).
14 Lane, Barbara Miller, *Interpreting Nazi Architecture: The Case of Albert Speer* (Bryn Mawr College, 1997).
15 Ibid.
16 Ibid.
17 Speer, Albert, *Inside the Third Reich* (Simon and Schuster, 1970), p. 27.
18 Gunston, David, 'Leni Riefenstahl', (*Film Quarterly* Vol. 14, No. 1 1960), p. 7.
19 Close Up, Territet, December 1929.
20 Bach, Steven, *Leni: The Life and Works of Leni Riefenstahl* (Little Brown, 2007), p. 77.
21 Gunston, p. 12.
22 Bach, p. 91.
23 Ibid, p. 92.
24 Gunston, p. 13.
25 Ibid.
26 *Daily Mail*, 3 February 1960.
27 Bach, p. 113.
28 Ibid, p. 123.
29 Spotts, p. 15.

Chapter 8: The Obsession with Antiquity

1 Diebold, W.J., 'The Politics of Derestoration: The Aegina Pediments and the German Confrontation with the Past' (*Art Journal*, 1995), p. 63.
2 Arendt, Hannah, *The Origins of Totalitarianism* (World Publishing, 1958), p. 262.
3 Chapoutot, p. 121.
4 Ibid, p. 26.
5 Krippendorf, p. 483.
6 Chapoutot, p. 102.
7 Ibid, p. 103.

8 Ibid, p. 114.
9 Schachermeyr, Fritz, *Die Aufgaben der Alten Geschichte im Rahmen der nordischen Weltgeschichte* (Vergangenheit und Gegenwart, 1933), p. 599.
10 Jekeli, Hermann, *Rasse ist Verpflichtung* (Nazi Party Publication).
11 Chapoutot, p. 33.
12 Ibid, p. 57.
13 Ibid, p. 70.
14 Ibid, p. 166.

Chapter 9: Propaganda through Architecture

1 Chapoutot, p. 7.
2 Schroeder, Christa, *He was my Chief: The Memoirs of Adolf Hitler's Secretary* (Kindle Edition), p. 219.
3 Spotts, p. 334.
4 Hinz, Berthold, *Art in the Third Reich* (Oxford University Press, 1979), p. 195.
5 Heiden, Konrad, *The Führer* (Castle Books, 2002), p. 283.
6 Spotts, p. 342.
7 Ibid, p. 336.
8 Diebold, p. 64.
9 O'Byrne, Darren M. and Christopher Young, *The Will of the Führer? Financing Construction for the 1936 Olympics* (University of Cambridge, 2022), p. 25.
10 Letter from Lewald to Pfundtner, 5 October 1933, Barch B R 1501/5608.
11 Chapoutot, p. 160.
12 Smith, Maggie L., *Germania: The Nazi Party and the Third Reich through the lens of Classical Architecture* (University of Mississippi, 2021), p. 31.
13 Hagen, Joshua and Ostergren, Robert, 'Spectacle, architecture and place at the Nuremberg Party Rallies: projecting a Nazi vision of past, present and future' (*Cultural Geographies*, Vol. 13, No. 2, 2006), p. 163.
14 Ibid, p. 167.
15 Spotts, p. 334.
16 Ibid, p. 318.
17 Ibid, p. 321.
18 Goebbels' Diaries, 14 March 1937.
19 Speer, Albert, *Spandau, the Secret Diaries* (Macmillan 1976).

Chapter 10: Germania

1 Goebbels' Diary, 8 March 1937.
2 Charles River Editors, *Albert Speer and Germania: The History of Nazi Germany's Lead Architect and His Plans for a Future German Capital* (Kindle Edition).
3 Spotts, p. 312.
4 Boehlert, Mumford Aaron, *Hitler's Germania: Propaganda Writ in Stone* (Bard College, 2017), p. 29.
5 Moss, Timothy, 'Hitler's Noxious Plan to "Restructure" Berlin' (thereader.mitpress.mit.edu/hitlers-noxious-plan-to-restructure-berlin 2021).
6 Speer, Albert, *Inside the Third Reich*, p. 158.
7 Spotts, p. 324.
8 Ibid, p. 360.
9 Boehlert, p. 65.
10 Speer, Albert, *Inside the Third Reich*, p. 138.
11 Jaskot, Paul B., 'Anti-Semitic Policy in Albert Speer's Plans for the Rebuilding of Berlin' (*The Art Bulletin*, Vol. 78, No. 4, 1996), p. 631.

12 Jakisch, Barry A., 'The Nature of Berlin: Green Space and Visions of a New German Capital, 1900–45' (*Central European History*, Vol. 47, No. 2, 2014), p. 331.
13 Irvine, David T., *Albert Speer* (Kindle Edition), p. 9.
14 Bukey, Evan B., 'Hitler's Hometown under Nazi Rule: Linz, Austria, 1938–45' (*Central European History*, Vol. 16, No. 2, 1983), p. 172.

Chapter 11: Propaganda through Film

1 Baird, Jay W., 'From Berlin to Neubabelsberg: Nazi Film Propaganda and Hitler Youth Quex' (*Journal of Contemporary History*, Vol. 18, No. 3, 1983), p. 495.
2 Hitler, p. 526.
3 Moritz, William, *Film Censorship during the Nazi Era,* (Harry N. Abrams, 1991), p. 186.
4 Baird, p. 495.
5 Ibid, p. 501.
6 Kater, p. 41.
7 Baird, p. 511.
8 Ibid, p. 496.
9 Gunston, p. 14.
10 Stupp, Vicki O'Donnell, 'Myth, Meaning, and Message in "The Triumph of the Will"' (*Film Criticism*, Vol. 2, No. 2/3, 1978), p. 40.
11 Sennett, Alan, 'Film Propaganda: Triumph of the Will as a Case Study', p. 45.
12 Gunston, p. 14.
13 Riefenstahl, Leni, *Hinter den Kulissen des Reichsparteitag* (International Historic Films, Inc., 1935).
14 Sennet, p. 51.
15 Ibid.
16 Stupp, p. 43.
17 Sennet, p. 54.
18 Bach, p. 121.
19 Kershaw, Ian, *Hitler 1889–1936: Hubris* (Penguin, 1999).
20 Bach, p. 166.
21 Sennet, p. 59.
22 McGilligan, Patrick, *Fritz Lang: The Nature of the Beast, a Biography* (St. Martin's Press, 1997), p. 175.
23 Lane, p. 3.
24 Mackenzie, Michael, 'From Athens to Berlin: The 1936 Olympics and Leni Riefenstahl's Olympia' (*Critical Inquiry*, Vol. 29, No. 2, 2003), p. 302.
25 Ibid, p. 306.
26 Downing, Taylor, *Olympia* (British Film Institute, 1992), p. 91.
27 Mackenzie, p. 317.
28 Spotts, p. 109.
29 Sontag, Susan, *Fascinating Fascism, Under the Sign of Saturn* (Penguin, 2013).
30 Mackenzie, p. 312.

Chapter 12: Propaganda through Music and Theatre

1 Abendroth, Walter, *Kunstmusik und Volstümlichkeit in Die Musik* (März, 1934), p. 57.
2 Levi, Erik, *Music in the Third Reich* (St. Martin's Press, 1994), p. 12.
3 Levi, Erik, *Atonality, 12-Tone Music and the Third Reich* (Tempo, 1991), p. 17.
4 Spotts, p. 4.
5 Ibid, p. 226.

6 Cathcart, Adam, 'Music and Politics in Hitler's Germany' (*Madison Historical Review*, Vol. 3, Article 1, 2006), p. 8.
7 Kater, p. 97.
8 Kyam, Wayne, 'The Nazification of Max Reinhardt's Deutsches Theater' (*Theatre Journal*, Vol. 40, No. 3, 1998), p. 360.
9 Ibid, p. 365.
10 *Rheinisch-Westfdlische Zeitung*, 11 June 1933, Wilhelm Tell in der Westfalenhalle.
11 Joseph Goebbels in Der Autor January 1934.
12 Kater, p. 47.

Postscript: Architectural Debate in Post-War Munich

1 Rosenfeld, Gavriel D., 'Architecture and the Memory of Nazism in Postwar Munich' (*German Politics & Society*, Vol. 16, No. 4, 1998), p. 140.
2 Ibid, p. 144.

INDEX